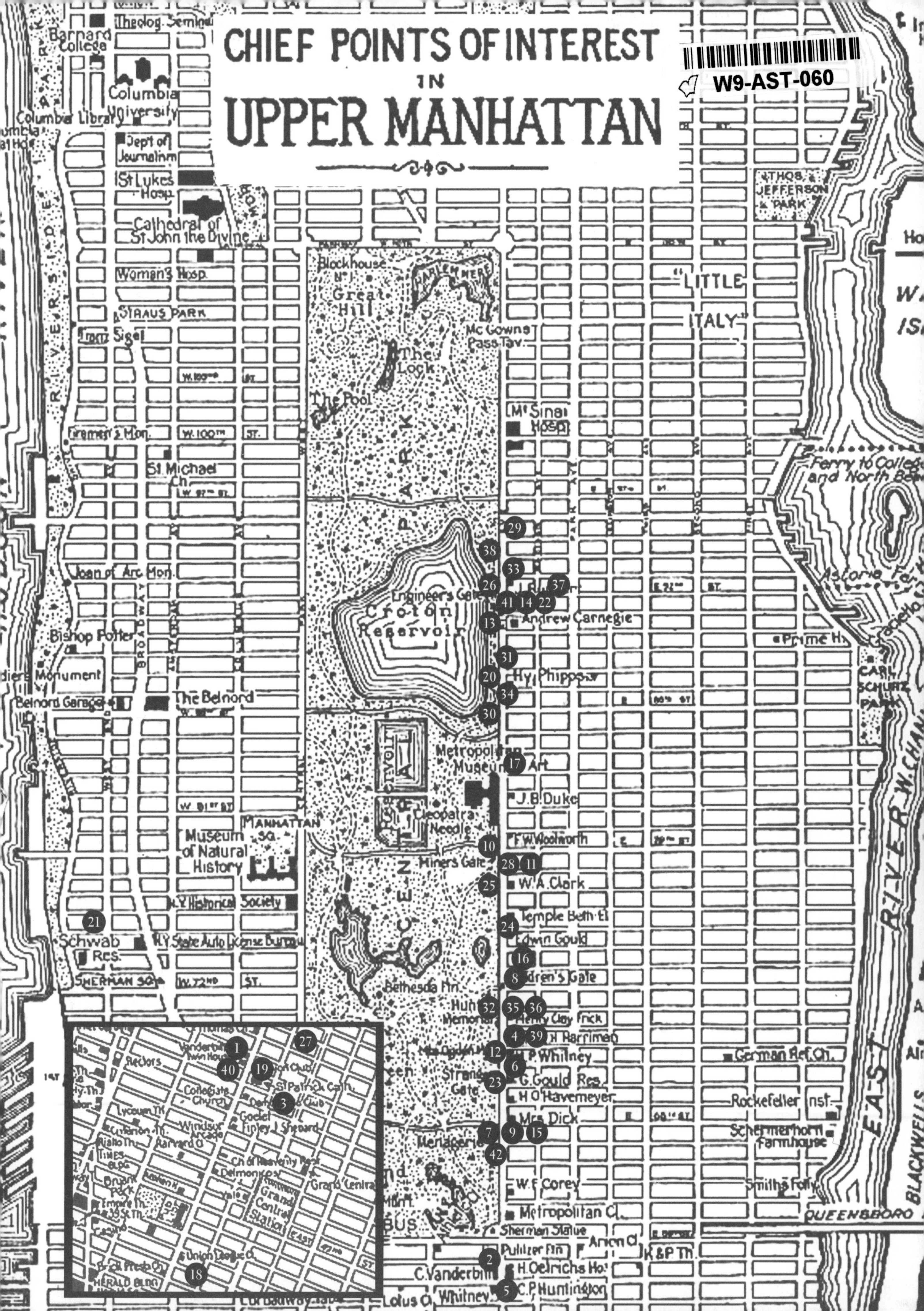

CHIEF POINTS OF INTEREST IN UPPER MANHATTAN
W9-AST-060
Barnard College
Theolog. Seminary
Columbia University
Columbia Library
Dept of Journalism
St Lukes Hosp.
Cathedral of St John the Divine
Woman's Hosp.
Straus Park
Franz Sigel
W. 100th St.
Firemen's Mon.
St. Michael Ch.
W. 97th St.
Joan of Arc Mon.
Bishop Potter
Soldiers Monument
Belnord Garage
The Belnord
Broadway
W. 81st St.
Museum of Natural History
Manhattan Sq.
N.Y. Historical Society
Schwab Res.
N.Y. State Auto License Bureau
Sherman Sq.
W. 72nd St.
Riverside
Blockhouse No 1
Great Hill
Harlem Mere
McGowns Pass Tav.
The Lock
The Pool
Central Park
Croton Reservoir
Engineer's Gate
Mt Sinai Hosp.
"Little Italy"
Andrew Carnegie
Hy. Phipps
Metropolitan Museum of Art
J.B. Duke
Cleopatra's Needle
F.W. Woolworth
Miners Gate
W.A. Clark
Temple Beth El
Edwin Gould
Children's Gate
Bethesda Ftn.
Hunt Memorial
Henry Clay Frick
Harriman
P. Whitney
G. Gould Res.
Stranger's Gate
H.O. Havemeyer
Mrs. Dick
Menagerie
W.F. Corey
Metropolitan Cl.
Sherman Statue
Pulitzer Ftn
Arion Cl.
K&P Th.
H. Oelrichs Ho.
C. Vanderbilt
C.P. Huntington
Whitney
Lotus Cl.
Thos. Jefferson Park
Prime H.
Carl Schurz Park
German Ref. Ch.
Rockefeller Inst.
Schermerhorn Farmhouse
Smiths Folly
Queensboro
East River
Blackwells
Ferry to College Pt. and North Beach
Astoria Ferry
Vanderbilt Twin Houses
St Patrick Cath.
Colleg. Church
Windsor Arcade
Gorham
Lyceum Th.
Times Bldg
Bryant Park
Delmonicos
Grand Central Station
Union League Cl.
Herald Bldg
Casino
Empire Th.
1 2 3 4 5 6 7 8 9 10 11 12 13 14 15 16 17 18 19 20 21 22 23 24 25 26 27 28 29 30 31 32 33 34 35 36 37 38 39 40 41 42

Great Houses of New York 1880–1930

Urban Domestic Architecture Series

Great Houses of New York 1880–1930

Michael C. Kathrens

ACANTHUS PRESS
2005

ACANTHUS PRESS LLC
48 West 22nd Street
New York, New York 10010
www.acanthuspress.com
800.827.7614

Library of Congress Cataloging-in-Publication Data

Kathrens, Michael C.
Great houses of New York, 1880-1930 / Michael C. Kathrens.
p. cm.
Includes bibliographical references and index.
ISBN 0-926494-34-1 (alk. paper)
1. Mansions–New York (State)–New York. 2. Historic buildings–New York (State)–New York. 3. Architecture, Domestic–New York (State)–New York. 4. New York (N.Y.)–Buildings, structures, etc. 5. Rich people–Homes and haunts–New York (State)–New York. 6. Rich people–New York (State)–New York–Biography. 7. Upper class–New York (State)–New York–History. 8. New York (N.Y.)–Biography. I. Title.

F128.7.K38 2005
974.7'104–dc22

2004030117

FRONTISPIECE: View up Fifth Avenue from 60th Street, c. 1925. (Author's Collection)

Book Design by Maggie Hinders
Printed in China

Acknowledgments

Research for this volume began 25 years ago, and within those two and a half decades I was fortunate in finding knowledgeable guides that made the journey substantially easier. Without their help this work would never have reached fruition. Many were friends and colleagues who offered much needed opinions and research paths, while others were associated with institutions whose archives are always instrumental in developing a work such as this. I am deeply indebted to them for their immense patience in dealing with my unending requests and for the uncompromising diligence that they each expressed in support of my goal.

Major sources for archival images were Mary Beth Cavanaugh at the New-York Historical Society, Melanie Bower and Marguerite Lavin, both at the Museum of the City of New York and Kathleen Kienholz of the American Academy of Arts & Letters. I also would like to acknowledge the staff of the New York Public Library, Lorna Gordon of the Society for the Preservation of New England Antiquities, and Lisa Bidell, of the Watson Library, Metropolitan Museum of Art.

I am grateful Richard Marchand, not only for his superb floor plans, but also for his continual encouragement in locating new sources of information and archival images. Other individuals who helped in acquiring images and floor plans are Gary Lawrance, William Morrison and photographer Juris Mardwig. Thanks also go to Janet Parks at the Avery Library at Columbia University, Sherry Birk at the American Institute of Architecture, Christopher Gray, Kelly Foster, Martha Frick Symington Sanger, Bora Moon at Cartier and Alex Wittenberg at the Jewish Museum. Thanks also goes to Stephen Van Dyke of the Cooper-Hewitt National Design Museum.

Among those that permitted me to tour extant structures were Margaret E. Maloney of the Commonwealth Fund, Joan Lebowitz at New York University's Institute of Fine Arts, Judi Counts at the House of the Redeemer, and the staff of the New York Academy of Sciences. Thanks also needs to be extended to Sister Pat Mier at the Convent of the Sacred Heart and Edgar Munhall of the Frick Collection. Many thanks to James Amodeo for his technical and indexing support. To Richard Johnson, Yael Lewin and Barry Cenower at Acanthus Press I perhaps owe my greatest thanks. Their talent, knowledge and sensitivity allowed the author to shine while they created this beautiful volume around me. Lastly, I would like to extend my gratitude to a dear friend and mentor, Marci McMillen, who was the first to encourage me to write about the houses I love.

Contents

Introduction

After the Civil War, the United States emerged as a leading economic power. Immigrant labor and the financial consolidation made possible by the transcontinental railroad generated vast personal fortunes not yet subject to income tax. By the 1870s, New York City had become the cultural and financial center of the burgeoning economy. Whether they were accepted or not within the well-established social order of the East Coast, pioneers rich from gold in California, copper in Montana, and steel in Pittsburgh came to the city, marking their arrival by building luxurious houses broadly modeled on the Great Houses of London.

In the 17th and 18th centuries, the landed aristocracy of England oversaw vast countryside estates and went annually to London for the social season. A sizable house to accommodate large banquets and the servants needed to mount them became an essential part of upper-class city life. By the third quarter of the 19th century, with the industrialization of England and the sharp decline in income derived from land, the aristocracy forged alliances outside the peerage with people who made their fortunes in banking and industry. The Prince of Wales, who led society with his Marlborough House Set, was particularly enamored of this new moneyed class because of his desire to be lavishly entertained.

With the advent of the luxury steamer, wealthy Americans traveled in record numbers to the capitals of Europe. The London social season remained a focal point of the American Grand Tour, with all the pomp and majesty of the Empire centered on brilliant events given in the Great Houses of the city. These aristocratic houses were more than just large; they were presentation stages for the spectacular trappings of the ruling class. A Great House in London embodied both the taste and prestige of the English aristocracy. The visiting Americans were impressed with the quality and scale of

GENERAL VIEW—MADISON AVENUE AND EAST 67TH STREET, C. 1900. (Courtesy of the Museum of the City of New York)

the English social events and had visions of duplicating them at home. It was not lost on Americans that to entertain on a grand scale required a commensurate setting. Newly rich Americans understood the potential to enhance their own social standing by emulating the lifestyle of the English ruling class.

• • •

In the late 1860s, New York society was concentrated along Fifth Avenue between Washington Square and Murray Hill. With the northward expansion of the city, and the willingness of people to sell their houses for substantial profit to commercial developers, the fashionable residential district continued its uptown migration another 20 blocks by the 1880s. This progression would continue until the beginning of World War I. Most of the American Great Houses were built on Fifth and Park avenues and the side streets connecting them from 50th to 95th streets, with the grandest houses being placed on the corner lots of the avenues. Unlike Fifth Avenue, which had been the residential street for the city's elite for well over half a century, upper Park Avenue became acceptable only after the electrification of the trains, which had previously billowed smoke out of an open trough. After the submerged tracks were covered, Park Avenue became the handsome and wide residential avenue we know today. Former Secretary of State Elihu Root was the first to build a house on upper Park Avenue when his Carrère & Hastings–designed house went up on the southeast corner of 71st Street in 1905.

UPPER FIFTH AVENUE AND CENTRAL PARK. (Courtesy of the Museum of the City of New York)

As the 19th century came to a close, the best architectural firms in the city participated in filling block after block with American interpretations of fluid Venetian palazzos, elegant French *hôtel particuliers*, and dignified Georgian mansions. All of the architects were trained at the Ecole des Beaux-Arts, or at least subscribed to its teachings. Many people associate the Ecole with the full-blown Modern French style of Garnier's Paris Opera House, but the school represents an important theory of spatial planning based on function. A Beaux-Arts trained architect could produce a building in any stylistic expression, from Byzantine to Art Deco, while striving to create the most lucid plan.

Of course, not every house was a success—certainly some were patently ugly—but overall the superb craftsmanship and infinite attention to detail gave these houses an overwhelming presence that embodied the power and stature of their owners. Sculptors, bronzers, wood carvers, painters, and decorative plasterers were brought from Europe in great numbers to ornament New York houses. Some owners had rooms constructed in Europe. These rooms, after a possible inspection by the owner during a tour abroad, were disassembled, crated, and shipped to New York along with workers needed to install them.

To give the sparkling new Great House a softer patina, as well as a feeling of age and permanence, Europe was ransacked for art, furniture, and period rooms. The wholesale exportation of European masterpieces to the United States was eventually halted by the enactment of laws to protect national treasures, but before those laws were put into effect,

Vanderbilt Row, c. 1890. (Courtesy of the Museum of the City of New York)

Leonard Jerome House, Madison Avenue and 26th Street. (Author's Collection)

ALEXANDER T. STEWART HOUSE, FIFTH AVENUE AND 34TH STREET. (Author's Collection)

American millionaires acquired the best in European and Asian art. From Henry Clay Frick's Fragonard panels commissioned by Madame du Barry, to Thomas Fortune Ryan's ducal collection of old masters, to Otto Kahn's 18th-century salon from the Hôtel d'Humières in Paris, the Great Houses were given distinction through remarkable private art collections.

• • •

Mr. and Mrs. William K. Vanderbilt officially opened their new house at 52nd Street and Fifth Avenue in the winter of 1882 with a costume ball for 1,200 people. The lavishness of this event, said to have cost a quarter of a million dollars, was on a scale never before attempted in a private house on this side of the Atlantic. The success of the party was directly related to the interest created by the house itself, as it was radically different from any other residence in the city. Designed to re-create the luxurious lifestyle of the great European town house, this Loire-inspired limestone chateau designed by Richard Morris Hunt affected the way wealthy New Yorkers lived for the next 50 years.

The Vanderbilt house was a dramatic departure from the interminable blocks of Italianate brownstones then lining the better residential sections of Manhattan. With its French Renaissance–inspired *tourelle* and steeply pitched roof with ornate copper cresting, the building relieved the monotonous box-like appearance of the typical New York town house. The white of the tooled limestone must have created a startling contrast to the unrelenting sea of chocolate brown.

Before the Vanderbilt house, there had been attempts to replicate European residential standards, the earliest being the Leonard Jerome house, completed on Madison Square in 1859. Jerome, a Wall

MARY MASON JONES HOUSE, FIFTH AVENUE AT 57TH STREET. (Courtesy of the Museum of the City of New York)

Street speculator, built his six-story house in the flamboyant French Second Empire style. It was in many ways stylistically similar to Brook House, built almost concurrently on Park Lane in London. The red-brick-and-limestone-trimmed Jerome house was topped by a tall mansard roof sprinkled with dormers of many shapes. Its use of cast iron in creating multiple verandas overlooking the square was a highly unusual feature for a New York residence. Its rich interiors included a large ballroom and a private theater that could reputedly seat 600 people. The Metropolitan Museum of Art was founded at a meeting at the house in 1869. Jerome's daughter Jennie, following the fashion for Anglo-American aristocratic alliances, married into the English peerage and was the mother of Winston Churchill.

A decade later, A. T. Stewart built a marble palace on the northwest corner of Fifth Avenue and 34th Street. Stewart, the owner of the largest department store in the city, built his house to accommodate his growing art collection and, some said, to advance himself and his wife socially. The mausoleum-like building contained dark, gloomy interiors that "good" society declined to enter. Mrs. Astor, who lived directly across the street, supposedly said of Stewart, "I buy my carpets from him but is that any reason I should ask him to walk on them?"

On the other hand, Mary Mason Jones, who came from an old and well-established New York family, dared to be adventuresome when she had Robert Mook design a row of French classical stone houses on the east side of Fifth Avenue between 57th and 58th streets. In 1869, the year they were completed, this area was considered to be far uptown. Her father had paid $1,500 for the

ELBRIDGE T. GERRY RESIDENCE, FIFTH AVENUE AND 61ST STREET.
(Byron Collection, courtesy of the Museum of the City of New York)

block-front property some 40 years earlier. Called "Marble Row," these houses were distinctly Parisian in feel with fewer of the Victorian excesses of contemporary American architecture. Mrs. Jones, who lived in the spacious 57th Street corner house, was portrayed by her niece Edith Wharton as Mrs. Manson Mingott in *The Age of Innocence:*

> It was her habit to sit in the window of her sitting room on the ground floor, as if watching calmly for life and fashion to flow northward to her solitary door. She seemed in no hurry to have it come, for her patience was equalled by her confidence. She was sure that presently the hoardings, the quarries, the one-story saloons, the wooden greenhouses in ragged gardens, and the rocks from which goats surveyed the scene, would vanish before the advance of residences as stately as her own—perhaps (for she was an impartial woman) even statelier; and that the cobblestones over which the old clattering omnibuses bumped would be replaced by smooth asphalt, such as people had reported having seen in Paris.

Notwithstanding these solid earlier attempts, the William K. Vanderbilt house is still considered the house to have ultimately ended the reign of the brownstone in New York City. The credit for this must be given to its architect, Richard Morris Hunt, an ardent Francophile with an affinity for the early French Renaissance. In an era when there were no architecture schools in the United States, Hunt was the first American to be trained at the Ecole des Beaux-Arts in Paris, the 19th century's most prestigious architectural school. The Vanderbilt house was the first of many designed by Hunt that subsequently graced Fifth Avenue. Others included the Ogden Mills house (1887), the Elbridge T. Gerry house (1893), and Mrs. William B. Astor's house (1895). All were beautifully executed, with meticulous attention paid to proportion and detail. Many of these houses' interiors were entrusted to the leading Parisian decorating firm of Jules Allard et Fils, who had decorated Alva Vanderbilt's influential French Régence salon.

Mrs. Vanderbilt worked very closely with Hunt on the stylistic aspects of her house, but the basic plan was always left in the architect's hands. The bedrooms had conveniently adjoining bathrooms and dressing rooms, the servants could work hidden from view, and the kitchen was close enough to the dining room so that meals could be brought to the table still warm.

A functional floor plan was developed to allow inhabitants the most prized of all luxuries: privacy. This was accomplished through an intelligent division of the house into four distinct areas of function. The first was the reception area, which included an entrance hall, lavatory, coat closet, and a reception room where guests would wait to be greeted by a member of the family.

The second area held the public rooms designed for entertaining on a grand scale and included the drawing room, dining room, library, music room, and ballroom. To be a member of the upper echelon in this era, one was obliged to "entertain." Because entertaining occurred almost exclusively in private houses, the grander entertainments demanded grander settings. By the 1880s, sit-down dinners for 50 people or more were not uncommon, and balls required rooms large enough to hold up to 500.

The third distinct section of the Great House comprised the family's private quarters, consisting of each member's bedroom and bath plus a communal sitting room and small family dining room in which to entertain intimate friends and family. Following European custom, husband and wife generally had separate but connecting bedrooms. This section also contained rooms for overnight guests.

The fourth and final area was dedicated to the service. Fully a third of the square footage of the Great House was allotted to staff and service areas, including the kitchen, pantry, servants' rooms, cellar, laundry, etc. In Europe, with its lack of technological advances, the service square footage could often exceed 50 percent.

New York houses were designed to not only uphold the strict social code of the Edwardian era, but to combine it with the latest American technological advances. These inventions are what made the New York house so comfortable. Central heating, electric lights, and plentiful baths were not common features in European houses of the time.

To run and maintain these properties, a large, well-trained staff of at least 12 was required, and they were often recruited from the vast numbers of immigrants entering the country. Most of the servants lived in the house and needed rooms in which to eat and sleep, all separate from but convenient to the family. Staff members were required to rise by six in the morning so as to have cleaning done before the family appeared at nine, and if there was a formal dinner that night they would be expected to work until after midnight.

A typical New York City family of two adults and three children might have a permanent household staff of 12. This included: a butler and two footmen to take care of the principal entertaining rooms; a chef, a scullery maid and a cellar man to take care of, respectively, the kitchen, pantry, and furnace room; three maids for the bedrooms and bathrooms; and one laundress, a personal maid for the lady of the house and a valet for the gentleman of the house. Having children would require the presence of a governess in the nursery, and there would be a coachman and two grooms to take care of the family's transportation. Last, there was a housekeeper. More elaborate households of the era easily could have staff requirements twice as large. Mrs. Ogden Mills, for example, had a staff large enough to accommodate 100 for dinner without calling in extra help.

• • •

The Great House era in New York lasted 50 years. It began with the opening of the Vanderbilt house in 1882 and ended in the first years of the Great Depression. Within this time, three distinct subsections mark its progression. The Development Years (1882–1900) was the period when wealthy New Yorkers were casting off old Knickerbocker social conventions and developing their own to reflect the new financial order. The local architectural community was also becoming aware of the power of the plutocrats and began to find suitable architectural expression for their abodes. Clients were seeking an evocation of permanence and stability inherent in the European Great House but adapted to the vastly different urban landscape of New York. The preferred styles used during these years were the Loire Valley chateau (Mrs. Willaim B. Astor, 1895); the flamboyant Beaux-Arts baroque (Henry Sloane, 1894); and the Italian Renaissance revival (Villard Houses, 1885). Desmond and Croly's *Stately Homes in America*, published in 1903, states:

> During the past fifteen years or twenty years there have been built in the United States a large number of expensive and magnificent private dwellings. These houses have had their predecessors, of course, but hardly any precursors. They are as different in size and magnificence from earlier types of American residences as the contemporary skyscraper is from the old five-story brick office. And since they are a comparatively new fact in American domestic architecture, it may be inferred that they are the expression of similarly new facts in American economic and social developments.

After the turn of the century, with great fortunes firmly established and the architectural community now understanding what was expected by new clients, the most prolific period of the Great House began. During the Mature Years (1901–18), houses being built in New York City generally surpassed anything then being constructed in Europe. Again, these American buildings were inspired by different historical styles, but they were designed with more authority, and attention was being given to more refined details. The favored style of the period was the Modern Renaissance, which was a synthesis of 18th-century French and Italian models. The James A. Burden (1902), George J. Gould (1907), and Oakleigh Thorne (1908) houses are all examples of this style. *Architecture* commented in 1909:

> ... at least in New York City houses we have found a style at once characteristic, suitable and beautiful, and most of the larger houses recently erected in this city have been designed in this style. It has its genesis in the French of the periods of Louis XV and Louis XVI, and is strongly affected by the admiration for the Italian Renaissance ever present in American architects of today. These influences have resulted in a style that at first glance appears French, and upon closer inspection evidences its

70TH STREET FROM MADISON AVENUE, 1920S. (Courtesy of the Museum of the City of New York)

> American genesis. The. . . decorative members. . . are kept very flat, with the result that the surface has sufficient play of light and shade to keep it from being tiresome without the exaggerated lines which result in restlessness.

Later in the Mature Years, there was a resurgence of the Anglo-American Georgian style with an emphasis on the Federal. These houses, such as the Williard Straight house (1914) and the Francis Palmer house (1918), were built on a much larger scale than any original model, but they were still proportionately correct. This revival was not fully explored until after World War I, being better suited to the smaller houses then being built.

Traditionally, the Great Depression is cited as the cause for the end of the Great House era. However, the economic collapse was merely the "coup de grâce" for an already defunct tradition. The Declining Years (1919–32) actually began around the end of World War I. Several factors contributed to the demise of the Great House: a shortage of servants was brought on by the severely restrictive Immigration Act of 1919; the first income tax was instituted in 1913; and immediately following the end of the war, escalating land values in Manhattan discouraged even the very rich from building single-family residences. Socially, with the acceptance of the luxury hotel, like the Plaza and the St. Regis, as settings for private functions and large dinner parties, there was less need to maintain a Great House in the city.

The smaller houses of the Declining Years had cozier floor plans that suited the less formal "Roaring '20s." Mott B. Schmidt, with his crisp colonial revival houses such as the Anne Vanderbilt

FIFTH AVENUE, LOOKING SOUTH FROM 60TH STREET, C. 1928. (Author's Collection)

residence on Sutton Place (1921), probably best expressed the domestic architectural feeling in post-war New York. Comfort and a simplified elegance were on the ascendancy, but the old standards were not completely dead. As late as the early 1930s, two extremely formal and elegant houses were completed on East 93rd Street—the Virginia G. F. Vanderbilt house at number 60 and the William Goadby Loew house at number 56. But these houses were anachronous structures exemplifying a lifestyle already gone.

• • •

After World War I, the East Side followed the model of the West Side and succumbed to apartment house living. Fine houses had been constructed after the Civil War along Riverside Drive and on the blocks along Central Park West, but only a handful of these ever attained Great House status. One reason was that socially dominant 19th-century families generally stayed on the East Side, where the establishment had always lived. Another reason was the earlier acceptance on the West Side of apartment building living. Affluent New Yorkers took to the convenience and economy of apartment houses such as the Dakota (1884) on Central Park West and the Osborne (1885) at Seventh Avenue and 57th Street. By the middle of the first decade of the 20th century, the West Side was populated by apartment houses for people of means, while the East Side remained the domain of the private house.

An early exceptional East Side apartment house was the McKim, Mead & White–designed building at 998 Fifth Avenue. At the time of its 1920–21 construction, the socially discerning heard a collective scream all the way from Murray Hill to the upper reaches of Fifth Avenue. The wall had been breached: the first high-rise apartment house on Fifth Avenue above 59th Street was being erected on the northeast corner of 81st Street. To make matters worse, one of their own—August Belmont II—had knowingly sold the property to developers for just such a project. Elihu Root, who had moved into his spacious Park Avenue house only four years earlier, was the first to sign a lease in 998. This lease was for a 20-room apartment with an annual rent of $15,000. Murray Guggenheim, Governor Levi P. Morton, and Mrs. Elliot F. Shepard quickly followed.

Wealthy New Yorkers could hardly have failed to perceive the demise of the Great House. Vanderbilt Row, on the 10 blocks of Fifth Avenue just below Central Park, was already decimated with hotels and retail establishments by 1920. Grace Vanderbilt at 640 was the last residential holdout on this part of the avenue. When she finally left in 1945, skyscrapers had totally engulfed her house, with Rockefeller Center being directly across the street. Those that began to inherit these houses generally chose a lifestyle that did not require the marbled splendor that their parents found so essential, and they showed far less regret in disposing of them than did the stoic Grace.

During the 1920s, the blocks on Fifth Avenue facing Central Park saw the destruction of one house after another for the erection of luxury apartment buildings. Park Avenue similarly took the form we recognize today, becoming an almost solid wall of apartment buildings from the Grand Central Building (now the Helmsley Building) to 96th Street. New houses did continue to go up in the city, but generally they were smaller in scale and were built on less valuable side-street lots rather than facing an avenue. But in 1922, Marcellus Hartley Dodge, the munitions heir who married the daughter of William Rockefeller, completed a large house on the northeast corner of Fifth Avenue and 61st Street. This rather nondescript red brick residence had the distinction of being the last mansion erected on Fifth Avenue.

• • •

Some of the best Great Houses of New York, such as the Duke, Warburg, Harkness, and Frick houses, still dominate the avenue that continues to pride itself on its residential exclusiveness. But these are exceptions, and as grand as these houses are, it is only on certain side streets that one can still experience the turn-of-the-century scale of the neighborhood. The entire block between 78th and 79th streets from Fifth Avenue to Madison Avenue is of particular interest. Because of certain deed restrictions placed on it by industrialist Henry H. Cook, who purchased it in the 1880s, there is not a single high-rise building on the entire block today. It is the only Fifth Avenue block that essentially looks the same as it did at the beginning of World War I.

The last flowering of the urban Great House here in New York followed the arc of so many American institutions. Whereas in Europe it took hundreds of years to define and refine the idiom, in New York there was only half a century to see it develop and disintegrate—hardly time to create a tradition whose passing would be mourned. Even the demolition of the William K. Vanderbilt house in 1926 elicited only one article from the architectural profession. This article, although lamenting the fact that we did not protect our architectural masterpieces, was permeated with resignation, stating that the house's destruction was "as irresistible as the commercial spirit that is reducing even our fine architecture to a simple matter of dollars and cents."

Author's Note

The Beaux-Arts preservation movement in the United States really began in 1963 with the demolition of McKim, Mead & White's Pennsylvania Station in New York. The building, completed in 1910, was only 53 years old. The public was outraged by the destruction of what many people felt to be one of the most eloquently monumental buildings that this country had produced, and for the first time leaders in the architectural profession, such as Phillip Johnson, joined in the general chorus of discontent.

In New York City, the public's appreciation of architecture has filtered down to less well-known buildings. Entire historic districts have been created to safeguard remaining structures. The Upper East Side has three such districts, which encompass an area from 59th Street to 94th Street, from Fifth Avenue to Lexington Avenue. Most of these preserved houses now operate as schools, consulates, and offices, while some, such as the Joseph Pulitzer house on East 73rd Street, have been divided into luxury apartments. A few actually remain as private homes.

In this work I have tried to give the reader a taste of the architecture and interior art that once prevailed. Almost exclusively using archival photography, I feel that the buildings are seen better as they were built. The houses are arranged in chronological order, so that the reader will be able to see the stylistic progression of the Great House in New York. Perhaps most importantly, I have attempted to make this book interesting and understandable for the general reader with descriptions of the buildings and their interiors while providing a glimpse into the social life of these wealthy New York denizens. Ultimately, I hope that this book helps develop a new-found appreciation for these incredible residential structures that have both fascinated me and given me such intense pleasure.

Michael C. Kathrens

Great Houses of New York 1880–1930

William K. Vanderbilt House
660 Fifth Avenue
Richard Morris Hunt, 1882

William K. Vanderbilt House

Fifth Avenue Facade. (Author's Collection)

At 11:30 P.M. on March 26th, 1883, guests began to arrive at 660 Fifth Avenue for the long-awaited official housewarming of Mr. and Mrs. William K. Vanderbilt's new residence. A dress ball given in honor of Mrs. Vanderbilt's childhood friend Consuelo Yznaga, now Lady Mandeville, celebrated the occasion. The police stationed outside the house restrained thousands of curious onlookers who ventured out on the cold night to watch the Vanderbilt guests arrive.

For weeks, the local papers had been full of articles about the ball and who would be attending it. The New York World speculated that the cost of the affair would run close to a quarter of a million dollars. Klunder, the society florist of the day, banked the house with orchids and American Beauty roses worth over $10,000. The cost of catering a midnight supper for 1,200, combined with the fee charged by the two attending orchestras, totaled well

Fifth Avenue Elevation Drawing. (Author's Collection)

over $65,000. The greatest expense, however, estimated to be close to $150,000, came from the costumes worn by the invitees. Fortunately, this was one bill the Vanderbilts shared with their guests, who paid for their own regalia.

As the procession of carriages with their liveried coachman discharged the costumed guests onto the maroon plush carpet that had been spread across the sidewalk, banker Henry Clews was overheard to say that this ball put the Vanderbilts "at the top of the heap in what is called good society in New York." That is precisely where Alva and William K. Vanderbilt wanted to be.

Even Mrs. William B. Astor, then the undisputed leader of New York society, attended; this was the first time she had ever deemed it necessary to step across the threshold of any house belonging to the vast and extremely rich Vanderbilt clan.

Legend had it that Mrs. Astor's daughter Carrie had been practicing a formal quadrille for the party with her friends. As it came closer to the date of the ball, it became apparent that an invitation to the affair was not forthcoming. A tearful Carrie, who did not want to miss what promised to be the party of the century, pleaded with her mother to intercede. Subsequently, Ward McAllister, Mrs. Astor's fashionable majordomo, was sent discreetly to ask

52nd Street View. (Author's Collection)

Mrs. Vanderbilt if there had been some mistake. McAllister returned with the ominous news that because Mrs. Vanderbilt had never been introduced to Mrs. Astor or to her daughter, it would be highly improper to invite either of them to her party. Mrs. Astor, so the story goes, immediately ordered her carriage, so she could drop her calling card at 660. Upon receipt, Alva Vanderbilt, in turn, dispatched a liveried footman to hand-deliver an invitation to the Astor household.

As distinguished as the guest list was, what really made the function a success was the building that showcased it. At the time, Manhattan was drowning in a sea of brownstone, and this limestone French Renaissance house represented a new era in residential splendor. New Yorkers had never seen anything quite like the Vanderbilts' "little Chateau de Blois." It was, for a brief moment, unique on this side of the Atlantic. American residential architecture was now on a par with the Great Houses of Europe.

Past an entrance vestibule lined in delicately carved stone drapery, the long main hall neatly bisected the house. Its walls of finely detailed Caen stone contrasted with the elaborate wood ceiling. Midway through the hall, on the right, an ornate stone arch opened onto the grand staircase. Around the rest of the hall, the principal entertaining rooms were arranged. A French Renaissance library and a reception room with intricate inlaid paneling faced Fifth Avenue; within a few years, the latter room was

52nd Street Elevation Drawing. (Author's Collection)

redecorated using a set of carved 17th-century Grinling Gibbons limewood pendants. On the 52nd Street side was a gold-and-white Régence salon with a ceiling painting by Paul Baudry and an ornate beamed-ceiling breakfast room that featured Rembrandt's portrait *The Noble Slav*. Across the rear of the house, a two-story stone banquet hall had lower walls paneled in carved, quartered oak. During the day, the large stained-glass windows surrounding the room's upper walls bathed the 35-by-50-foot space in soft colors. The last room on this level was the exotic Moorish billiard room tucked behind the staircase. All the rooms could be thrown open on gala nights to accommodate the large throngs the Vanderbilts entertained.

Facade Detail. (Author's Collection)

VESTIBULE. (Author's Collection)

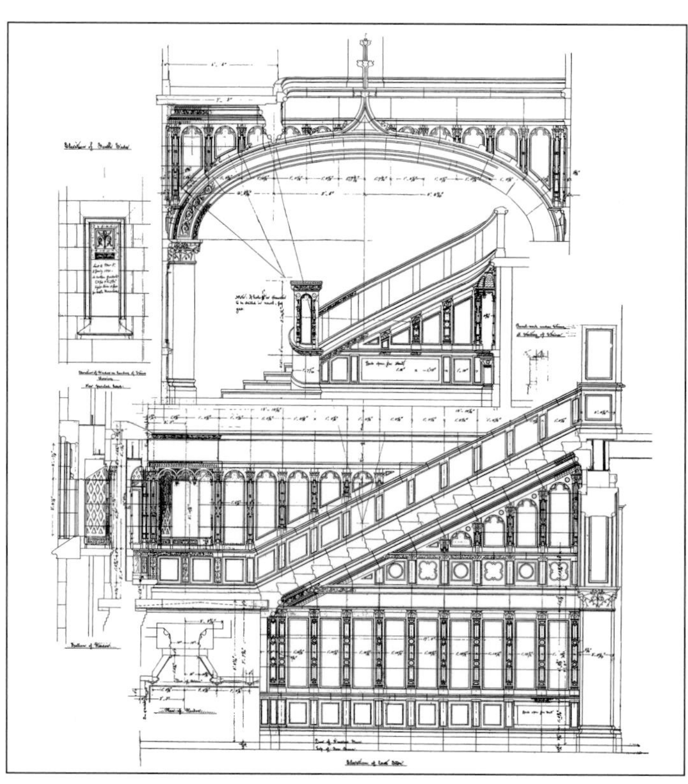

STAIRCASE DRAWING. (Author's Collection)

Suites for Mr. and Mrs. Vanderbilt and for their three children occupied the next two floors. Mirrors, hand-painted with blossoming cherry trees, paneled Mrs. Vanderbilt's bathroom. On the third floor above the great hall, a gymnasium was later converted into an Elizabethan-style supper room.

During the couple's messy 1895 divorce proceedings, one of the first involving a prominent New York society family, William offered 660 to Alva, who declined, stating that it would be far too expensive to maintain on her now much-reduced income. So William retained the New York City house while Alva received the $11 million Newport, Rhode Island, cottage, Marble House. A few years later, he purchased two lots immediately north of 660 as a site for the house of his son William K. Jr. and his new wife, Virginia Fair, the daughter of Comstock Lode millionaire James Fair of San Francisco. Richard Morris Hunt, who had designed 660, was now dead, so William chose Stanford White to design the adjacent new house in similar French Renaissance style.

Although William K. Vanderbilt Sr. now began spending a considerable part of each year abroad, particularly at his racing stables in France, he continued to purchase surrounding Fifth Avenue properties to protect the family residential enclave from commercial intrusion. He finally gave up this losing battle in the mid-teens when he allowed the jeweler Cartier to move into the former Morton F. Plant mansion directly across the street. This decision bothered him very little because by 1916, the multimillionaire rarely returned to the city of his birth—only when his duties at the New York Central offices made it necessary. Because these trips were of short duration, Vanderbilt generally stayed at one of his clubs rather than incur the tremendous expense of opening the house.

In the winter of 1919, Vanderbilt arrived in New York for the last time and became so weakened

GRAND STAIRCASE. (Author's Collection)

Entrance Hall. (Author's Collection)

during his stay that he had to literally be carried aboard the steamer that returned him to France. In April of the following year, he collapsed amid the fashionable crowd at the races at Auteuil. Bedridden for three months, he died on July 23 with his daughter, Consuelo, then the Duchess of Marlborough, and younger son Harold in attendance. He was 70 years old.

After the choicest pieces from William's collection were removed to The Metropolitan Museum of Art—including *The Noble Slav* and Boucher's *Toilet of Venus* as well as two pieces of French 18th-century furniture made by master ébéniste Jean Henri Reisener in 1785 for Marie Antoinette's private apartments at Saint-Cloud—his children put 660 Fifth Avenue on the market. An idea to preserve it as a museum collapsed, and the family called in the American Art Galleries to sell whatever architectural embellishments could be safely removed from the superstructure of the building. The Vanderbilt house sat empty for the next four years, until the heirs finally agreed to sell the stripped building to a developer for $3.75 million. An article in *The American Architect* entitled "Scrapping an Architectural Masterpiece" prophesied that the entire city would be the real loser with 660's destruction.

In February 1926, wreckers leveled Richard Morris Hunt's beautiful early French Renaissance chateau and carted the remains to an anonymous landfill. Today, a rather mundane office building stands on the site where Alva and William K. Vanderbilt once conquered society's "400."

Grinling Gibbons Parlor Room. (Author's Collection)

Dining Hall. (Author's Collection)

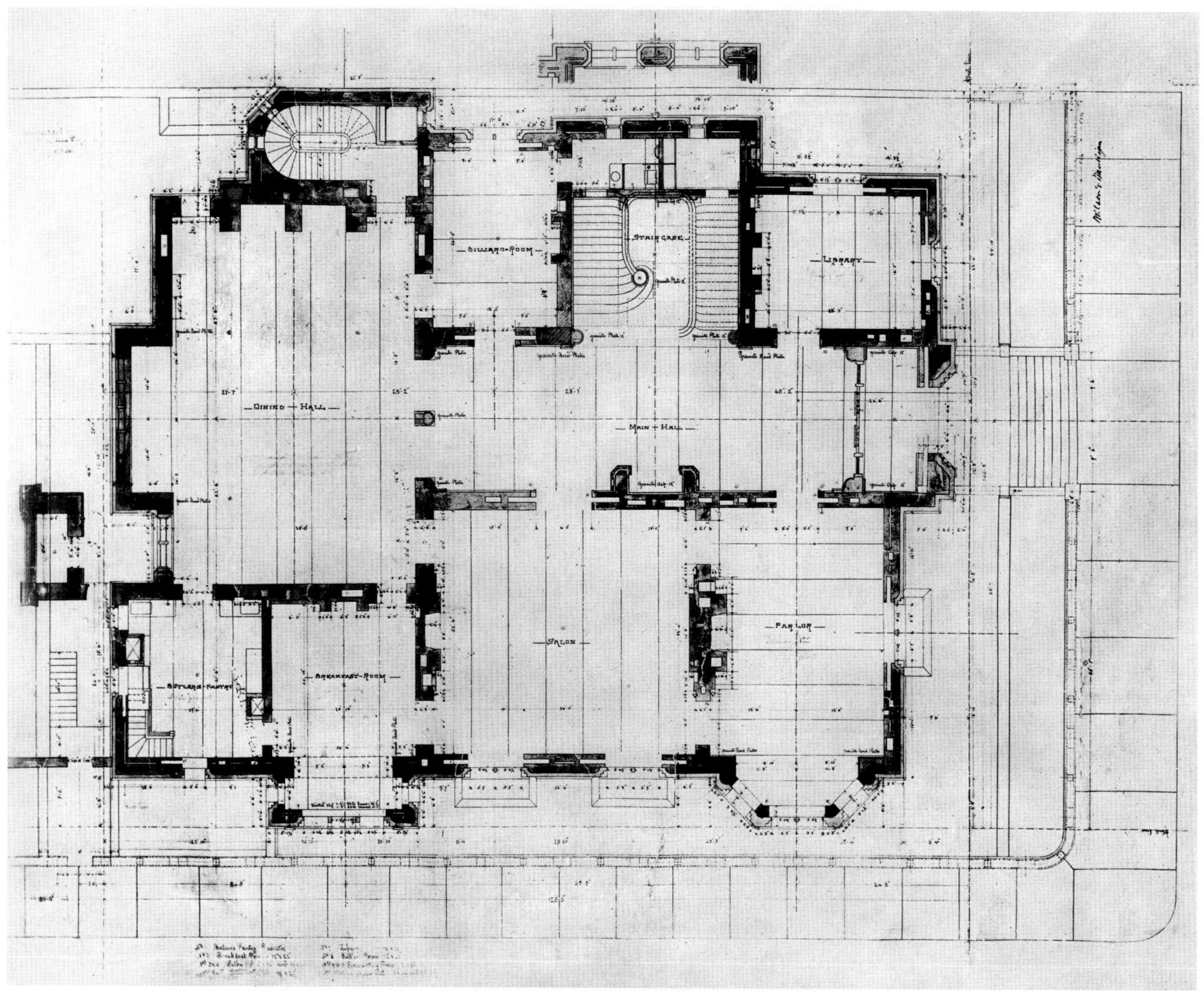

FIRST FLOOR PLAN. (Author's Collection)

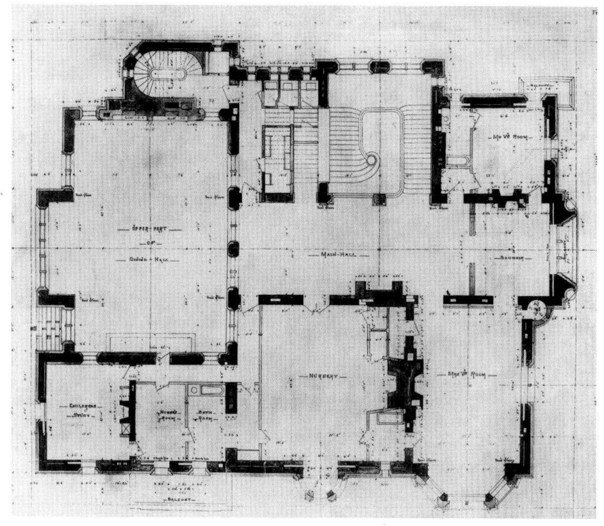

SECOND FLOOR PLAN. (Author's Collection)

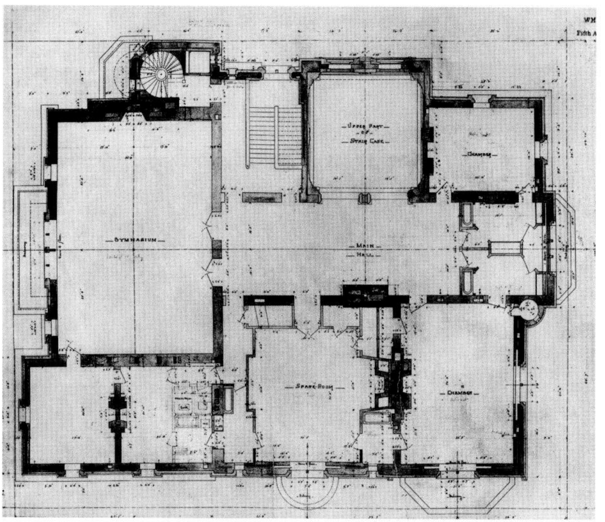

THIRD FLOOR PLAN. (Author's Collection)

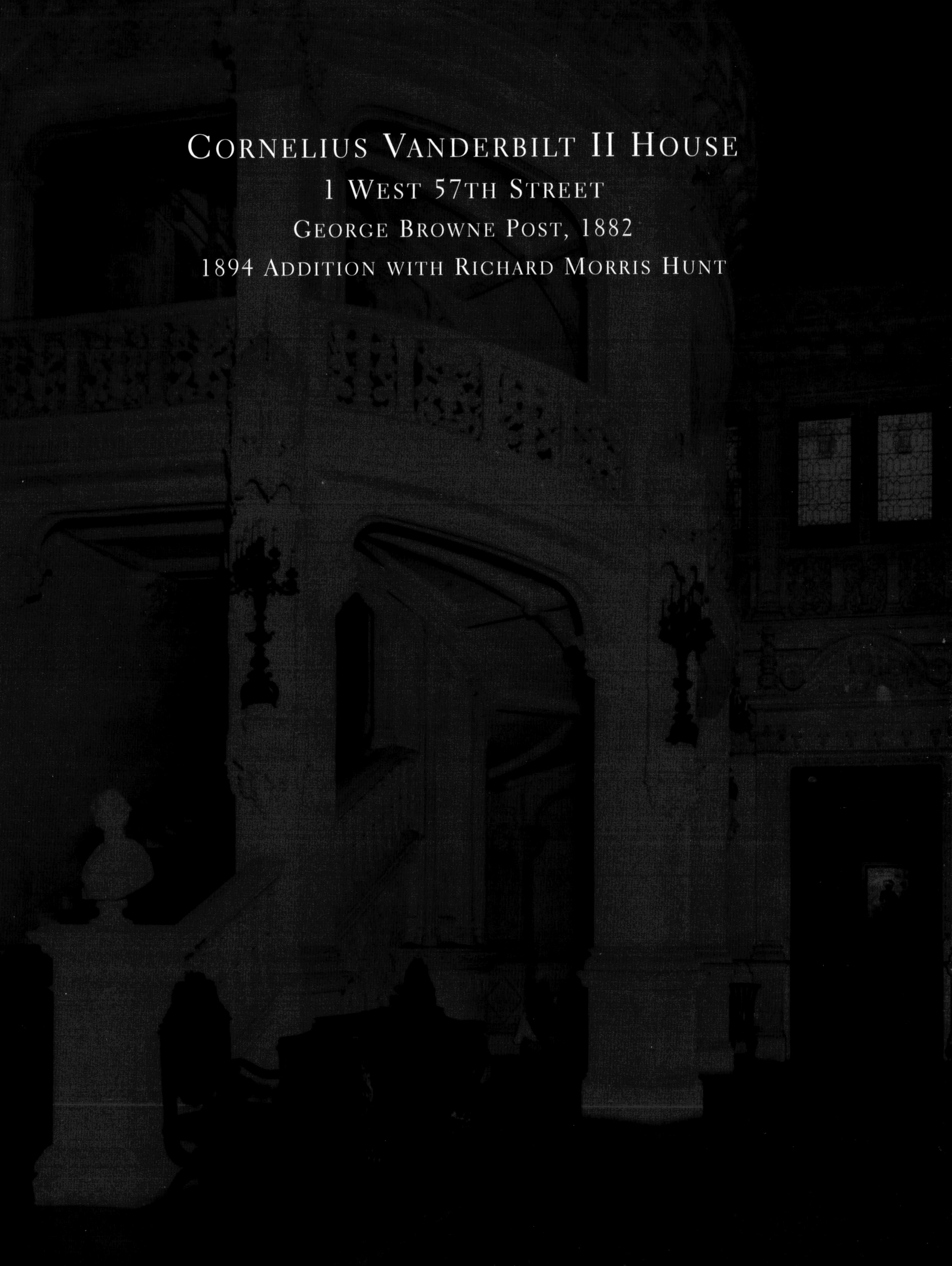

Cornelius Vanderbilt II House

1 West 57th Street

George Browne Post, 1882

1894 Addition with Richard Morris Hunt

Cornelius Vanderbilt II House

Exterior from Grand Army Plaza. (Courtesy of the New-York Historical Society)

As his parents and siblings were populating midtown Fifth Avenue with palatial mansions, the late Commodore Vanderbilt's favorite grandson, Cornelius II, was throwing his architectural hat into the ring with a George Browne Post–designed house on the northwest corner of 57th Street. Cornelius had purchased three brownstones on this Fifth Avenue corner in 1877, the year after his grandfather's death. After demolishing them, Post erected an early French Renaissance chateau–style building of red brick and limestone. Although receiving favorable professional comment in 1883 at the time of its completion, it never did make the eloquent statement of brother William's house at 660 Fifth Avenue. The building was ill-proportioned and appeared top-heavy because of its huge dormers and over-abundance of picturesque chimney stacks.

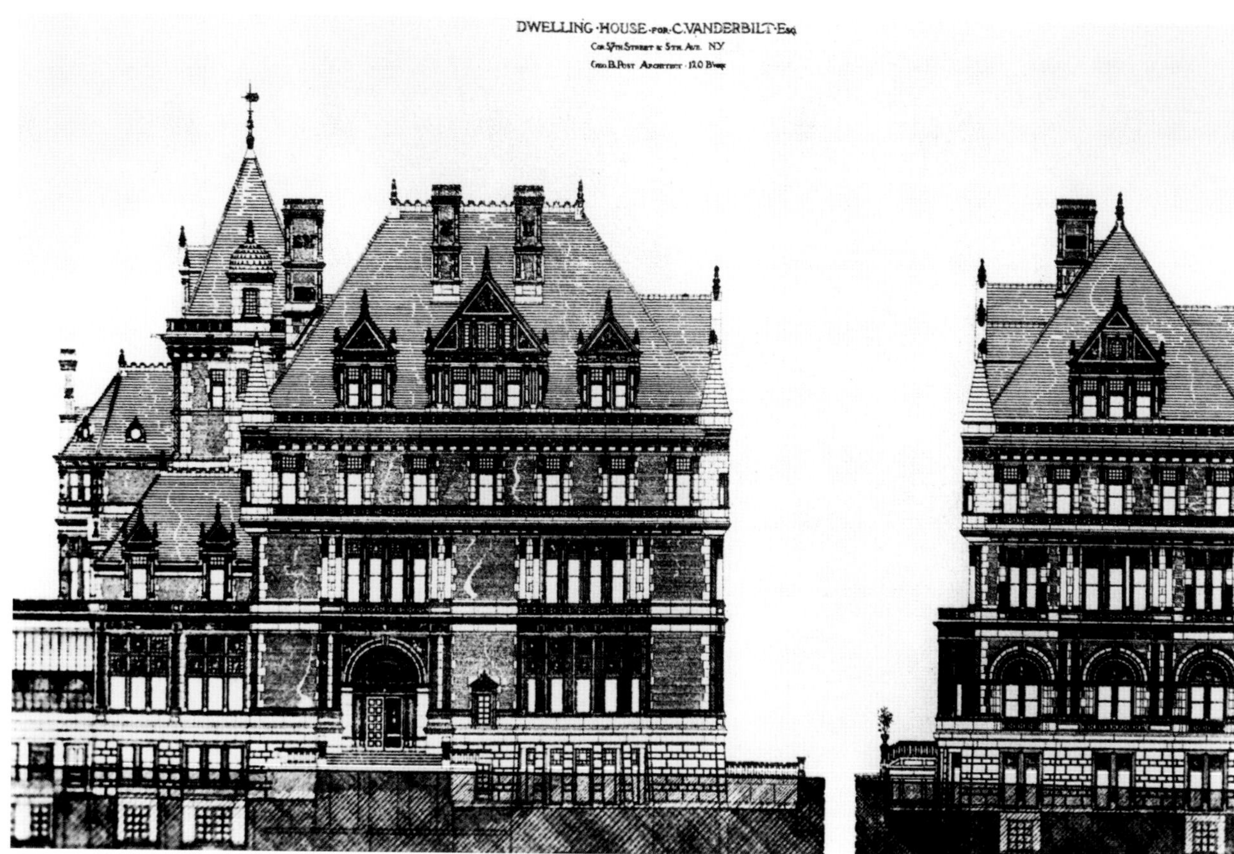

FACADE RENDERING. (Author's Collection)

57TH STREET FACADE, C. 1890. (Author's Collection)

Three years after moving into the house, Cornelius' father, William Henry Vanderbilt, died, leaving him as the official head of the "House of Vanderbilt." By the early 1890s, Cornelius became aware that others were trying to equal—if not surpass—the Vanderbilt houses in size and splendor. Feeling that this impinged on the family honor, he decided to purchase and raze the six houses that stood between his house and Grand Army Plaza. He then commissioned an enormous addition to 1 West 57th Street that he hoped would permanently dominate both the plaza and New York society. Post was again hired as architect, but this time, Cornelius and his wife, Alice, also brought in Richard Morris Hunt as a consultant. Construction began in March 1892 on the $3,000,000 addition. Vanderbilt, who wanted it completed posthaste, authorized as many as 800 workers at a time to labor through the night under enormous electric lights. It is not recorded what his affluent neighbors thought of the nocturnal

Main Hall and Staircase.
(Courtesy of the New-York Historical Society)

Detail of the Augustus Saint-Gaudens Fireplace.
(Author's Collection)

noise, but work was completed on the vast project in less than two years.

When finished, the new and improved mansion quickly became one of the most important tourist attractions in the city. With 130 rooms, the house was, and would remain, the largest single-family residence ever erected in New York. The large and easily distinguished square tower on the northeast corner of the building marked Hunt's most important contribution to the design of the new addition; he often used this device on his Fifth Avenue houses to unite two major, but not uniformly architecturally treated, facades. The northern front of the structure, facing the plaza and Central Park, had a monumental ceremonial porte cochere set in a small, fenced park. The family entrance remained on 57th Street, whereas this important new state entrance was used for weddings, funerals, balls, and large receptions. *Valentine's Manual of Old New York* espoused that "Visitors lucky enough to be on this spot during a social function will never forget the procession of smart equipages, drawn by blooded horses, and manned by liveried footmen and grooms, discharging passengers, each of them a Society member of high standing."

Inside, the grand new rooms were decorated by the best international decorating firms. Jules Allard decorated the Louis XVI music room, fellow Parisian Gilbert Cuel was responsible for the immense ballroom. The Moorish smoking room by Louis Comfort Tiffany had walls lavishly inlaid with mother-of-pearl. A mahogany-paneled library featured large windows overlooking both Fifth Avenue and 57th Street, while the oak-trimmed banqueting hall held no windows at all, but was instead illuminated by a long, stained-glass skylight, electronically backlit at night. All of the first-floor rooms were

Grand Salon. (Courtesy of the New-York Historical Society)

centered on a three-story Caen stone-sheathed hall that boasted a curving staircase adapted from the principal staircase at the Chateau de Blois in the Loire Valley. This immense house required a live-in staff of over 30.

Vanderbilt suffered a severe stroke within two years of completion of the house. Society speculated that this illness was brought on by overwork, and, more importantly, by his eldest son Neily's defiant marriage to society beauty Grace Wilson. The daughter of prominent New York banker Richard T. Wilson, Grace was thought to be a little "fast" by Cornelius and Alice Vanderbilt because of her and her family's association with the elegant and fun-loving Prince of Wales set in England. This, combined with what the elder Vanderbilts felt to be an all-too-obvious Wilson campaign to snare one of their sons, made them withhold their approval of the match.

Neily, on the other hand, felt that he had already compromised Grace Wilson and was therefore duty-bound to marry her. A quiet ceremony eventually took place in the home of the bride's family with no Vanderbilts in attendance. Neily's father promptly disinherited him. Even though Cornelius and Alice were eventually proven right about the unsuitability of a social butterfly like Grace marrying a shy and introspective boy like Neily, the collective Vanderbilt family became the ultimate loser in this fracas. Neily was the only fourth-generation member of the family who had any dynastic feelings or genuine interest in the family's transportation empire. His departure from the New York Central marked the beginning of a long decline in the family fortune.

On the morning of September 12, 1899, Cornelius Vanderbilt II sat up in bed exclaiming, "I think I am dying!" and within five minutes, he

Ballroom. (Gary Lawrance)

expired from a cerebral hemorrhage. His widow went into deep mourning from which she never fully emerged, and the great Fifth Avenue house sat silent and shuttered except for infrequent small family gatherings. The ceremonial entrance gates remained locked, opened only for funerals. One son, Alfred, went down on the *Lusitania* in 1915, and another son, Reginald, drank himself to death 10 years later.

With yearly real estate taxes mounting to almost $130,000 by the early 1920s, Alice Vanderbilt decided to sell the property in 1925. Holding no illusions about the structure's survival, she knew that the developers had paid a hefty $7.1 million for the choice 200-by-125 foot site and not for the building that stood on it. Her home of over 40 years came down to make way for high-end retail establishments such as Bergdorf Goodman and Van Cleef & Arpels.

Feeling that the family's lofty position precluded her from living in an apartment house, Alice acquired the home of the late George J. Gould at 1 East 67th Street. Immediately following her 10-block move uptown, the 57th Street palace was opened for seven days to an eager citizenry. Thousands of awestruck visitors paid a small donation to the New York Association for the Improvement of the Conditions of the Poor to view the remnants of what was once the most exclusive house in the city.

In 1927, the house was demolished. A few items went to The Metropolitan Museum of Art, but most of the mansion's salvageable interiors were purchased by movie moguls to be used either as sets for forthcoming costume dramas or as smoking and ladies' rooms in the great motion picture palaces being constructed during the late 1920s. One set of gates, saved from the 58th Street ceremonial entrance, continues to grace Fifth Avenue as the entrance to the Central Park Conservatory Gardens at 104th Street.

Petit Salon. (Courtesy of the New-York Historical Society)

Dining Room. (Courtesy of the New-York Historical Society)

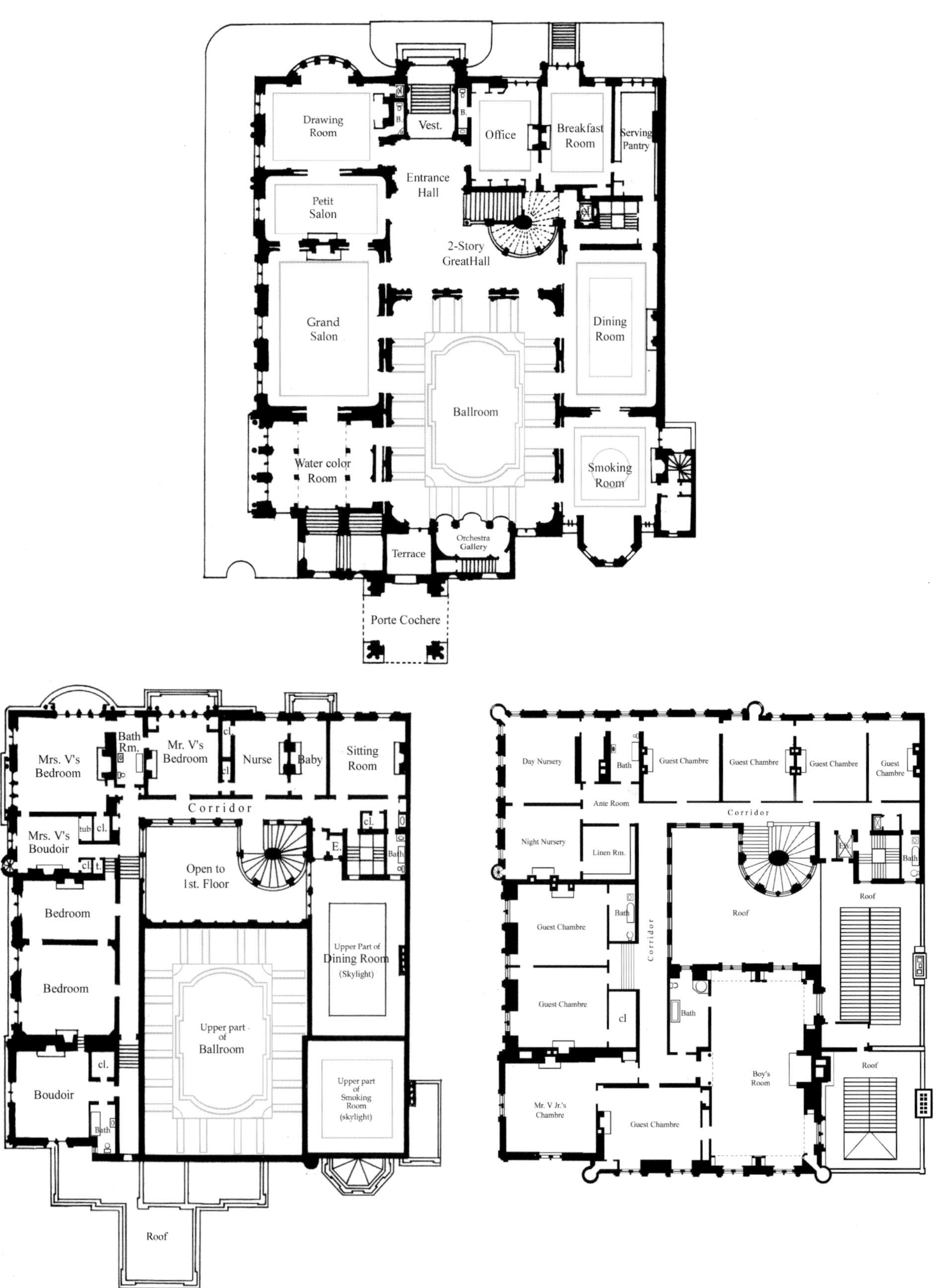

First, (top), Second, and Third Floor Plans. (Richard Marchand)

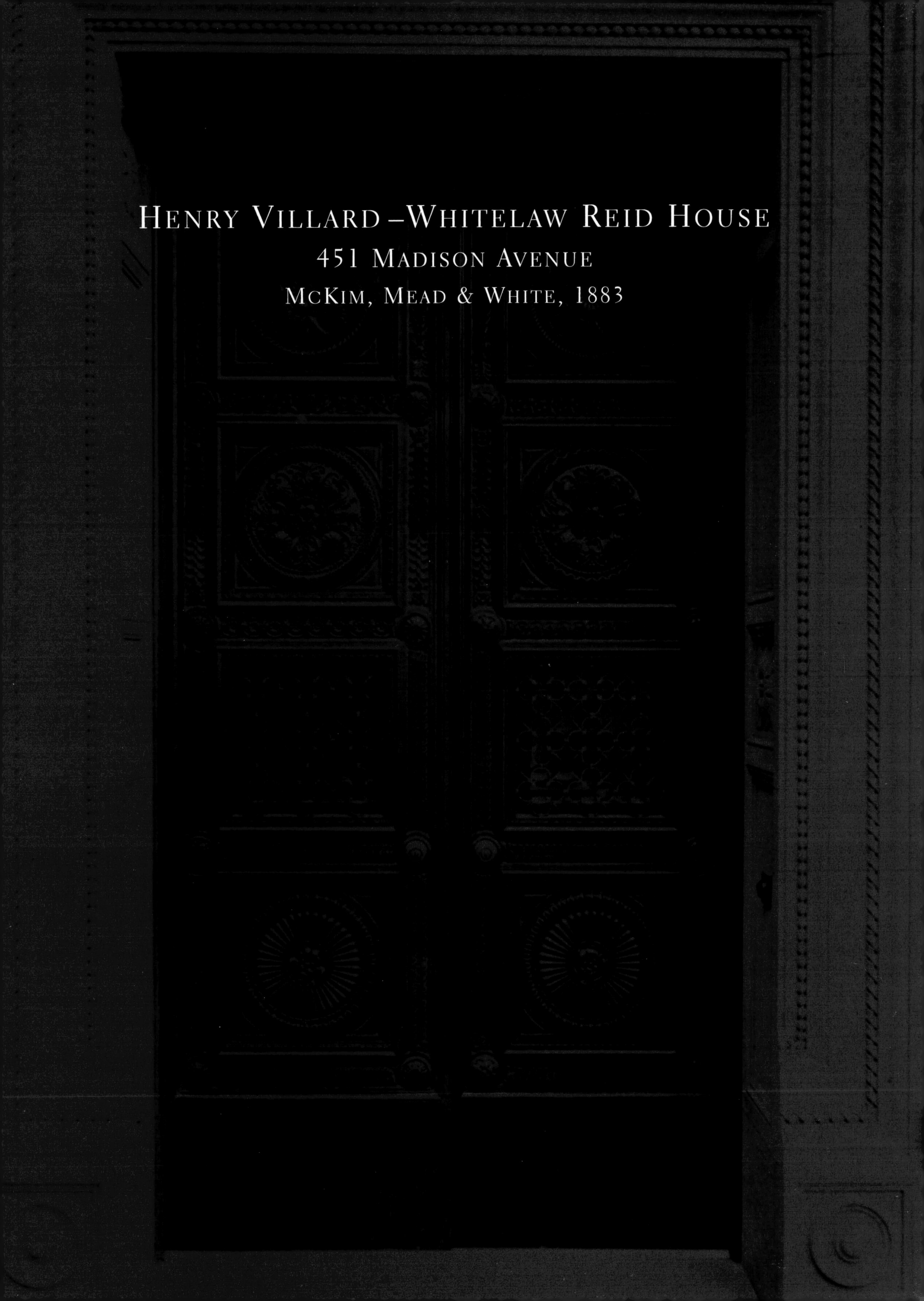

Henry Villard–Whitelaw Reid House

451 Madison Avenue

McKim, Mead & White, 1883

Henry Villard–Whitelaw Reid House

Facade. (Author's Collection)

In 1881, Bavarian-born railroad tycoon Henry Villard purchased the 200-foot block front on Madison Avenue directly behind St. Patrick's Cathedral between 50th and 51st streets. He then commissioned McKim, Mead & White to design a complex of six houses around a central courtyard. The then-fledgling firm received this high-profile project because Villard's brother-in-law was married to Mead's sister. The firm had previously remodeled and enlarged the house at Villard's estate, Thorwood, in Dobbs Ferry, New York.

Joseph Morrill Wells, a talented designer in the office of McKim, Mead & White, is considered responsible for the exterior of the Villard complex. The buildings were inspired by the Cancelleria and Farnese palaces, both in Rome. Villard and Wells became good friends during the design stage of the houses and disagreed only on the material to be used for the exterior finish: Wells wanted to use a more expensive limestone, while Villard favored the then more traditional brownstone, which is how the building was faced. Wells, who was highly regarded in the office, was also known for his clever wit. One day, while the designer-was eating lunch, Stanford White burst into his office, waving a drawing in front of his face and

TOWER ADDITION. (Courtesy of the Museum of the City of New York)

saying, "Look at that! In its way, this is as good as the Parthenon." Wells dryly replied, "Yes, and so too, in its way, is a boiled egg."

Under almost any criteria, the Villard houses are masterpieces of refined interpretation. It may have been these buildings that prompted Le Corbusier to say that he preferred the Renaissance as interpreted in New York to the originals in Florence. Although the complex was designed as a group of large houses, the interior emphasis was always focused on Villard's own house in the southern wing. The lavish interiors that Stanford White designed for this house made his reputation. Italian yellow Siena marble, with a warmth and fire totally

DRAWING OF WEST ELEVATION. (Author's Collection)

ENTRANCE DOORS. (Author's Collection)

VESTIBULE. (Author's Collection)

unexpected in stone, sheaths the entrance hall and the grand staircase. The dining room, with its carved frieze, fine wood paneling, and Augustus Saint-Gaudens–designed fireplace wall, created a rich, invigorating environment that became typical of the high caliber of work generated by White.

Due to financial setbacks, Villard was forced to move out of his luxurious hotel suite and into the incomplete mansion in 1883. Early in 1886, he sold the still-unfinished house to Elizabeth Mills Reid for $350,000. Reid was the wife of *New York Tribune* editor and publisher Whitelaw Reid, who had received the newspaper as a wedding present from his father-in-law, Darius Ogden Mills, the California banker and financier.

The Reids, who took possession of the house at the end of the year, immediately hired Stanford White to complete the interiors. In addition, they commissioned John La Farge to paint two large lunette pictures representing music and drama at opposite ends of the music room. La Farge began painting these to coordinate with the decoration being applied to the room's large barrel-vaulted ceiling. Unfortunately, just as La Farge was completing his work, White decided to change the color scheme from blue to gold, thereby requiring the painter to redo the colors on his almost-finished work.

In 1905, Whitelaw Reid was appointed United States ambassador to England, a post he held until his death. Even though the Reids began spending the greater part of each year in London, it was decided in 1910 that more space was needed in the Manhattan house. McKim, Mead & White was called in and they erected a tower extension on the

ENTRANCE HALL. (Courtesy of the New-York Historical Society)

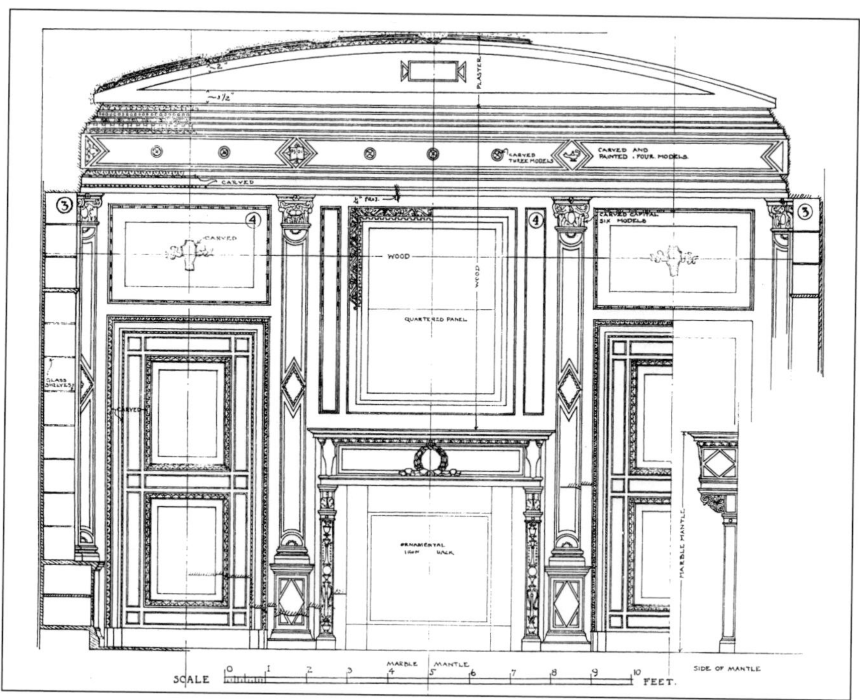

DRAWING OF FIREPLACE WALL IN MR. REID'S STUDY. (Author's Collection)

Dining Room Mantel. (Courtesy of the New-York Historical Society)

DINING ROOM. (Courtesy of the New-York Historical Society)

MUSIC ROOM. (Author's Collection)

PANTRY. (Courtesy of the New-York Historical Society)

eastern end of the building. This expansion added service rooms in the basement and extended the first-floor dining room by 20 feet. On the second floor, Ambassador Reid acquired a new paneled study next to his library. These improvements might have been prompted by an expected New York visit of the Duke of Connaught, the third son of Queen Victoria, who was then governor-general of Canada. He and his party were sumptuously entertained at 451 Madison Avenue in January 1912. Later that year, Whitelaw Reid died while attending to official duties in London.

Elizabeth Reid continued to live in the Madison Avenue residence and, after a suitable mourning period, proceeded with her grand scale of entertaining. The last large party to be held in the house was a ball given in 1919 to honor Edward Albert, Prince of Wales. The prince had dined earlier with the Cornelius Vanderbilts and arrived at 451 at 10:30 P.M. His hostess and her daughter, Lady Ward, greeted him in the drawing room. Two orchestras were on hand to entertain the prince and the cream of New York and international society.

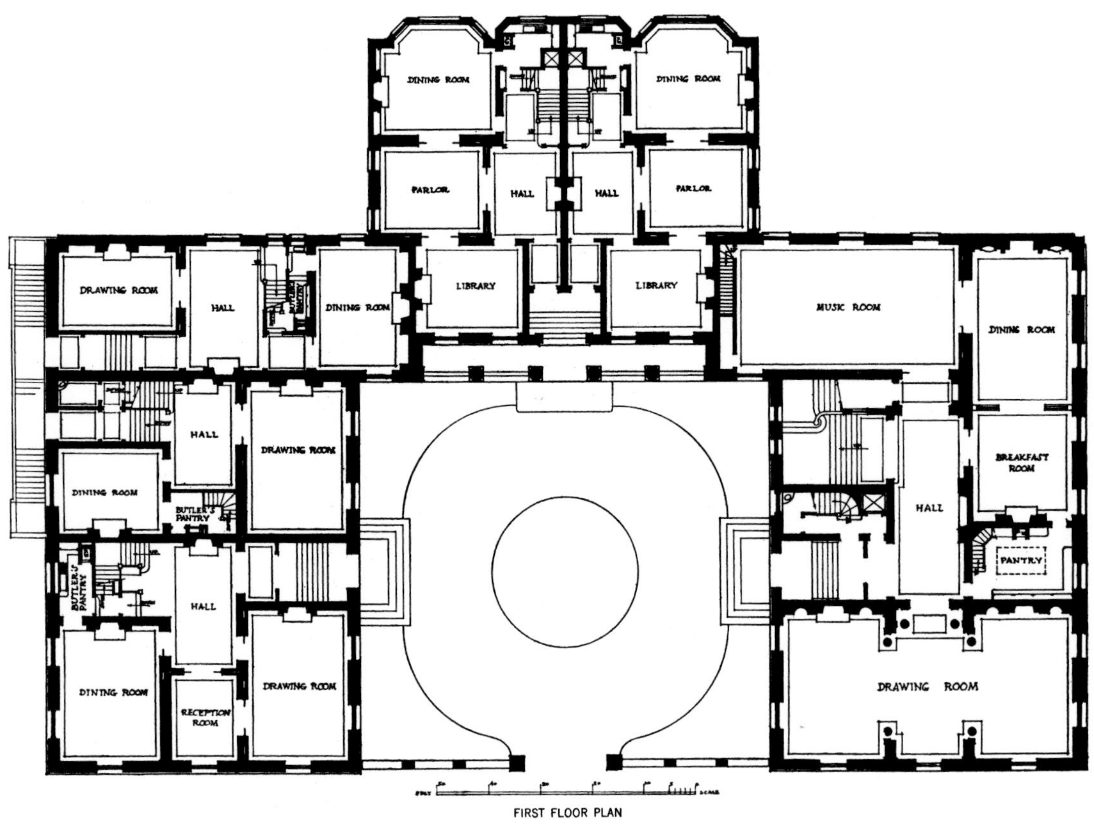

First Floor Plan. (Author's Collection)

Although living another 11 years, Elizabeth Reid spent most of that time at her 1,000-acre Westchester estate, Ophir Hall, while the New York house remained shuttered. After her death, the furnishings were auctioned in May 1935, ending the private residential life of the 50-year-old house. The building served different organizations during the World War II and was later purchased by the Archdiocese of New York. In 1974, Harry Helmsley began a hotel development scheme that maintained most of the original exterior of the Villard complex and all of the important interior spaces of the Villlard-Reid house. Today, the house, minus the 1910 addition, is part of the New York Palace Hotel.

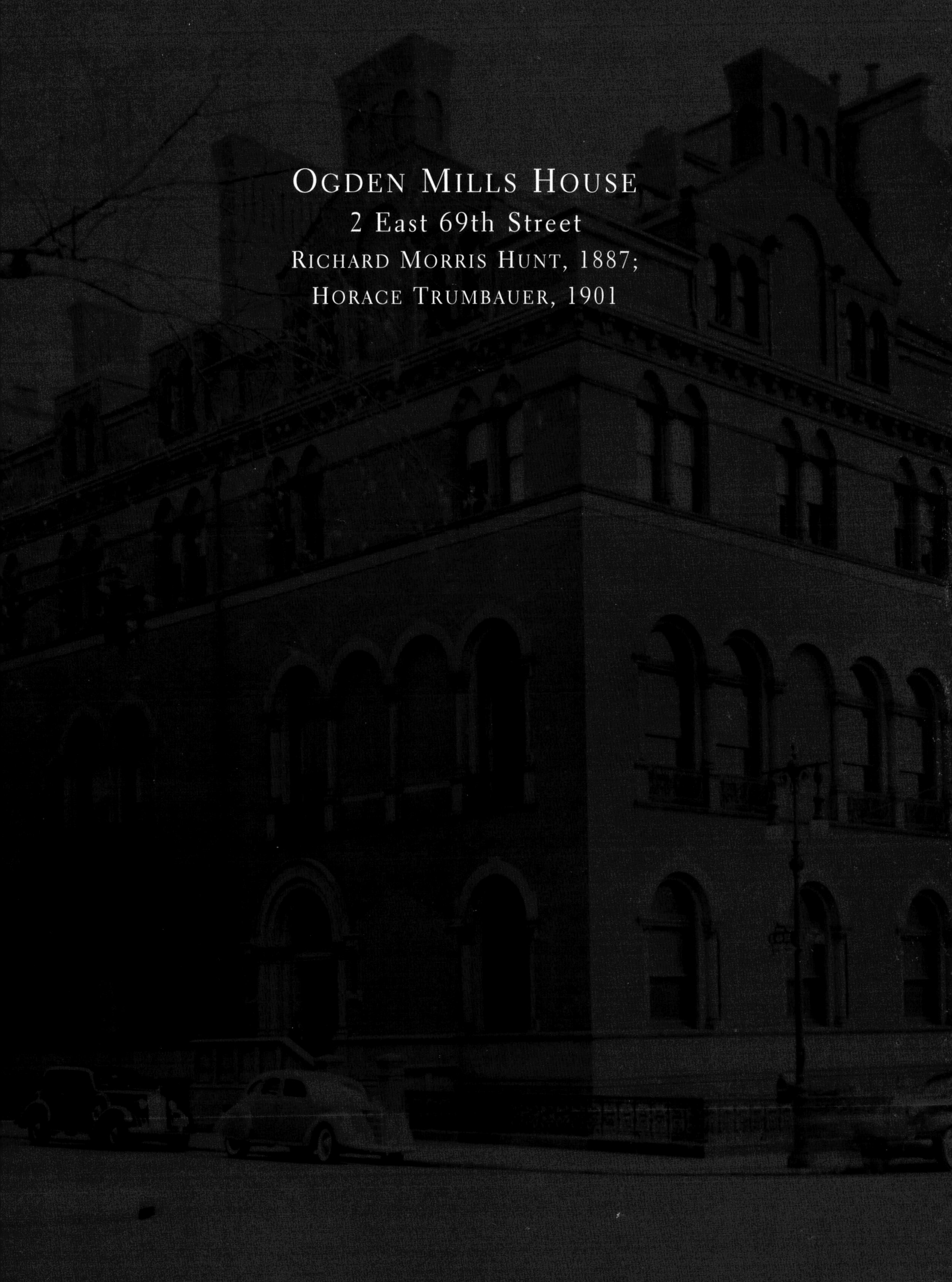

Ogden Mills House

2 East 69th Street

Richard Morris Hunt, 1887;
Horace Trumbauer, 1901

OGDEN MILLS HOUSE

EXTERIOR, C. 1930. (Courtesy of the New York Historical Society)

IF THERE IS SUCH A THING as an American aristocratic hierarchy, then the Livingston family would be found somewhere near the top of it. The founder of the dynasty, Scottish immigrant Robert Livingston, first arrived on this side of the Atlantic in 1674. Within a short period, this merchant became powerful enough to establish himself as the first lord of Livingston Manor. With succeeding generations, this Hudson River estate grew to encompass over 1 million acres, while the family continued to produce an unending stream of illustrious statesmen and merchants. Robert Livingston, the founder's great-grandson, helped write the Declaration of Independence and administered the presidential oath of office to George Washington. With all this good fortune and favorable notoriety, the Livingstons had come to hold a very high opinion of themselves and their position in

BALLROOM. (Author's Collection)

American society. So it was not surprising that the family looked askance when 100 years later, one of Robert's descendants, Ruth Livingston, married out of her social milieu.

The unworthy bridegroom was Ogden Mills, son of the enormously wealthy Darius Ogden Mills. It seems that most of the Livingstons, while fully appreciating the importance of the Mills' millions, felt that the fortune was too new and unrefined for their tastes. The elder Mills was born in 1825 to a poor, upstate New York family. As a young man he moved to Buffalo, where a relative found him a job in a local bank. Although successful, becoming chief teller within just a few years, Mills decided to go out west to make his fortune during the California Gold Rush. This fastidious "forty-niner" did not see himself working in the mines, but rather as a banker and adviser to those lucky few who did strike it rich. Eventually, he became head of the Bank of California in San Francisco and thus dominated the West Coast's most important source of money. His riches multiplied when he wisely invested his early profits in railroads and timberland.

Through all this, Mills remained an Easterner at heart. In 1880, he moved himself and his family to New York City, basing his financial empire there. Within two years, son Ogden met and married the very correct Miss Ruth Livingston. With her

GRAY SALON. (Author's Collection)

GREEN SALON. (Author's Collection)

Drawing Room. (Author's Collection)

pedigree and the Mills fortune to back her, Ruth elevated her husband's family into proper society by becoming one of the most elegant and stately hostesses of her time. To advance her campaign, she commissioned Richard Morris Hunt to design a new house on the southeast corner of Fifth Avenue and 69th Street. The Millses moved into their Venetian Gothic mansion in 1887. Ruth entertained lavishly, and it was said that she could accommodate 100 guests for dinner without calling in extra help. Her ceremonious entertainments were always chillingly correct and attended by only the very best people. However, Mrs. Mills generally had a difficult time keeping a large following, always essential to any hostess, because she had reduced society in her own mind to a mere 20 families. She was ultimately defeated by her own exclusiveness in her bid to reign over New York.

In 1901, the Millses hired Horace Trumbauer to enlarge 2 East 69th Street because Ruth's widowed mother, Mrs. Maturin Livingston, was coming to live with them. While Trumbauer respected Hunt's rather austere Gothic exterior and matched its fenestration in his extension, most of the original interiors were redecorated into a more accurate version of French 18th-century classicism. Antique boiseries, carved marble mantelpieces, and masterpieces of cabinetmaking were imported from

STUDY. (Author's Collection)

France to accomplish this. The house, when completed, became one of the most refined in the city.

Ruth Mills died in 1920 follow by her husband nine years later. Their son, Ogden Livingston Mills, then moved in to 2 East 69th Street. Carrying on in the Livingston family tradition of public service, he had become a successful politician and was eventually appointed Secretary of the Treasury during the Hoover Administration. Soon after his death, Parke-Bernet held a three-day auction of the home's contents, beginning on March 31, 1938. The house was demolished soon after, and with it, the last vestiges of Ruth Livingston Mills' bid for social supremacy in New York City.

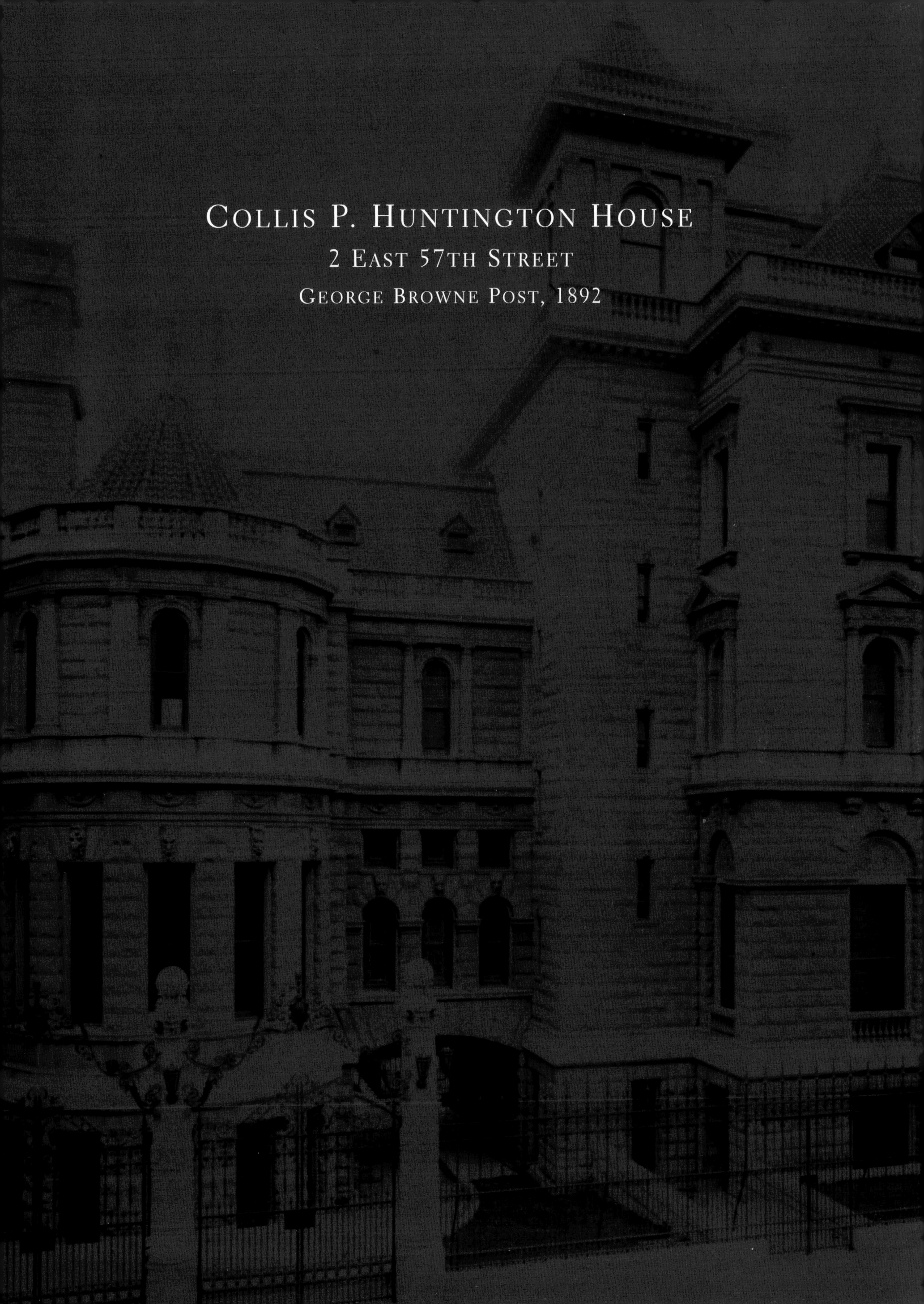

Collis P. Huntington House

2 East 57th Street

George Browne Post, 1892

Collis P. Huntington House

Exterior. (Courtesy of the New-York Historical Society)

Collis P. Huntington was born in New England but decided as a young man to head west to make his fortune. Moving to California during the peak gold rush year of 1849, the newly minted entrepreneur opened a hardware store. Five years later, he entered into a lucrative partnership with fellow merchant Mark Hopkins. In 1861, Huntington and the other California "Big Four"—Hopkins, Leland Stanford, and Charles Crocker—incorporated the Central Pacific Railroad, which, for the first time, brought direct rail service from the East Coast. This feat was instrumental in the development of the country west of the Mississippi, and all four investors subsequently reaped substantial profits from the endeavor. Huntington, who was considered the strongest of the group, later branched off into shipbuilding and finance.

GREAT HALL. (Courtesy of the New-York Historical Society)

As with many transplanted easterners, Huntington moved his headquarters to New York. By 1867, he and his wife Elizabeth had established themselves in a house at 38th Street and Park Avenue. Four years later, Collis took the comely young Arabella Yarrington Worsham as his mistress and established her in a luxurious town house on East 54th Street. Elizabeth Huntington died of cancer in 1883, conveniently leaving the way open for Arabella and her benefactor to marry. After the nuptials, the couple temporarily moved into 65 Park Avenue while the bride looked for a suitable site for a new Fifth Avenue mansion.

The purchase of six adjoining lots on the southeast corner of Fifth Avenue and 57th Street completed Arabella's quest in 1889. They were all bought from the estate of Robert Bonner, the late editor of the *New York Ledger*. Since the site was catercorner from the Cornelius Vanderbilt II house designed by George Browne Post, this could have been the reason the Huntingtons decided to hire Post to draw up plans for their new home. The architect's initial proposal was rejected on the grounds that it was too large. Then Arabella approached Richard Morris Hunt, who declined to accept the commission, stating that the Huntingtons had already compromised themselves with another architect. The honorable Hunt suggested that they give Post another chance, and several proposals later, his plans were finally accepted.

SALON. (Courtesy of the New-York Historical Society)

Construction began toward the end of 1889 and was completed a little over two years later. In looking at photographs of the building, it was indeed unfortunate that Hunt did not have a hand in it. Post tried to impose classical manners on a Richardsonian Romanesque revival mass, with the end result being that it looked more like what writer James Maher called "a wayward railroad station" rather than an upper-class residence. *The Dictionary of American Biography* stated that Post was "interested primarily in the engineering side of architecture and had much more success with commercial and civic buildings." His houses tended to be ponderous and lacking a definitive style.

The rough stone building had a wide set of stairs that led up to the 57th Street entrance. The base of this staircase ran between two unattached decorative columns that were distinctly reminiscent of the pair found in front of Hunt's William K. Vanderbilt house. At the eastern end of the building, twin carriage gates led to an entrance beneath the house. A tall wrought-iron fence protected both street frontages.

Post designed the interiors, often just as heavy in appearance as the exterior, with the help of the decorating firms of Herter Brothers and Wm. Baumgarten & Co. The plan of the structure was centered on a three-story great hall that featured a beautiful frieze carved by Austrian sculptor Karl

Dining Room. (Courtesy of the New-York Historical Society)

Bitter. The Huntington collection of 18th- and 19th-century paintings hung on the lower walls of this immense space. A French Régence salon, an Italian Renaissance reception room, and a Byzantine dining room adjoined the hall. The library, in a separate wing, had a large Carrara marble fireplace with a shelf supported by carved male figures. The second floor functioned as the private domain of Mr. and Mrs. Huntington and the floor above was devoted to seldom-used guest accommodations.

Collis Huntington died in 1900, leaving a large part of his estate, including the Fifth Avenue mansion, to his widow. With this vast inheritance at her disposal, Arabella soon began acquiring paintings and works of art that were substantially better, and far more expensive, than those she had collected with her late husband. For assistance, she had the guiding hand of the famous art dealer Joseph Duveen. Her walls were soon filled with an impressive collection of pictures by artists like Corot, Gainsborough, Hals, Rembrandt, Reynolds, Romney, Velázquez, and Vermeer. Arabella became so enraptured with 18th-century French culture and art that she purchased an enormous Parisian *hôtel particulier* at No. 2 rue de l'Elysée and filled it with fine examples of French 18th-century artistry.

In 1913, after a dozen years of widowhood, she surprised everyone by marrying her late husband's nephew, Henry E. Huntington. Since he had also inherited a large chunk of Collis' empire, this marriage reunited the fortune. The younger Huntington built his famous house and library in San Marino, California, to entice Arabella to move out west. Although she did manage to make a few trips there, primarily to inspect the construction of the house, Arabella preferred to spend most of her time in New York and Paris. During one of her last trips abroad, she went to see the art dealer Germain Seligman at his gallery:

> She had just dropped in to say hello, she said, as she was no longer in a buying mood and had everything she wanted to own. She was in her seventies by then, but still carried her unusual height with a splendid bearing. . . . I showed her a number of objects of a type that I knew she enjoyed, among them a delightful little marble Venus by Falconet. Looking at me somewhat reproachfully through thick-lensed glasses, she said, "You really shouldn't go to so much trouble for me. You know my sight has become so bad that I can hardly see anything." Whereupon she leaned forward for a closer view of the little figure, not over a foot high overall, and exclaimed, "What a lovely thing. Isn't it a shame that the little finger of the left hand is broken!" I couldn't help bursting into laughter as I congratulated her upon her bad eyesight, for the whole hand was certainly not over half an inch long. Almost before I did, she threw her head back in a hearty laugh.

The 77-year-old Arabella Huntington died at her New York home on September 14, 1924. Three years later, 2 East 57th Street was demolished, and the jewelers Tiffany & Co. eventually occupied the site.

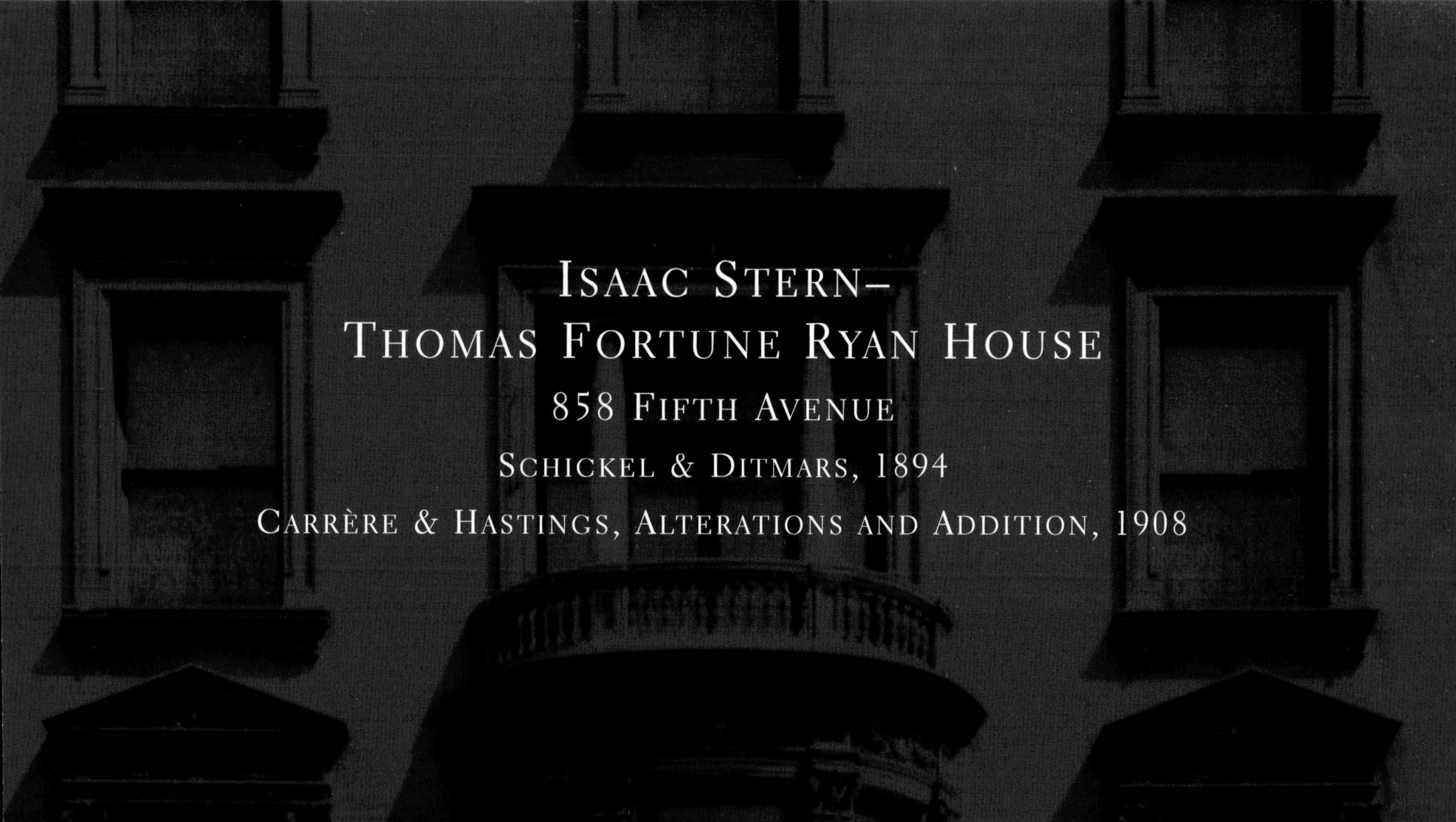

Isaac Stern–Thomas Fortune Ryan House

858 Fifth Avenue

Schickel & Ditmars, 1894

Carrère & Hastings, Alterations and Addition, 1908

Isaac Stern–Thomas Fortune Ryan House

Exterior. (Courtesy of the Museum of the City of New York)

In 1816, Isaac Stern and his German-born family immigrated to Albany, New York, where his parents opened a small jewelry store. While still in his teens, Isaac's older brother Louis was sent to West Virginia to learn merchandising in an uncle's shop. On returning, he suggested to Isaac that they jointly should open a dry-goods store in New York City. Soon the brothers were the proprietors of a small shop at 22nd Street and Sixth Avenue. By 1878, the brothers moved to a large building on 23rd Street, between Fifth and Sixth avenues, where the firm continued to prosper. Following commerce's uptown migration, the Sterns hired Snook Brothers in 1913 to design a giant structure on West 42nd Street, opposite Bryant Park and the New York Public Library. This store was one of the principal reasons for the commercial success of this major cross-town thoroughfare.

STAIRCASE. (Courtesy of the New-York Historical Society)

In 1893 Isaac called in the architects Schickel & Ditmar, who had designed his brother's Gothic revival mansion located at 993 Fifth Avenue seven years earlier, to design a house for the Fifth Avenue lot between 67th and 68th streets that he had recently purchased. The limestone-finished early Renaissance–styled house at 858 Fifth Avenue was completed the following year. The rusticated first floor had a set of double windows on either side of an arched entrance portal. On the second floor, between two pedimented windows, a large, curved oriel window supported a small balustraded terrace above. On the fifth floor, the most elaborate exterior decoration appeared as a carved frieze with floral swags and oval windows surrounded by molded wreaths. Over this, a bracketed and dentiled cornice was surmounted by a stone balustrade.

Wrought-iron entrance doors led to an eclectic mixture of first-floor rooms designed in European styles from the 16th through the 18th centuries. On either side of the center hall, reception rooms were finished in Louis XV style. The banquet-size dining room at the rear, decorated in the style of Louis XIV, had oak paneling with decorative details picked out in gold. On the ceiling was a painting by Gabriel Ferrier, a noted Parisian artist of the period. Up a flight of curved marble steps, a Francis I library ran the entire width of the house. The walls

RECEPTION ROOM. (Courtesy of the New-York Historical Society)

here were hung with red and green silk damask, and the decorative plaster ceiling was divided into sections by carved beams. A white and gold Louis XV ballroom filled the rear of this level. Mr. and Mrs. Stern's private suite occupied the third floor; it included a domed den for Mr. Stern, and a boudoir for Mrs. Stern painted and draped in an Edwardian floral fantasy.

Several years after moving into the new mansion, Mrs. Stern died, and Isaac Stern moved to a suite at the St. Regis Hotel. In 1905, he sold 858 Fifth Avenue to traction magnate Thomas Fortune Ryan, who hired Carrère & Hastings to renovate the 11-year-old house. The largest structural change was the gutting of the ballroom, replacing it with an art gallery to house Ryan's acclaimed collection of Renaissance art. In fact, the burgeoning Ryan collection necessitated an additional gallery that wrapped around the rear of the house and stretched to the 67th Street frontage just east of the George Gould house. Because of the importance of Ryan's collection, the house soon became known as an American Louvre. Experts felt the art housed there was in many ways superior to that in the Morgan and Frick collections, and Ryan's Limoges enamels were the finest in the world. One of the most important pieces in the collection was the 1475 bust of Beatrice of Aragon by Francesco Laurana.

A chapel with a four-ton altar from a 15th-century Italian palazzo was installed adjacent to Mrs. Ryan's suite. The devout mistress of the house convinced her husband to donate $1 million to construct the church of St. Jean Baptiste at Lexington Avenue and 76th Street. Ultimately, $20 million of the almost $200 million Ryan fortune went to the Catholic Church, and Mrs. Ryan was made a countess of the Holy Roman Empire by a grateful Pope Pius X.

SALON. (Courtesy of the New-York Historical Society)

DINING ROOM. (Courtesy of the New-York Historical Society)

RYAN GALLERY ADDITION. (Collection of the American Academy of Arts and Letters)

RYAN GARDEN. (Collection of the American Academy of Arts and Letters)

Mr. Ryan, who enjoyed gardening almost as much as making money, had created a small flower-filled spot behind his new house. This space did not satisfy his gardening ambitions, so he purchased the empty Charles Yerkes mansion addition to the north for $1,239,000 and had it razed to make way for the more spacious Eden he envisioned. The only items he retained from the Yerkes mansion were an antique Venetian staircase and 32 marble columns upon which his roses and vines could climb. Ryan often would be seen happily puttering around his garden wearing an old Chinese robe and carpet slippers with a floppy straw hat perched on his head.

VENETIAN STAIRCASE.
(Collection of the American Academy of Arts and Letters)

In 1908, when the additions and alterations were completed, Ryan announced that he would be

RYAN GALLERY. (Courtesy of the New-York Historical Society)

retiring from business so he could enjoy his remaining years in privacy. He purchased a 4,000-acre farm in Lovingston, Virginia, his hometown. The highly touted retirement never occurred, though, because he could not keep from acquiring additional railroads and public utilities, and Ryan trusted no one else to run them. Around 1910, King Leopold II of Belgium appointed him as the head of a syndicate to exploit the diamond, copper, and gold resources of the Congo. The millions kept pouring in.

Twelve days after Mrs. Ryan's death in 1917, the 66-year-old widower shocked his family and business associates by marrying the twice-divorced Mrs. Mary Townsend Cuyler. Although the new bride came of excellent family, Ryan's children were understandably put off by the haste of the union. His eldest son, Allen, said it was "one of the most disrespectful, disgraceful, and indecent things I've ever heard of." This unguarded remark cost him a large inheritance, for after his father's death in 1928, the will revealed that Allen was left nothing except two pearl shirt studs. Ryan's youngest son, Clendenin, who had not been so openly judgmental, received many millions plus the Fifth Avenue mansion. He inhabited the house until 1939, when he stuck his head in one of the many gas fireplaces and killed himself. Clendenin was typical of many unlucky inheritors who were crushed by the accompanying burdens of great wealth. After his death, 858 Fifth Avenue was torn down to make way for an apartment tower.

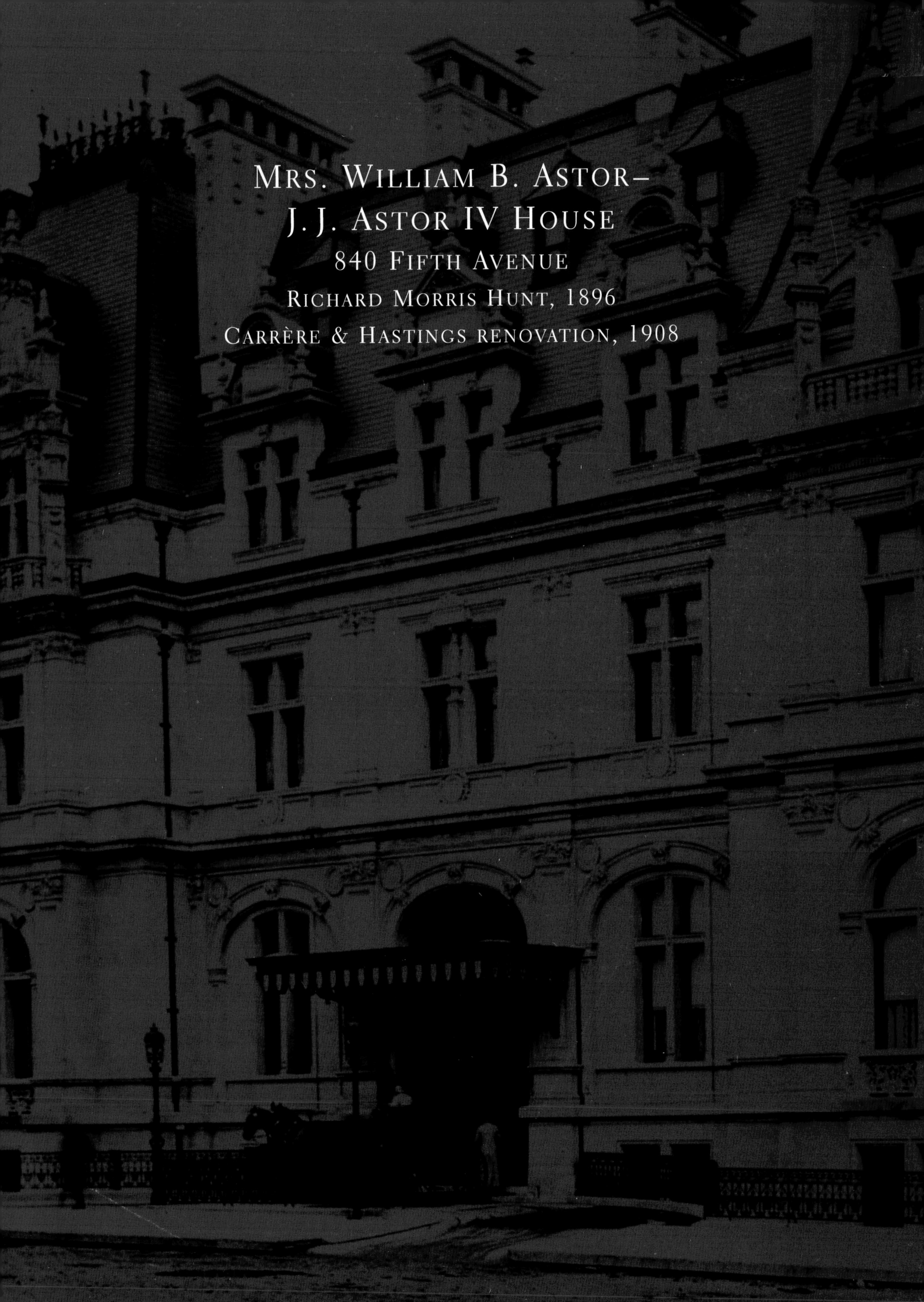

Mrs. William B. Astor–J. J. Astor IV House

840 Fifth Avenue

Richard Morris Hunt, 1896

Carrère & Hastings renovation, 1908

Mrs. William B. Astor–J. J. Astor IV House

EXTERIOR. (Byron Collection, courtesy of the Museum of the City of New York)

MRS. WILLIAM B. ASTOR'S move uptown to 65th Street was directly related to a feud with her new nephew, William Waldorf Astor. Their disagreement began at the death of Waldorf's father, John Jacob Astor III, who had occupied the house next door to Mrs. Astor at the corner of Fifth Avenue and 33rd Street. Waldorf, as he was known, being the eldest son of the eldest son, naturally thought that his wife should be the reigning Mrs. Astor and queen of the "400." Caroline Astor, who had been ruling New York society for more than two decades, did not agree and refused to retire into social oblivion. In 1892, Waldorf, in a fit of pique, tore down his father's house and built the Hotel Waldorf on the site. He believed that the traffic and noise generated by this new establishment would soon drive his aunt out of her own home. Then Waldorf, declaring "that America was no fit place for a gentleman to live," moved permanently to England.

GREAT HALL, C. 1910. (Avery Library, Columbia University)

To escape the neighboring hubbub, Caroline surveyed the family's extensive real estate portfolio in search of a suitable Fifth Avenue location for her next mansion. Originally she considered a 55th Street site but found it uncomfortably close to commercial development. Caroline settled on a choice 100-by-100-foot plot on the northeast corner of 65th Street overlooking Central Park. She then commissioned Richard Morris Hunt, who had created mansions for the Vanderbilts, to design a double house: the northern half was for herself, and the 65th Street side was for her son, John Jacob Astor IV, and his family. A giant ballroom, extending across the rear of both houses, was to be shared.

Immediately after moving into the new house, she had the 34th Street house torn down and replaced by a hotel that would merge with her nephew's to create the original Waldorf-Astoria Hotel. Family feuds are one thing, but business, after all, is business.

Born Caroline Webster Schermerhorn, Mrs. Astor started her social campaign in 1871 when she began planning to bring out her four daughters and did not want them to meet the wrong sort of suitors. She complained, "People seem to be going quite wild and inviting all sorts of people to their receptions. I don't know what has happened to our taste." To protect her daughters, Mrs. Astor set out to discipline New York society, and with the help of her majordomo, Ward McAllister, she created the

Ballroom. (Author's Collection)

Patriarchs' Ball. McAllister organized a ball committee of 25 patriarchs who had the right to invite five gentlemen and four ladies—all to be preapproved by Mrs. Astor. Because they were small and select, the balls were an instant success.

McAllister was once asked how many people made up society. He replied, "Why, there are only about 400 people in fashionable New York society. If you go outside that number, you strike people who are either not at ease in a ballroom or else make other people not at ease." Was it merely a coincidence that 400 was the exact number that Mrs. Astor could comfortably hold in her ballroom at the 34th Street house? She accommodated considerably more at 840 Fifth Avenue.

At 840, Richard Morris Hunt designed a French Renaissance chateau, which stylistically dated from the time of Henri II in the middle of the 16th century. It was a synthesis of elements Hunt freely adapted from several Loire Valley chateaux, including Azay-le-Rideau, Amboise, and Serrant, yet it was distilled through the regularizing effect of the Italian classical manner found in the later Renaissance. There were no vestiges of the Gothic as found in Hunt's earlier Renaissance revival town house work in the city, and it showed none of the asymmetrical inventiveness of the William K. Vanderbilt house of 1882 and the Elbridge T. Gerry residence of 1894.

The balanced tripartite Fifth Avenue elevation of 840 was sheathed in Indiana limestone. Three stories ascended from a raised basement, and a fourth floor was located in its high mansard, copper-crested roof, which was enlivened with carved and

DINING ROOM, C. 1910 (Avery Library, Columbia University)

molded dormer windows. The large stone-mullioned divided windows were a further exploration of themes Hunt used on the Lenox Library of 1877, located on Fifth Avenue just five blocks north of the Astor site. The facade was divided at each level by entablatures and sill-level stringcourses, while the linear mass was divided by pilasters capped by composite capitals. On the 65th Street elevation the corner pavilion was still paramount, but it was balanced a by a tripartite rear extension. Overall, it was a solid and well-articulated design that, although handsome, was somewhat ponderous in its effect.

The interiors were designed by Jules Allard et fils and were typical of the lavish rooms of the 1890s. They were predominataly sheathed in boiserie inspired from the French 17th and 18th centuries.

DINING ROOM DETAIL, C.1910.
(Collection of the American Academy of Arts and Letters)

John Jacob Astor IV Salon. (Avery Library, Columbia University)

Mrs. Astor took possession of her new house in January 1896 after three years of construction. She welcomed society just two weeks later with a gala ball, her first since the death of her husband in 1892. "Life could have no more bitter mortification," wrote Elizabeth Drexel Lehr, "than not to receive the slip of cardboard; 'Mrs. Astor requests the pleasure'; there remained only one course open to them: to hide the shameful truth from their friends. Doctors were kept busy during the week of the ball, recommending hurried trips to the Adirondacks for the health of perfectly healthy patients, maiden aunts and grandmothers living in remote towns were ruthlessly killed off to provide alibis for their relations . . . any and every excuse was resorted to." The palace had changed, but Queen Caroline continued to rule.

In the reception room, arriving guests were greeted by their hostess standing in front of her imperious, full-length portrait by Carolus-Duran; they then moved into the gold-and-white ballroom, the walls of which were covered with the Astor art collection. These balls were stately affairs with Caroline ensconced on her throne-like banquette, surveying the elect. There was always fierce competition involving who would sit with her on this banquette, as it was considered a badge of distinction to be chosen. After a Lucullan midnight supper, the 600 guests were invited to dance until dawn.

In January 1905, Caroline Astor gave her last ball. At the end of the year, she suffered a severe stroke that compelled her to give up public life entirely. There were rumors that she spent her final years wandering through her grand gilded reception

John Jacob Astor IV Library. (Avery Library, Columbia University)

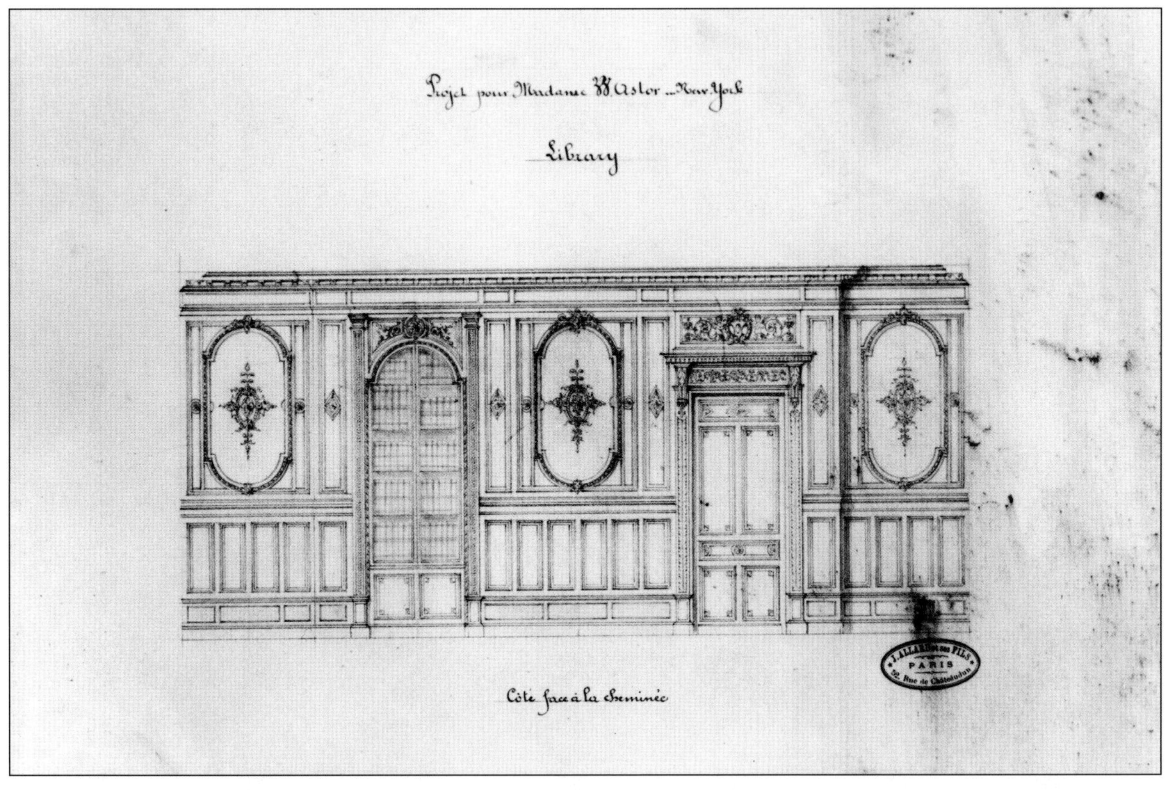

Allard Drawing of Library for Mrs. Astor. (Avery Library, Columbia University)

Mrs. Astor's staircase. (Author's Collection)

MRS. ASTOR'S SALON. (Avery Library, Columbia University)

rooms greeting imaginary guests of the highest social distinction. Mrs. Astor died in 1908.

After his mother's death, Colonel Jack Astor hired Carrère & Hastings to convert the double house into a single residence. This was accomplished by eliminating the two center halls with their monumental staircases and replacing them with a bronze-and-glass-roofed central court finished in Caen stone. A smaller and less conspicuous staircase in the rear of the house substituted for the originals. The new dining room had polychrome marble walls and a carved wooden ceiling. In 1910, Colonel Astor hosted a dinner-dance for 250 people to inaugurate the mansion's new interiors.

Along with the alterations to his house, Astor rearranged his private life. He divorced the beautiful, but cold, Ava Willing Astor and married Madeleine Force, the granddaughter of a former mayor of Brooklyn. Society was shocked to learn that the new 18-year-old bride was a year younger than Astor's only son, Vincent, and they found Madeleine a poor replacement for the elegant Ava. The newlyweds decamped to Europe to let the scandal subside.

Wishing to return to the United States in April 1912, Astor booked passage for himself, Madeleine, a maid, and a manservant on the maiden voyage of the luxurious White Star Liner *Titanic*. When the ship sank, Astor was among the over 1,500 people who died. Madeleine, who was then pregnant with John Jacob Astor V, survived.

Jack Astor's will revealed that, except for a $3 million trust for the unborn baby and a $5 million trust for his daughter, Alice, the bulk of Astor's estate, some $87 million went to his son, Vincent. Madeleine, who had previously waived her dower rights for a cash settlement of $1,695,000, also received the income from a $5 million trust and the use of the Fifth Avenue and Newport houses as long as she did not remarry. This arrangement lasted until 1919, when, at the age of 26, Madeleine married stockbroker William Dick, thereby forfeiting her benefits. Both the houses and the trust reverted to her stepson.

After Madeleine's departure, Vincent and his first wife, Helen Huntington Astor, felt duty-bound to live in the family mansion and give a major ball every January in remembrance of grandmother Caroline. Prince Serge Obolensky, who married Alice Astor in 1925, said that the house was "the most imposing mansion in New York if not the New World. Facing the great hall, we passed through huge bronze gates, and came into a reception room whose walls were paneled with canvases patterned after Brussels cartoons. Facing the entrance was a big sculptured fireplace. Beyond it lay the ballroom which was also the art gallery . . . statues were everywhere. The marble stairs and the enormous, heavily gilded drawing room created an impression of almost overpowering solidity and permanence."

Vincent sold the house in 1925 for $3.5 million and moved to a much smaller one on East 80th Street designed by Mott B. Schmidt. As a tribute, he had his father's bedroom and bath reinstalled there. Eight hundred forty Fifth Avenue—the social mecca for two generations of New York society—was eventually demolished to make way for Temple Emanu-El.

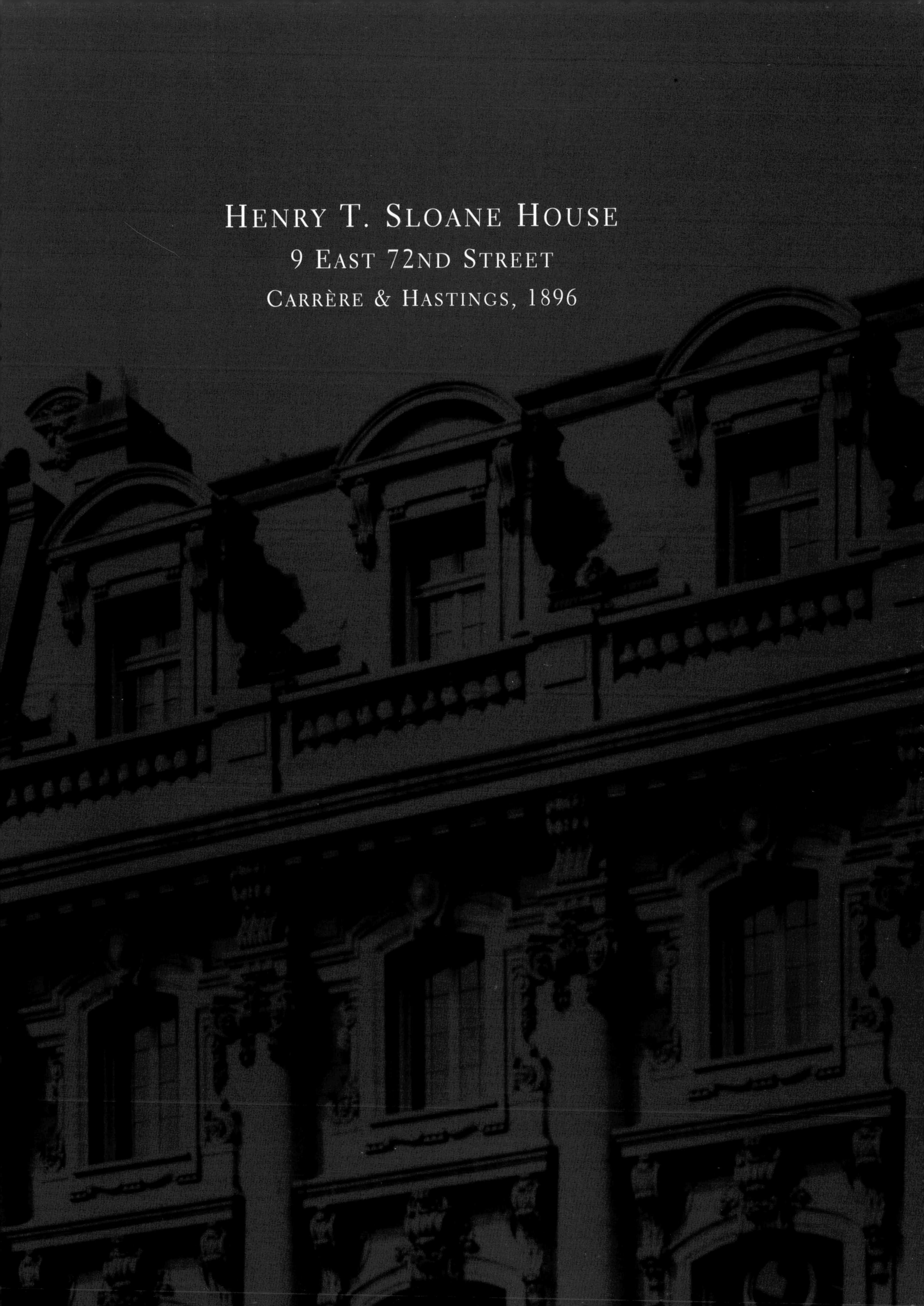

Henry T. Sloane House

9 East 72nd Street

Carrère & Hastings, 1896

HENRY T. SLOANE HOUSE

ELEVATION. (Author's Collection)

THIS FRENCH-INSPIRED TOWN HOUSE was Carrère & Hastings' third major residential commission in the city. Henry Sloane, who commissioned the house, was a son of one of the founders of W. & J. Sloane, the fine furniture and carpet emporium. After graduating from Yale University in 1869, Henry joined the family business and was immediately sent to San Francisco to oversee the opening of a new branch. In the early 1880s, after returning to New York, he married society beauty Jessie A. Robbins, the daughter of Daniel Robbins of Brooklyn, a founding partner of the wholesale drug firm of McKesson & Robbins.

The newlywed couple initially lived in a brownstone just off Fifth Avenue on West 54th Street, but in 1896 they moved to their considerably more spacious neoclassical mansion at 9 East 72nd Street. During their first season in the house, the Sloanes gave an elaborate house-warming ball to show off the building to their family and many friends. Soon the well-connected couple found themselves hosting an endless succession of dinner parties and formal receptions in their new abode.

Soaring columns, convoluted consoles, intricate garlands, and other sculptural details adorn the house's facade, a beautiful example of what was contemporarily called "Modern French." An ornate two-story colonnade created by the use of engaged Ionic columns rests on a plain rusticated ground floor, and low stone balustrades guard the large, ornamented glazed French doors on the second floor. Consoles above the column capitals support a heavily dentiled cornice and roof balustrade, while stone dormers project from a low mansard roof.

The cartouche, a prominent decorative element employed in the building, is used above the third-floor windows and in massive form above the main entrance. It may have been the Sloane house that prompted the negative article on the use of the cartouche in architecture in *The Architectural Review*: "Originating from an abnormal and dropsical development of the keystone and the medallion, or heraldic escutcheons, it has invaded the field of architectural ornament like a bubonic plague. The cartouche is even more offensive than the perpetual garland in that it can and does appear in so many places." The article notwithstanding, its use remained popular well into the new century.

Originally, large wooden front doors surmounted by a bronze marquee led to a classically designed entrance hall that had windows overlooking a columned courtyard. The elliptically shaped staircase ascended to a 50-foot-long salon that extended across the entire front of the building. A large dining room and a conservatory filled the rear of the second floor.

The Sloanes did not long enjoy their stylish new house. Perry Belmont, a son of August Belmont, the American representative of the Rothschild banking family, fell madly in love with the unhappily married Mrs. Sloane. Henry Sloane, who professed undying love for his wife, tried to salvage the floundering marriage by indulging Jessie with fine homes, beautiful jewels, and costly Worth gowns from Paris. Nonetheless, this wasn't enough because Mrs. Sloane continued to see, quite openly, the handsome and gallant Mr. Belmont. In their intimate social circle, the Sloanes and Perry Belmont had become mockingly known as "The Triangle." In desperation, Henry threatened his spouse with divorce and disgrace if she continued to see her lover. Not believing him, and trusting in her husband's morbid fear of open scandal, Jessie continued her liaison with Belmont. She obviously underestimated Henry's resolve because in 1899 he filed for divorce. Jessie, who hadn't even bothered to contest the suit or try to retain custody of her two daughters, had the further audacity to

EXTERIOR. (Courtesy of the City of the Museum of New York)

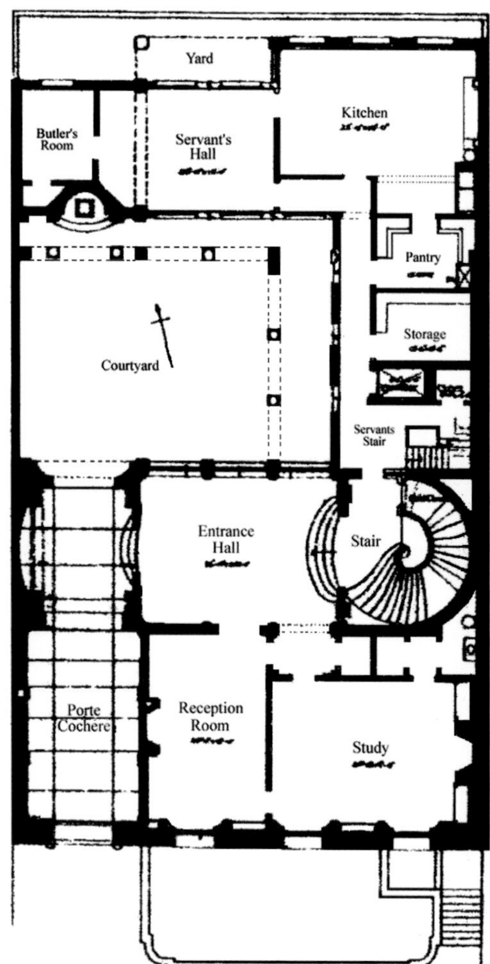

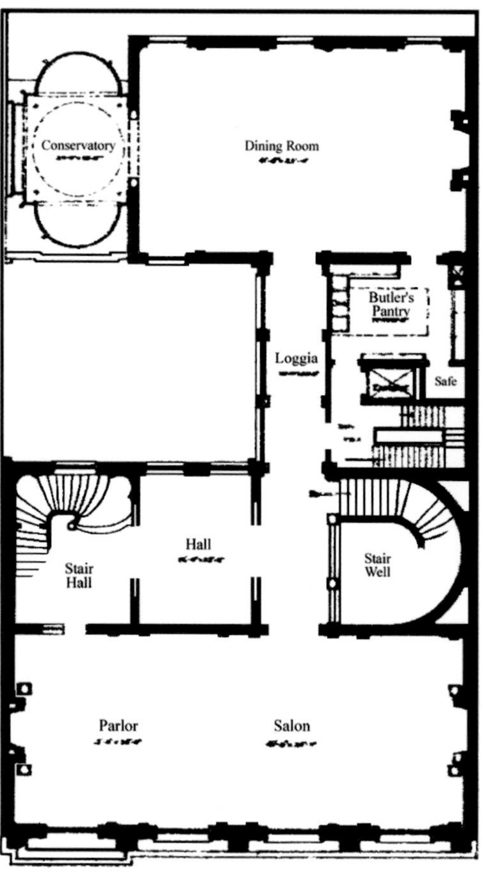

First (left) and Second Floor Plans. (Richard Marchand)

marry Belmont within hours of obtaining the divorce decree. The Belmonts settled in the somewhat less hostile environs of Washington, D.C.

Sloane never remarried, and his two daughters remained with him until they married. One tied the knot with Philadelphia traction magnate George Widener Jr., while the other married into French nobility. Before his death in 1937, Henry Sloane had the satisfaction of outliving Jessie by two years, but the dashing Perry Belmont outlived them both when he died in 1947 at the age of 97.

Not wanting to live in the mansion after the divorce, Henry Sloane first leased it to Joseph Pulitzer, after the publisher's house on East 55th Street was destroyed by fire. In 1901, Sloane sold it to First National City Bank president James Stillman. For many years, it was occupied by the Lycée Français de New York, but it was sold at the beginning of the 21st century to new owners who may return it to residential use.

Edward J. Berwind House

2 East 64th Street

Nathan C. Mellen, 1896

Edward J. Berwind House

Exterior. (New York Public Library)

President Abraham Lincoln appointed 17-year-old Edward Julius Berwind to the United States Naval Academy in 1865. This highly ambitious young man was one of five sons born in Philadelphia to parents of German birth. Because his father had started a moderately successful coal company, the family led a comfortable existence. Berwind went on to serve as a naval aide in the White House during the Grant administration, and the political connections he acquired during his tenure there greatly enhanced his success in later years. In 1886, the 37-year-old lieutenant married Herminie Torrey, the daughter of an American diplomat stationed in Leghorn, Italy.

Soon after this marriage, Berwind relinquished his naval commission and returned to Philadelphia to found the Berwind-White Coal Mining Company with his brother Charles and Judge Allison White. When White retired

ENTRANCE DETAIL. (New York Public Library)

a few years later, Berwind brought in his younger brothers as partners. The company flourished and soon became a leader in the production and marketing of coal, as well as the largest owner of bituminous coal mines in the world. At one time, Berwind-White controlled all the steamship coal used in both New York and Boston harbors, and because of Berwind's Washington contacts, it also supplied most of the coal used by the United States Navy. The company became so large and so well organized that it began to profitably export coal to South America, the West Indies, and even Europe.

Edward Berwind, who remained chairman of the board of Berwind-White until his death, also acquired important interests in allied industries like railroads, steel, utilities, and lumber. At some point, he was the second-largest investor in International Telephone and Telegraph. During the 1890s, Berwind decided to move his headquarters to New York, leaving his brothers to run the Philadelphia office. He and his wife, a member of the Strawbridge department store family, soon became social leaders in their adopted city as well as at their summer cottage, The Elms, in Newport, Rhode Island. The Berwinds, who later became patrons of the Metropolitan Opera, had already begun collecting fine paintings, tapestries, and decorative arts to adorn their homes.

In 1895, Berwind purchased a choice piece of property at 2 East 64th Street, directly across from

BALLROOM. (Juris Mardwig)

SECOND FLOOR HALL. (Juris Mardwig)

Boudoir, 1990s. (Lazlo Hege)

the Central Park Armory. He then hired architect Nathan C. Mellen to design an eclectic quasi-Byzantine-Renaissance house for the site. The first floor, faced in boldly coursed limestone, has round-topped windows and an entranceway defined by marble columns supporting a richly carved chancel-style arch. The floor above is also veneered in limestone, but in a smoother finish that is embellished by multiple paired stringcourses. The square-headed windows of this level have decorative lunettes enclosing a decorative rondel. The third floor, of red brick with limestone detailing, includes a small stringcourse at the sill level. Another stone stringcourse separates the third and fourth floors. The latter has round-topped coupled windows based on those found on the Palazzo Medici-Riccardi in Florence. At the top of the structure, paired rectangular windows sit under a full limestone entablature.

The opulent interiors of the Berwind house used many European design inspirations, but they were all executed in a highly fastidious manner under the direction of Jules Allard. The first floor had a large salon that overlooked the park and a dining room and pantry at its eastern end. A drawing

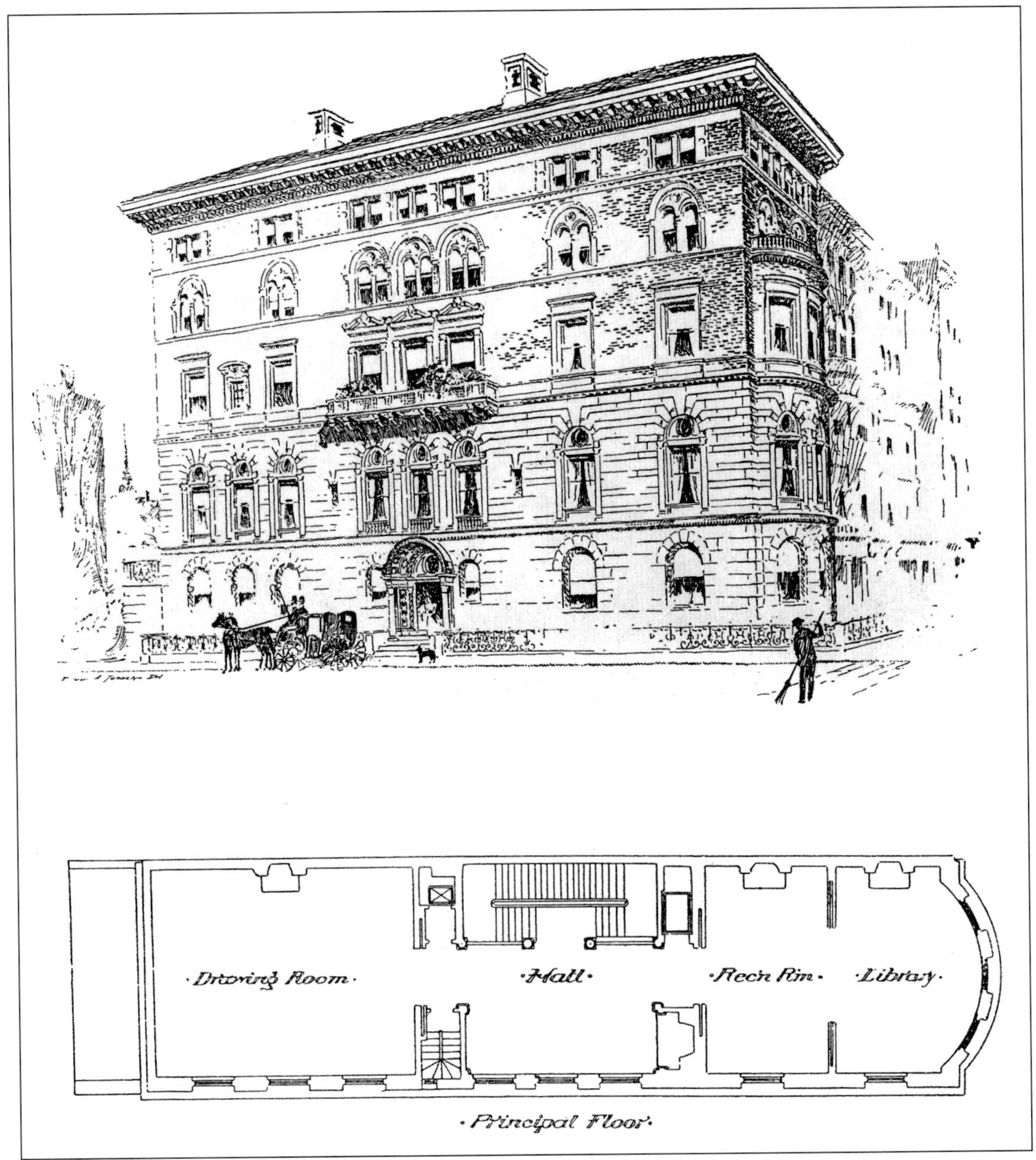

ELEVATION DRAWING AND SECOND FLOOR PLAN. (Author's Collection)

room that doubled as a ballroom, a reception room, and the library filled the second floor. Bedrooms and sitting rooms were on the next two levels, while the top floor held the usual complement of sewing rooms and staff bedrooms.

After Herminie Berwind's death in 1922, the childless widower asked his unmarried sister, Julia, to act as hostess at both of his homes. After her brother's death, Julia sold the 64th Street house and moved to a suite at the Savoy Plaza, although she did continue to summer at the Newport mansion until her own death in 1961. Eventually, the Institute of Aeronautical Sciences purchased 2 East 64th Street and maintained it well for many years. During the 1980s, a conversion of the house into very expensive cooperative apartments was sensitively accomplished without having to alter much of the interior finish. Over a dozen people now reside in what was once a palatial house.

Isaac D. Fletcher House

975 Fifth Avenue (now 2 East 79th Street)

C. P. H. Gilbert, 1899

Isaac D. Fletcher House

Exterior, c. 1950. (Courtesy of the New-York Historical Society)

This neo-Loire-Valley, chateau-style residence was constructed primarily to house the art collection of its connoisseur owner. Isaac D. Fletcher, who made his fortune in manufacturing and as president of the New York Coal Tar Company, had been acquiring important works of art for many years. His famous collection represented works by such renowned artists as David, Gainsborough, Rembrandt, Reynolds, and Rubens. In 1897, needing more space, Fletcher purchased the Fifth Avenue corner lot at 79th Street from Henry Cook for $200,000. Cook had purchased the entire block from 78th to 79th street between Fifth and Madison avenues in 1880 for $500,000 and soon began selling off lots for the development of first-class single family dwellings. To safeguard the area, Cook put iron-clad restrictions on each deed specifying that all future building must be to residential scale.

ENTRANCE HALL, C. 1950. (Courtesy of the New-York Historical Society)

These restrictions are directly responsible for the lack of any high-rise development on the block. It is the only Fifth Avenue block that still wholly retains its residential feeling and continues to look much as it did just prior to World War I.

After Fletcher purchased the 32-by-100-foot site, he spent another $200,000 on the construction of a C. P. H. Gilbert–designed house. The building has many similarities to the William K. Vanderbilt house that Richard Morris Hunt had completed 17 years earlier. Gilbert later used this same florid French Gothic style in designing Fifth Avenue mansions for F. W. Woolworth and Felix Warburg.

Set back from the street behind a fenced moat, the limestone Fletcher mansion was entered by traversing a wide stone "drawbridge." Just inside the massive decorative wrought-iron doors, a small glass-enclosed vestibule led into the entrance hall. The hall's most important feature was an intricately carved wooden staircase balustrade. The park end of the first floor contained a paneled reception room, and the kitchen and service area filled its eastern portion. A dining room and a Louis XVI–style drawing room occupied the next level. Adjacent to the dining room at the east end of the house was a small, glass-domed conservatory. The third floor contained a library that overlooked Central Park, an oval-shaped music room, and Mrs. Fletcher's bedroom. Curiously, Isaac Fletcher's room was not located on this floor

Reception Room, c. 1950. (Courtesy of the New-York Historical Society)

Drawing Room, c. 1950. (Courtesy of the New-York Historical Society)

Library, c. 1950. (Courtesy of the New-York Historical Society)

Bedroom, c. 1950. (Courtesy of the New-York Historical Society)

Master Bedroom, c. 1950. (Courtesy of the New-York Historical Society)

Master Bathroom, c. 1950.
(Courtesy of the New-York Historical Society)

but on the fourth floor, directly above that of his wife. He shared this level with guest accommodations and a small sewing room. A labyrinth of small servant bedrooms occupied the top floor. Isaac Fletcher died in 1917, predeceased by his wife several years earlier. Their art collection, with a $3 million bequest, was left to the neighboring Metropolitan Museum of Art. Henry T. Sinclair, an oilman remembered for his involvement in the notorious Teapot Dome scandal, then occupied the house and lived there until 1929. The building was then purchased by the last direct male descendant of Peter Stuyvesant, Augustus Van Horne Stuyvesant Jr., who resided there until his death in 1953. The pinnacled Gothic structure now houses the Ukrainian Institute of America.

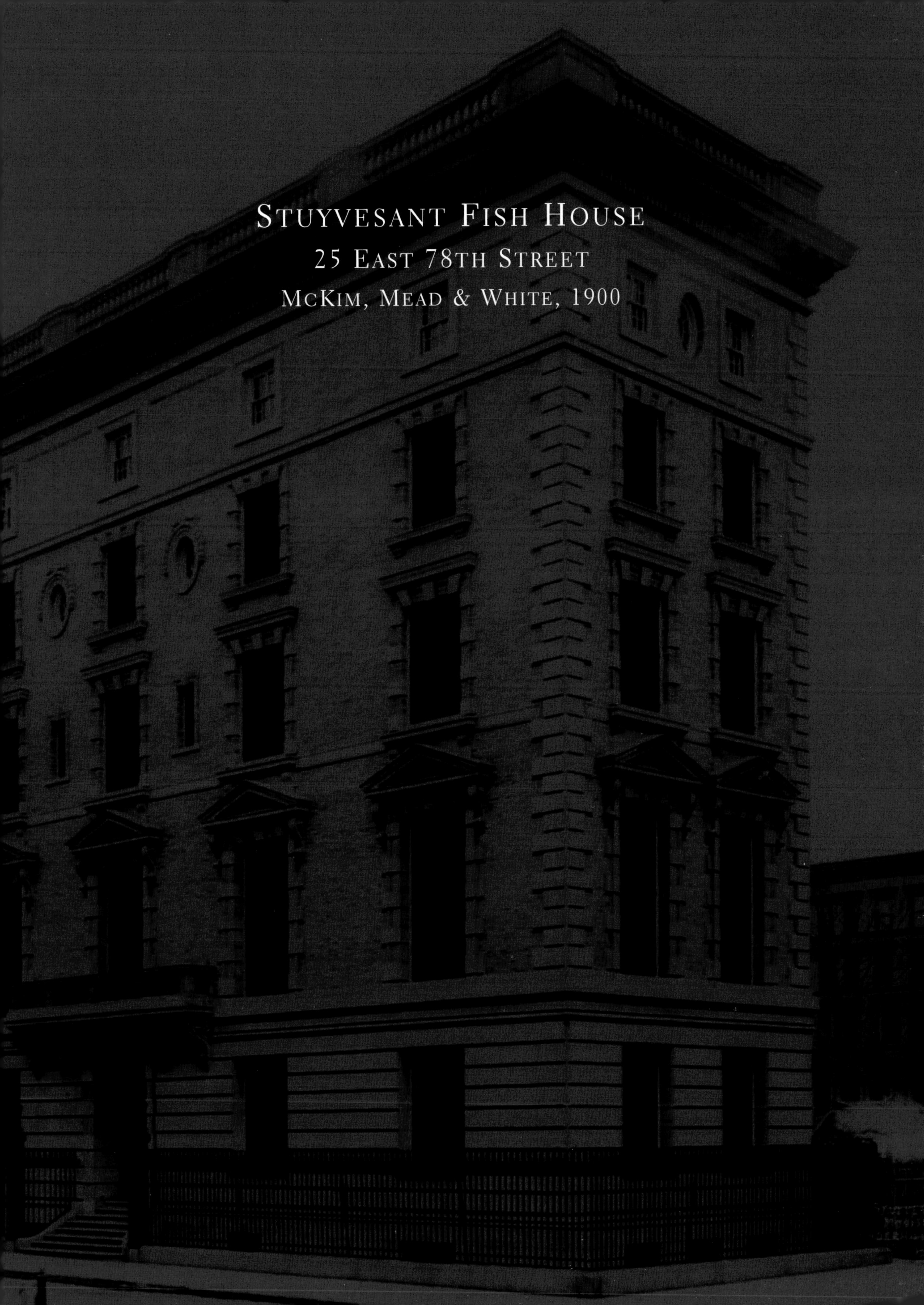

STUYVESANT FISH HOUSE

25 EAST 78TH STREET

MCKIM, MEAD & WHITE, 1900

Stuyvesant Fish House

Exterior. (Author's Collection)

Stuyvesant Fish, president of the Illinois Central Railroad, was the son of Hamilton Fish, who had been a governor of New York, a United States senator, and secretary of state under President Ulysses S. Grant. His wife, Mamie, the former Mary Ann Anthon, daughter of lawyer William Henry Anthon, was society's enfant terrible, known for her sharp wit and extravagant parties.

Mamie had once told her daughter-in-law that it didn't matter what one decides to do with one's life, but one must do it better than anyone else. As there were not many acceptable choices then available to a lady of good family, Mamie Fish decided to become a leader of society. That she succeeded is attested to by the fact that it is impossible to pick up a social chronicle of the era and not learn of her exploits.

SECOND FLOOR HALL. (Courtesy of the New-York Historical Society)

Mamie, who never attended school, had a difficult time spelling, and she read little more than *Town Topics*, the social rag of the day. She was asked to co-write a book, but she declined, saying that if it were good, everyone would know she hadn't written it, and if it were bad, she'd be mortified. Her sharp tongue was considered a sort of social baptism by fire. Once, at the start of a new season, she greeted her guests with, "Well, here you all are, older faces and younger clothes." She could not abide a banal question. A gentleman who had been abroad for a few years remarked on seeing a new bridge, "Well, how did that get there?" Mrs. Fish answered, "That bridge? Why, I had it and it was most painful." Upon greeting her guests, she would say things like, "Make yourselves perfectly at home, and believe me, there is no one who wishes you were there more heartily than I." To Tony Shaw-Safe, an Englishman who came to the United States as a polo team manager, married a very wealthy socialite, and then pretentiously hyphenated his name, she said: "Howdy-do, Mr. Safe. I'm so sorry to call you Mr. Safe, but I've forgotten your combination." Never able to remember people's names, she came up with the solution of calling everyone "lamb," "sweet pet," or some mixture of the two.

Always bucking the traditions of American society, she could not endure the three mortal hours at table that formal dinners of the time required, so she had hers served in less than an hour. Her record

BALLROOM. (Courtesy of the New-York Historical Society)

was an eight-course meal served in just under 30 minutes. Guests were required to hold their plates down with one hand while simultaneously eating with the other. She also liked to serve champagne with meals, saying, "You have to liven these people up, wine just makes them sleepy."

In 1887, with broadening social horizons, the Stuyvesant Fish family purchased the house at 20 Gramercy Park South, and Stanford White was called in to complete $120,000 worth of improvements. A decade later, Mamie, finding her surroundings still not grand enough, commissioned White to design a completely new house on the corner of Madison Avenue and 78th Street, which was completed in 1900.

The Fishes were only moderately rich by the standards of many of their friends. Even with a somewhat restrained budget, White was able to construct an imposing Italian Renaissance palazzo with distinctly American Renaissance details such as the copper-sheathed cornice and roof balustrade. In building the new house, a substantial amount of money was saved by facing the majority of it in buff Roman brick, while reserving the more expensive limestone veneer for the ground floor and the decorative trim found above. The 78th Street facade, because of its size, must have been very impressive to arriving guests, but venturing around the corner, one realizes it is just a stage front, as the house is actually quite narrow. Money was spent where it could be seen, and for best effect.

The ground floor consisted of a marble paved entrance hall, a paneled reception room, and a dark 17th-century-style dining room. The largest room of this very social house was the ballroom, which was on the second floor and decorated in Louis XVI style. The only other room on this floor, with the exception of the large stair hall, was the Red Salon, which

SALON. (Courtesy of the New-York Historical Society)

DINING ROOM. (Courtesy of the New-York Historical Society)

MRS. FISH'S BEDROOM. (Courtesy of the New-York Historical Society)

overlooked Madison Avenue. On the third floor was Mrs. Fish's Gothic bedroom. Elizabeth Drexel Lehr wrote that Mrs. Fish felt her bedroom was too perfect to disturb, so she slept in an adjoining dressing room. Mamie always thought that her house was "an uncomfortable place for anyone without breeding." The house was Mrs. Fish's New York residence until her death in 1915. Sometime later, the house was put to commercial use, and in the 1980s the interiors were completely removed. As of late 2003, the house stood empty, yet the exterior facade still reflects Stanford White's vision.

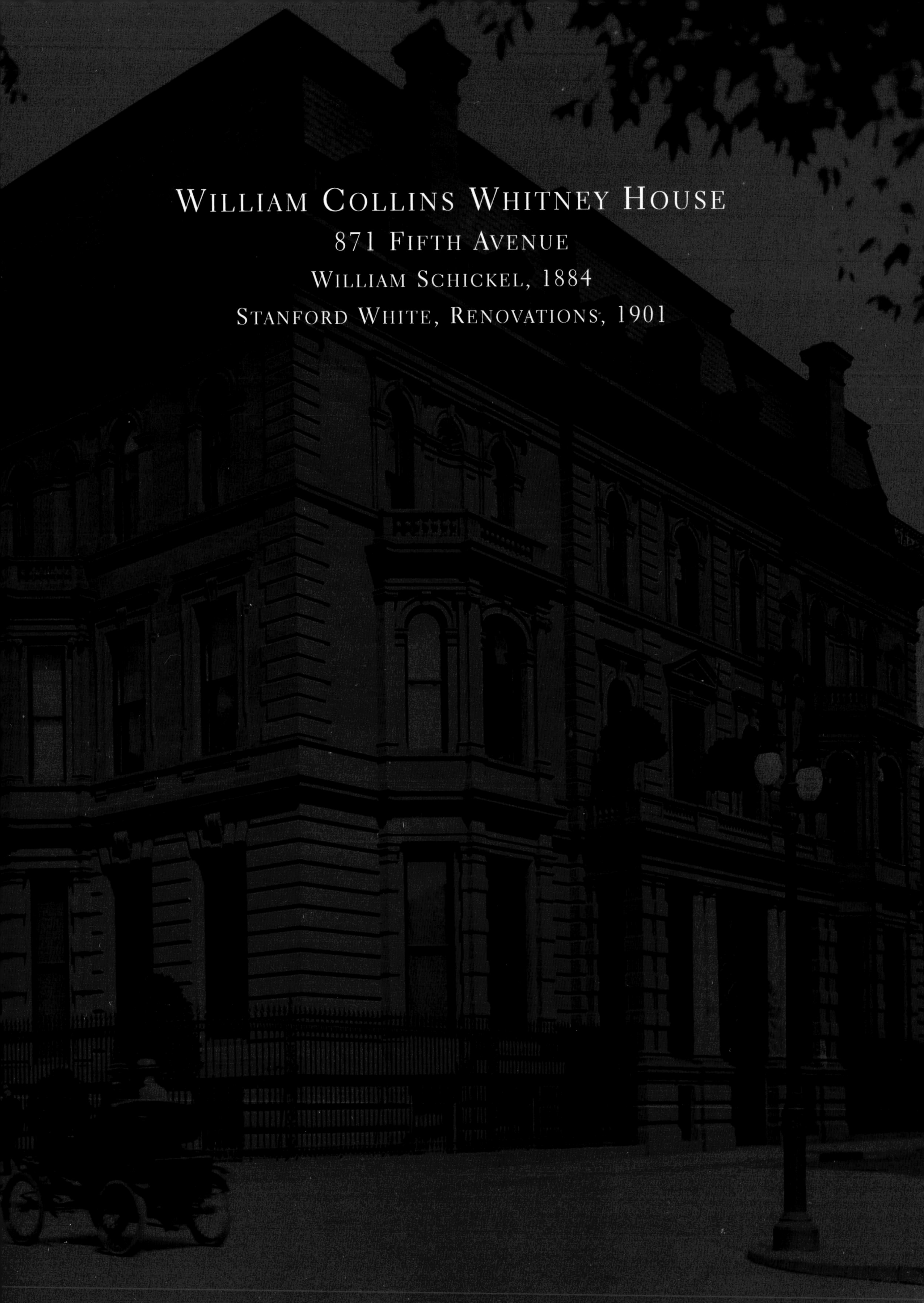

William Collins Whitney House

871 Fifth Avenue

William Schickel, 1884

Stanford White, Renovations, 1901

William Collins Whitney House

Exterior. (Byron Collection, Museum of the City of New York)

Three years after the death of his wife, Flora Payne Whitney, traction magnate William Collins Whitney decided to remarry. The popular bride-to-be, Mrs. Edith S. Randolph, came from a respectable Baltimore family and was the widow of a prominent British army officer. She was also 15 years younger than Whitney. Their marital plans were marred by Flora's sanctimonious bachelor brother, Oliver Payne. Having made an enormous fortune with John D. Rockefeller in Standard Oil, Payne thought William Whitney should remain in perpetual mourning for Flora. When Whitney went ahead with his second marriage, Payne disowned him. His vindictiveness did not end there, as Payne also insisted that any of the four Whitney children who did not side with him would be permanently cut off from his $50 million fortune. Already possessing riches estimated at $40

BALLROOM. (Courtesy of the New-York Historical Society)

million, this created little financial hardship on Whitney, but it did create a schism with his second son, Payne, and his eldest daughter, Pauline. Harry Payne Whitney and his teenage sister, Dorothy, remained by their father.

A rare bird among New York plutocrats, William Whitney was both highly cultured and of well-bred demeanor. A contemporary writer stated that he had "a tall, handsome grace that is the despair of men and the admiration of women." In anything he did, "mediocrity was unthinkable." A connoisseur of art and horses, Whitney was considered by many to be a genius. Born to a distinguished, if not well-heeled, New England family, he attended Yale, where he shared a room with Oliver Payne. On a visit to Oliver's well-to-do family in Ohio, he met and fell in love with his sister, Flora. They were married in 1869. Whitney soon began his professional career as the corporation counsel of the City of New York. He then became a corporate attorney for the Vanderbilts. From there, Whitney took an active interest in the development of urban transit in New York and was one of the organizers of the Metropolitan Street Railway Company. In this lucrative field that was rife with corruption, he began to amass his fortune.

In 1884, newly elected president Grover Cleveland asked Whitney to become the country's next secretary of the navy. During the four years of the Cleveland administration, the Whitneys enjoyed the Washington social whirl. Flora blossomed into an accomplished hostess. After their

Drawing Room. (Courtesy of the New-York Historical Society)

Dining Room. (Courtesy of the New-York Historical Society)

LIBRARY. (Courtesy of the New-York Historical Society)

return to New York in 1888, Oliver Payne gave the couple a new house at Fifth Avenue and 57th Street. It sat directly across the street from the residence of Cornelius Vanderbilt II, whose daughter Gertrude would marry the Whitneys' eldest son, Harry. A few years after Flora's death in 1893, William Whitney gave this house to Harry and his new bride.

In 1896, Willliam purchased from the estate of Robert L. Stuart a house on the northeast corner of 68th Street and Fifth Avenue. The late sugar refiner's house had been constructed 12 years earlier to the designs of William Schickel. Whitney paid $650,000 for the building and hired Stanford White to perform a $3 million basement-to-attic renovation. He wanted nothing less than a perfect setting where he and his new wife could mount their grand entertainments.

Fourteen months into the four-year project, Edith had a severe riding accident on their Aiken, North Carolina, estate. After being in a coma for months, she was brought north in April 1898 on a specially fitted railroad car. A private ambulance met Edith and her medical entourage at the 42nd Street ferry, and William Whitney walked beside the horse-drawn conveyance as it made its slow progress up to the 57th Street house. After experiencing only fleeting improvements, Edith Whitney died in the spring of 1899, long before renovations were completed on the 68th Street house.

When 871 was finished, it was proclaimed by the press to be another triumph for the decorating skill of Stanford White. The only exterior changes to the 55-by-200-foot-long house were the erection of a new entrance, using antique iron and bronze gates taken from the Doria Palace in Rome, and the

SECOND FLOOR HALL. (Courtesy of the New-York Historical Society)

THIRD FLOOR HALL. (Author's Collection)

LOUIS XVI BEDROOM. (Author's Collection)

LOUIS XVI SITTING ROOM. (Author's Collection)

Boudoir. (Author's Collection)

addition of a new ballroom wing at the eastern end of the 68th Street facade.

Exquisite objects taken from three continents filled the interiors. A green onyx vestibule led to a white marble-walled entrance hall that had dark green pilasters and columns. A staircase of Istrian marble led up to a main hall that had a stone floor inlaid with 10,000 pieces of bronze and a fireplace from the chateau of the Sieur France de Conseil at Argenes-Marter. Over this staircase hung important tapestries bearing the entwined monograms of Henri II and Diane de Poitiers. The walls of the adjoining drawing room were covered in antique Italian embroidery, and the floor was covered with Persian prayer rugs. On the wall hung Hoppner's *Dancing Girl*. In the dining room, below a ceiling painted by Bordini that was taken from an old Genovese palazzo, the walls were resplendent with Brussels tapestries. Often 100 people dined in this room while using the famous Whitney gold dinner service. Antique Renaissance bookcases encircled the coffered-ceilinged library.

The largest of the house's 54 rooms was the 60-foot-long ballroom in the new addition. Its gilt-trimmed antique boiseries came from a chateau outside of Bordeaux that once belonged to Baron de

Kitchen. (Author's Collection)

Pantry. (Author's Collection)

Servants' Entrance. (Author's Collection)

Laundry. (Author's Collection)

Foix, a field marshal under Louis XIV. Over the mantel hung Reynold's *Portrait of a Lady*. On January 4, 1901, this room hosted the official opening ball for the house, which also marked the debut of William Whitney's niece, Helen Tracy Barney. One of the 700 invited guests was the 70-year-old Caroline Astor.

After William Whitney's death three years later, the house was sold, complete with furnishings, to James Henry Smith, who had recently inherited a large fortune from an elderly uncle. Smith died in 1909, and the executors of his estate put 871 and its artwork back on the market. Harry Payne Whitney, not wishing to see his father's house and collection dispersed, bought it back for $2 million. At Harry's death in 1930, life tenancy of the house was given to his widow, Gertrude. She lived in the mansion during the famous custody trial of her niece Gloria Vanderbilt in 1934. By 1940, Gertrude was spending most of the time at her Westbury, Long Island, estate, so she closed 871. Two years later, after having given many of its treasures to her children and grandchildren, she planned to auction the mansion's remaining contents. Before the sale took place, Gertrude Whitney died, leaving many millions to be shared by her children and the Whitney Museum of American Art. Later that year, 871 fell to the wrecker's ball.

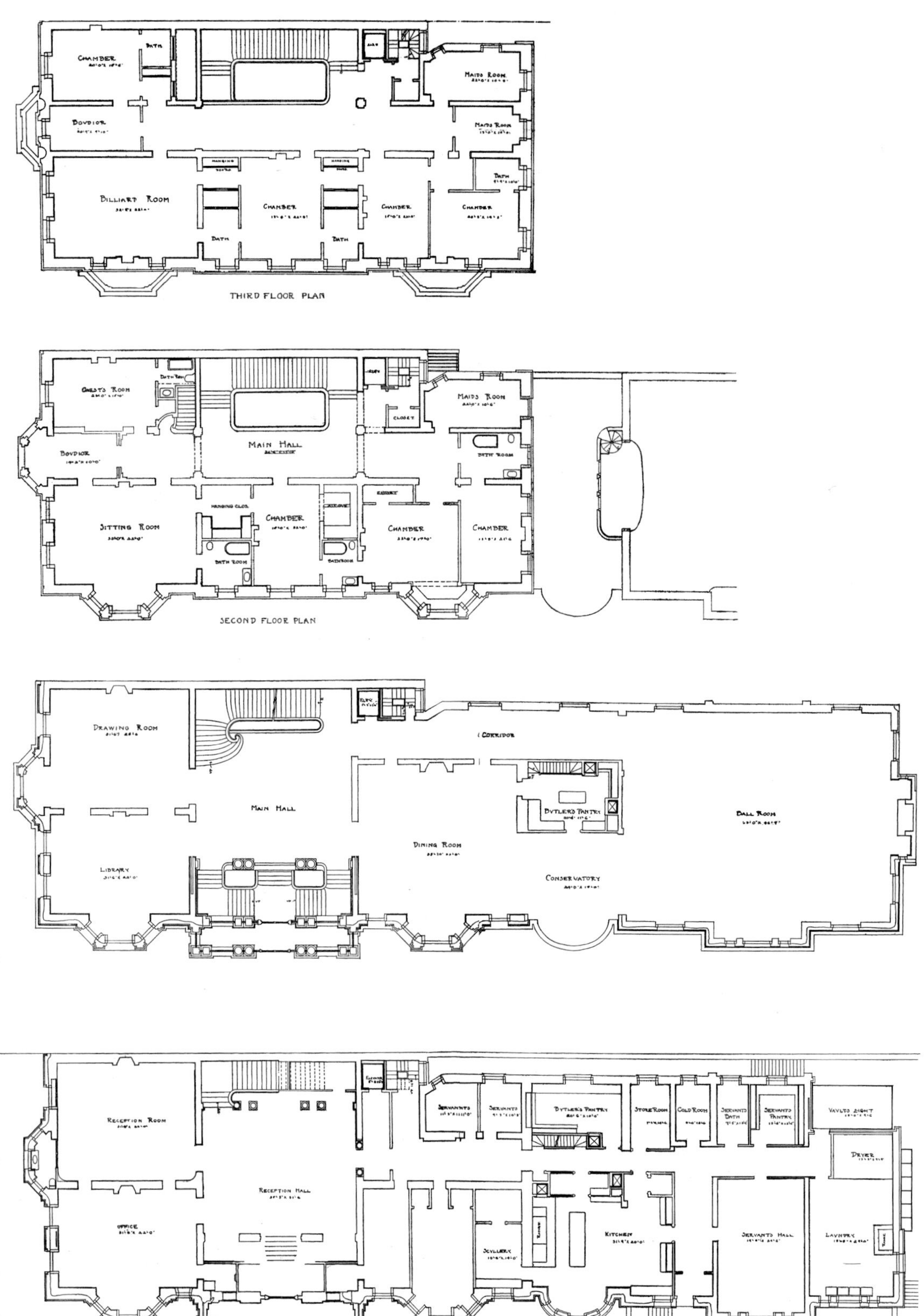

Ground through Third Floors Plans (bottom to top). (Author's Collection)

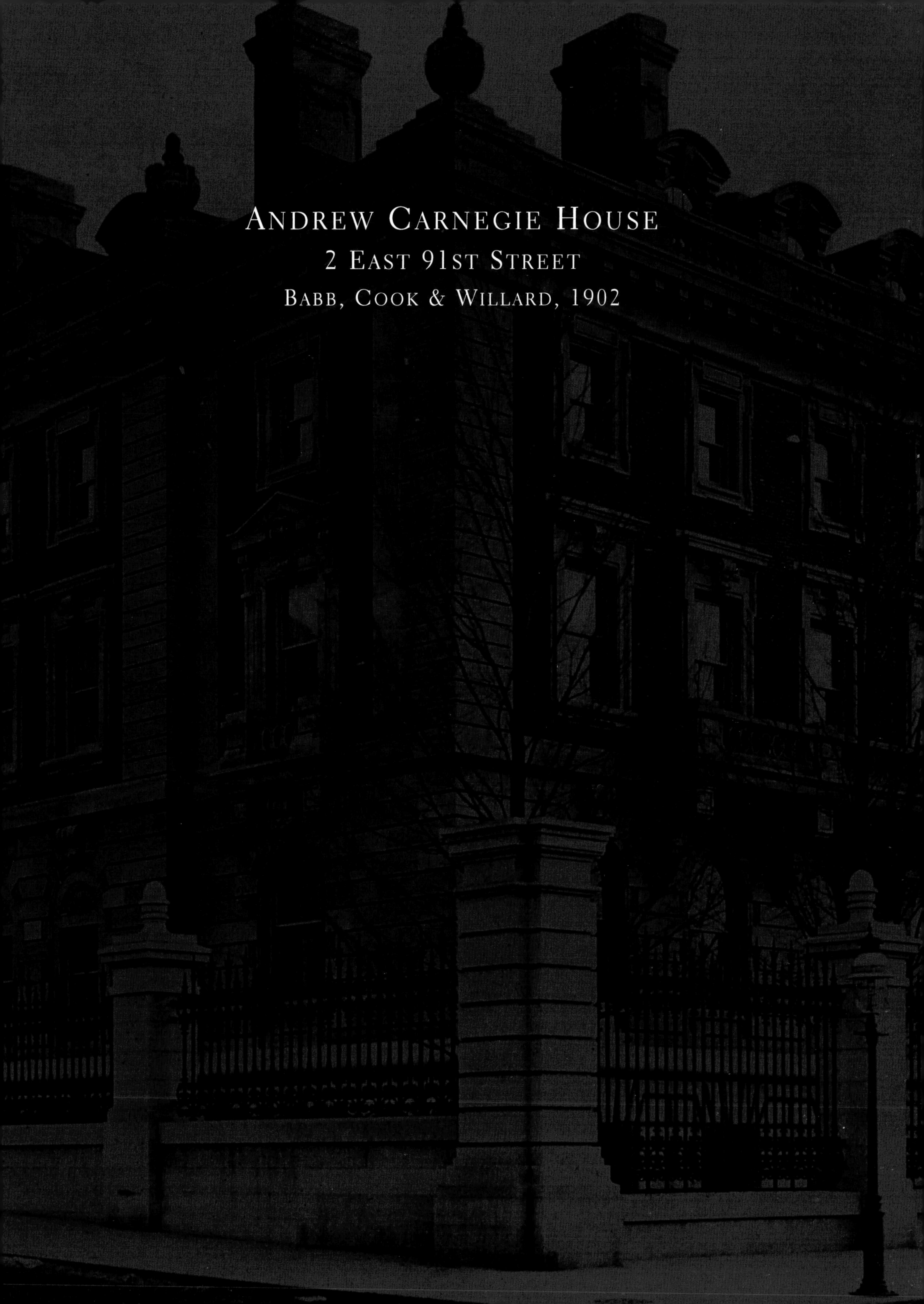

Andrew Carnegie House

2 East 91st Street

Babb, Cook & Willard, 1902

Andrew Carnegie House

Entrance Facade. (Collection of the New York Public Library)

When Andrew Carnegie purchased the Fifth Avenue block between 90th and 91st streets with the intention of building a new house, some thought he was more than just a little crazy. In 1898 the neighborhood primarily consisted of middle-class brownstones interspersed with parcels of land that was mostly occupied by shanties—Carnegie's site was partially occupied by the Fifth Avenue Riding Academy. The fashionable crowd had not yet ventured above 79th Street. Carnegie explained his move to the highest point on the avenue by saying, "The little life that has come to us needs the park and sunshine, and it is for these reasons that we have not only concurred in the advice of our physician, but deemed it a duty to remove to the highest ground and where there is plenty of room."

Only five feet four inches tall, Carnegie was once described as "a mite of a man, but all of it a dynamo." He was born in 1835 in Dunfermline,

GARDEN FACADE. (Collection of the New York Public Library)

Scotland, to a poor family that immigrated to Allegheny, Pennsylvania, in 1847. After the death of his father, the 14-year-old Carnegie became the sole support of his family. The young man wrote in his diary that "whatever I engage in, I must push inordinately." He persevered until he became the Pittsburgh steel king as head of the Carnegie Steel Corporation. In 1899, Carnegie Steel showed a profit of $40 million.

Carnegie had often been ruthless in his business practices. In fact, he had once been described as "the most cruel taskmaster American industry has ever known." This may be true, but posterity will more likely remember Andrew Carnegie as a philanthropist without equal in the United States.

This dutiful Old World son had vowed he would never marry while his mother was still alive, and within five months of her death in 1886, the 51-year-old Carnegie married 28-year-old Louise Whitfield. He had already been seriously courting her for seven years and was lucky that Louise held out for him, as this pretty young lady had many admirers.

In 1892, Carnegie built a castle in Scotland as a summer home. The 40,000-acre estate was called Skibo, and the locals liked to call Carnegie "The Star-Spangled Scotsman."

In 1901, he wanted to retire and so decided to sell Carnegie Steel to the J. P. Morgan interests for $487,566,160, out of which he kept $300 million. Morgan, who later made Carnegie Steel the

STAIRCASE. (Courtesy of the Museum of the City of New York)

DRAWING ROOM. (Courtesy of the Museum of the City of New York)

DINING ROOM. (Courtesy of the Museum of the City of New York)

Library. (Courtesy of the Museum of the City of New York)

nucleus for his giant U.S. Steel monopoly, told Carnegie that this sale would make him the richest man in the world.

Little did the stalwart banker know what Carnegie intended to do with that money, along with his already considerable fortune. Between 1901 and his death 18 years later, the Scotsman assiduously gave away over $350 million. He believed, "He who dies rich, dies disgraced," and that he was merely a trustee to his immense fortune. His plan was to give away the entire fortune with the exception of 10 percent, which he kept for his family. When his secretary came to him early in the process, warning that he had already used up the annual interest on his fortune and was now invading capital, Carnegie responded by saying, "Delighted to hear it, my boy. Let's keep it up."

The philanthropist is best remembered in New York by Carnegie Hall, but his largest benefaction was the library buildings that he had constructed in North America, England, and Scotland. These libraries eventually totaled 2,811 in number and cost him $60,364,808. Carnegie donated only the buildings themselves, expecting each community to contribute the books to fill the shelves, according to his philosophy: "I do not wish to be remembered

MR. CARNEGIE'S STUDY. (Courtesy of the Museum of the City of New York)

for what I have given, but for what I have persuaded others to give."

His new Fifth Avenue house became the headquarters for his philanthropic work. On Carnegie's enormous 200-by-276-foot plot of land, Babb, Cook & Willard designed a 64-room Georgian revival house reminiscent of Hertford House in London. The Carnegies asked landscape architect Richard Schemerhorn to lay out the grounds in an informal English garden design. Completed in 1901 at a cost of just under $2 million, the house set the tone for what ultimately became known as Carnegie Hill.

The residence, although obviously derived from Georgian precedent, has French Beaux Arts detailing. The massiveness and solidity of the quoins, window surrounds, and urn-topped roof balustrade show none of the delicacy one would expect in original Georgian models but more of the voluptuousness found in mid-19th-century reinterpretations. The use of the glass and metal marquee over the entrance and the ponderous granite piers of the surrounding wrought-iron fence help confirm this. The mixture of the Flemish bond brickwork and the limestone decorative detailing are the only elements that truly speak to the structure's 18th-century Georgian ancestry.

Mrs. Carnegie's Bedroom. (Courtesy of the Museum of the City of New York)

The first floor contained an oak-paneled transverse entrance hall with a deeply coffered ceiling of the same material. At one end was placed a fireplace, while the other contained a console and the pipes of an Aeolian organ. To the left was the staircase, while straight ahead, on axis with the entrance vestibule, was a reception room with windows by Louis Comfort Tiffany. Flanking this was a parlor (music room) with ornate Louis XV plaster detailing, and the dining room with its paneled carved wainscot and elaborate ceiling treatment. It was a tradition with the Carnegies that at important formal dinners guests would be asked to sign their names in ink on the damask table linen where they were seated. A seamstress would later embroider these signatures in white thread. Beyond the dining room was a breakfast room that was decorated in a similar manner and a glass enclosed conservatory where Mrs. Carnegie could enjoy her plants and flowers year round. A door on the north wall led to the skylighted gallery where the family's rather undistinguished collection of academic art was hung. But the real center of activity for the house was Carnegie's library and adjoining office on the western end of the first floor overlooking the park. Above the library fireplace was the owner's favorite

MRS. CARNEGIE'S BOUDOIR. (Courtesy of the Museum of the City of New York)

BATHROOM. (Courtesy of the Museum of the City of New York)

BOILER ROOM. (Courtesy of the Museum of the City of New York)

motto, "The Hearth Our Altar, Its Flame Our Sacred Fire." When informed by his architect that this motto had too many words to fit on the mantelpiece, Carnegie replied, "Then tear down the house and build it with a larger library and a bigger fireplace." The chastened architect subsequently found a way to make the motto fit.

On the second floor, individual suites for Mr. and Mrs. Carnegie and their daughter, Margaret, each had their own sitting room, bedroom, dressing room, and bath. The third floor held guests' rooms, a small gymnasium, a schoolroom for Margaret, and a suite for Stella Whitfield, "Mrs. Carnegie's sister.". The fourth floor, behind the roof balustrade, was exclusively staff quarters.

The house was quite advanced mechanically for its day and included one of the first central air-conditioning systems in the country. Large attic fans

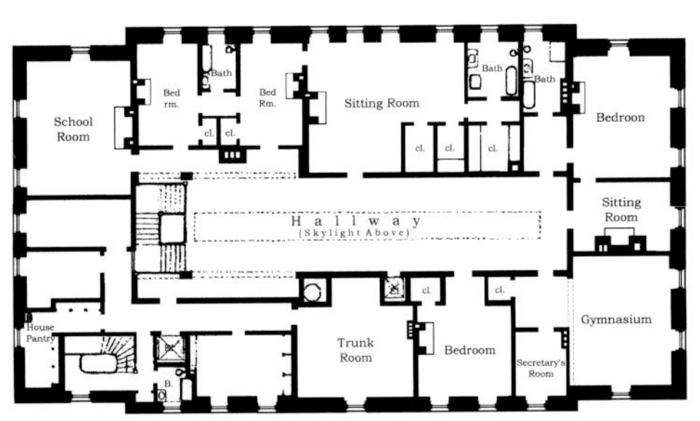

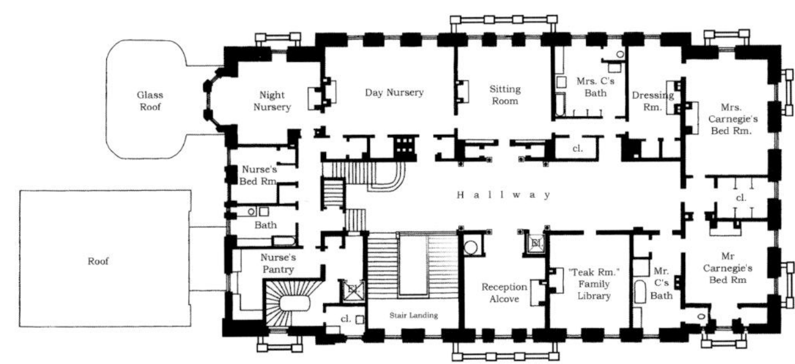

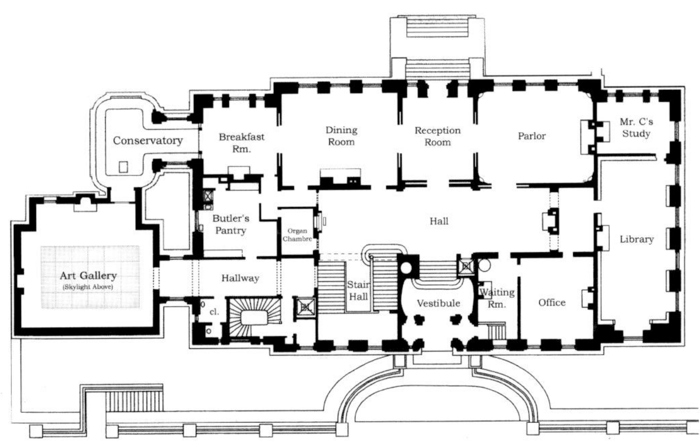

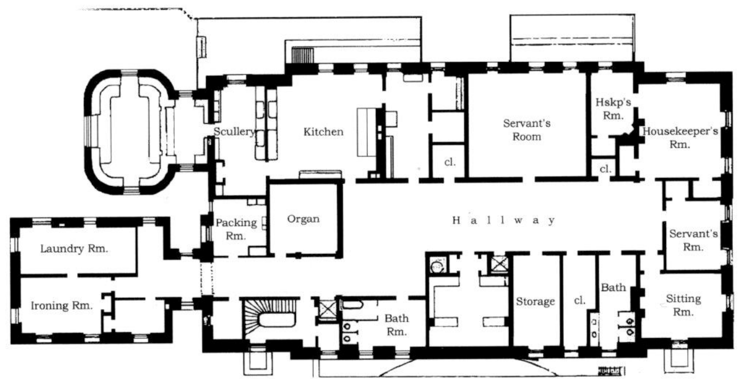

BASEMENT (BOTTOM) THROUGH THIRD FLOOR PLANS. (Richard Marchand)

pulled in air, which was filtered through stretched cheesecloth above tanks of water. The cooled air then was circulated throughout the house.

An ornate wrought-iron fence set on a granite base surrounded the large garden. Carnegie would often walk up to this fence and talk to people passing by. Unlike many of the public-shy millionaires of the era, Carnegie liked to talk to strangers, and he was said to have had quite a sense of humor.

The house was never as sophisticated or as elegant as many of the houses on the avenue. It was neither filled with great works of art nor thronged by the socially elect, but it did fully express the wishes of its owner. In 1898, when he first announced that he was building the new house, Carnegie said he wanted to erect "the most modest, plainest, and roomiest house in New York." By the standard of his day, this is precisely what he got.

Andrew Carnegie died in 1919, and his widow continued to occupy the house until her death in 1946. After the furnishings were auctioned, the building became the Columbia University School of Social Work. In 1972, the Carnegie Corporation purchased the property and generously donated it to the Smithsonian Institution as a home for the Cooper-Hewitt Museum.

James A. Burden Jr. House

7 East 91st Street

Warren & Wetmore, 1902

James A. Burden Jr. House

Exterior. (Author's Collection)

Henry Burden, the founder of the family fortune, was known as the iron master of Troy, New York. Henry had immigrated to the United States from Scotland in 1819, and three years later, the stockholders of the fledgling Troy Iron and Nail Factory asked this ambitious newcomer to take over the management of the company. An inventor, Henry developed a way of making wrought-iron spikes that all American railroads subsequently adopted for track laying. But his most profitable invention was the making a horseshoe out of an iron bar in only four seconds. This allowed him to become the leading producer of horseshoes in the world, and he eventually became the sole stockholder in what developed into the Burden Iron Company.

After Henry's death in 1871, the company was inherited by his two oldest sons. Each of these men sired sons who, by marrying Vanderbilt heiresses,

DINING ROOM. (Courtesy of the Museum of the City of New York)

dramatically enhanced the family fortune. I. Townsend Burden's son, William A. M. Burden, married Florence Twombly, a granddaughter of William Henry Vanderbilt. Another Vanderbilt granddaugher, Florence Adele Sloane, married James A. Burden's namesake son, always referred to in the family as "J." Adele was the daughter of Emily Vanderbilt and William Douglas Sloane, the son of a founder of W. & J. Sloane, the prestigious carpet and furniture emporium that had branches in major cities across the country. The Sloane nuptials took place in 1895 at the bride's parents' estate, Elm Court, in Lenox, Massachusetts. Among her many gifts, the bride received a diamond and sapphire necklace from her mother, a diamond sun brooch from her father, an elaborate diamond stomacher from her uncle Cornelius Vanderbilt II, and a tiara of the same stones from her husband. Diamonds and important pieces of jewelry seemed to be the appropriate gift of choice for Vanderbilt heiresses.

James Burden Jr. continued to work in Troy several days a week managing the family business, leaving his wife and growing family in New York. In 1901, his in-laws, seeing that the Burdens needed larger quarters, purchased from Andrew Carnegie a 135-by-100-foot mid-block site, 147 feet east of Fifth Avenue on the north side of East 91st Street. On the western half of this property, they

Family Living Room. (Courtesy of the Convent of the Sacred Heart)

built a limestone neoclassical mansion which the Burdens moved into in 1902.

This freestanding building designed by Warren & Wetmore has three visible and architecturally treated sides. A unique feature of the building is that it is entered through a large pair of decorative wooden carriage doors that give access to an interior drive-through courtyard. A small concierge cubicle on the right side was always staffed when any member of the family was in residence. A little farther along on the left are the large iron-and-glass entrance doors to the house.

Upon entering, a magnificent oval staircase with a wrought-iron balustrade comes into view. A dome over this staircase has a skylight surrounded by a mural, painted by d'Espousy, depicting the arts. Other spaces on the first floor include a large wood-paneled office, a small reception room, and a billiard room. Inserted between this floor and the second floor, a cozy entresol contains what was Mr. and Mrs. Burden's private suite as well as a comfortable living room and family dining room.

Whereas the entresol could be used for small gatherings of family and friends, the second floor was reserved for grand and formal occasions. With their high ceilings and marble decor reminiscent of the State Apartments at Versailles, these rooms were designed for the large balls and receptions that were typical of the era. The 50-foot-long ballroom, located at the front of the house, is separated from a dining room of almost the same size by a paneled reception room with ornate gilt detailing. The third floor held five bedrooms plus a large playroom for the three children: James A. III, William Douglas, and Sheila. At the top of the house was an infirmary. The house required a staff of 27 to keep it running smoothly.

The Burdens entertained such diverse people as the composer Giacomo Puccini and the American

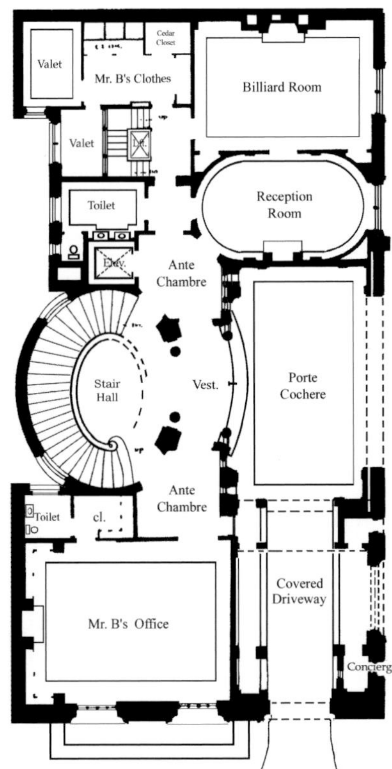

FIRST FLOOR PLAN. (Richard Marchand)

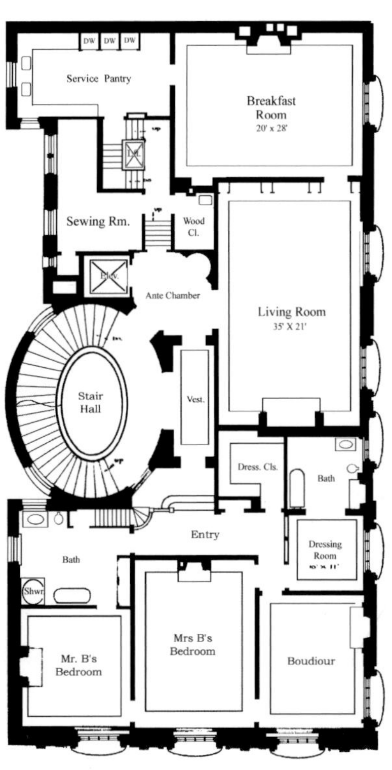

ENTRESOL PLAN. (Richard Marchand)

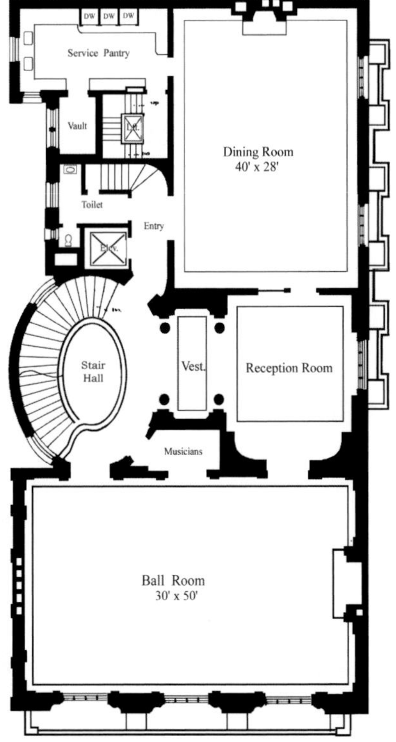

SECOND FLOOR PLAN. (Richard Marchand)

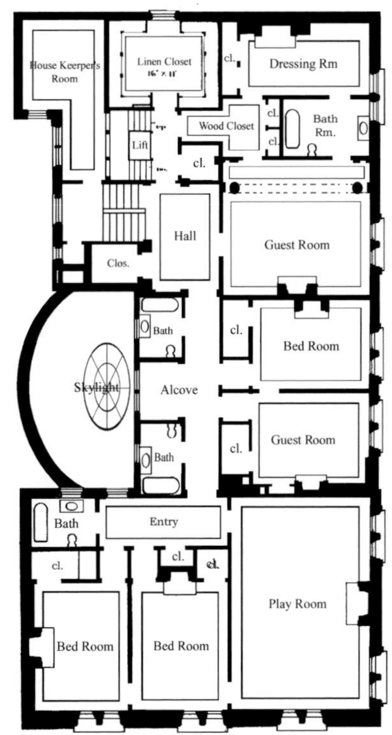

THIRD FLOOR PLAN. (Richard Marchand)

BALLROOM. (Author's Collection)

writer Mark Twain. Adele Burden, who appreciated the beauty of classical music, used her large ballroom more often for recitals than for dancing. In 1917, feeling the need for a country place, she built Woodside Acres in Syosset, Long Island. The extensive gardens there became famous in horticultural circles. She was also a founder and early president of the Colony Club. Adele was social by nature and loved to entertain her many friends. Being somewhat capricious, she often threw impromptu entertainments and took impulsive trips, whereas her husband had a quite a different temperament. As Louis Auchincloss wrote, "J. Burden had a more disciplined nature; his life was strict and orderly, perhaps too much so. He clung tenaciously to a failing business without any personal economic motive, and he always organized his pleasures, like his household, with meticulous care." James realized early in life that, to not be completely overwhelmed by enormous inherited wealth, one had to keep a firm grip on the intended direction of one's life.

The Burden house is now occupied by The Convent of the Sacred Heart, which also owns and beautifully maintains the neighboring Otto Kahn house. A with many other New York mansion owners, the sisters at Sacred Heart, in order to raise much-needed funds, rent the principal entertainment rooms of the house for parties, receptions, and fashion photography shoots.

Marshall Orme Wilson House

3 East 64th Street

Warren & Wetmore, 1903

Marshall Orme Wilson House

Exterior. (Author's Collection)

Caroline Schermerhorn Astor, queen of the "400," was initially very much against her youngest daughter's choice of a husband. This otherwise blameless child, who was also named Caroline, had fallen in love with Marshall Orme Wilson, the son of banker Richard T. Wilson. The elder Wilson was a southern gentleman from Georgia who, during the Civil War, had been sent to Europe with Confederate gold to buy supplies for the army. When the war was over, he did not return to the ravaged South but moved his family to New York, along with what appeared to be an enormous profiteering fortune. Mrs. Astor, who didn't care for the Wilsons, father or son, was said to have acquiesced only after seeing the young couple leaving church one Sunday hand in hand and obviously very much in love. She told a friend, "I felt that I could not stand in the way of their happiness a day longer." The marriage took place in 1884.

Reception Room. (Courtesy of the New-York Historical Society)

Dining Room. (Courtesy of the New-York Historical Society)

STAIRCASE. (Courtesy of the New-York Historical Society)

This was the beginning of an illustrious family matchmaking career that to this day has been unsurpassed by that of any other American family. They were dubbed the "Marrying Wilsons" by capital "S" society. A contemporary joke of the time was, "Why did the Diamond Match Company fail?" The reply: "Because the Wilsons beat them at making matches." Orme's oldest sister, May, married Ogden Goelet, scion of a New York real estate fortune second in size only to the Astors', while another sister, Belle, married into the old and aristocratic Herbert family of England. But the most sensational of the Wilson alliances was the 1896 marriage of the youngest sibling, Grace, to Cornelius Vanderbilt III. In the next generation, May Wilson Goelet's daughter was married to the Duke of Roxburghe. No New York family had ever before been this well connected.

The Orme Wilsons assumed a prominent position in New York society. Caroline Wilson became a particularly adept hostess, and as her mother's health deteriorated, she began to take on more and more of Mrs. Astor's duties.

This new responsibility created a need for a larger house. The Wilsons purchased a triple lot on East 64th Street in 1896 and hired the architectural firm of Warren & Wetmore. They designed an extremely wide Modern Renaissance town house finished with a finely detailed limestone facade. This building represents a turning away from the more vigorous elements found in houses of a decade earlier, with the effect of creating a simpler and more restrained composition. Decidedly French in inspiration, the five-story building has been shortened visibly by creating a main body of

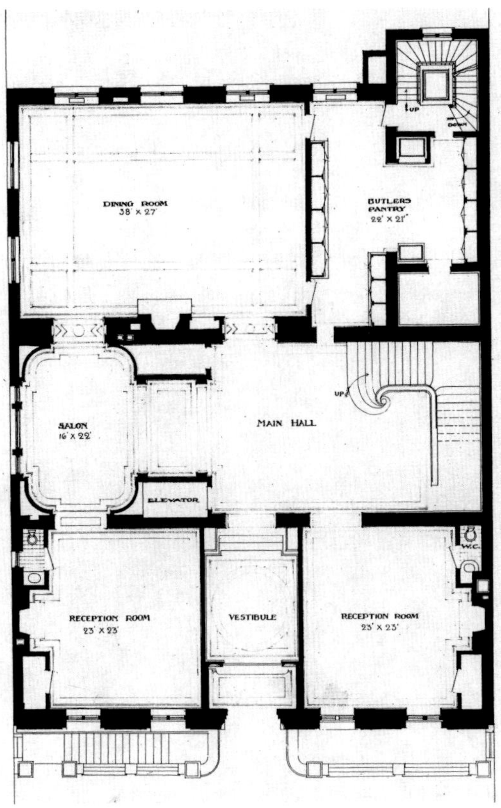

FIRST FLOOR PLAN. (Author's Collection)

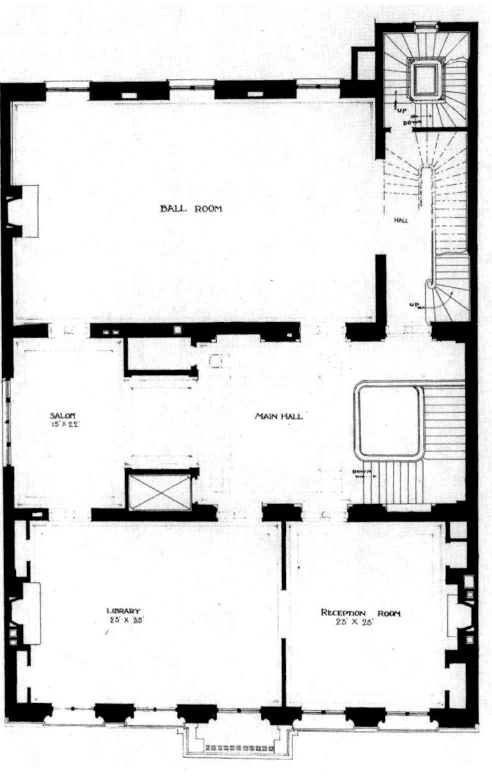

SECOND FLOOR PLAN. (Author's Collection)

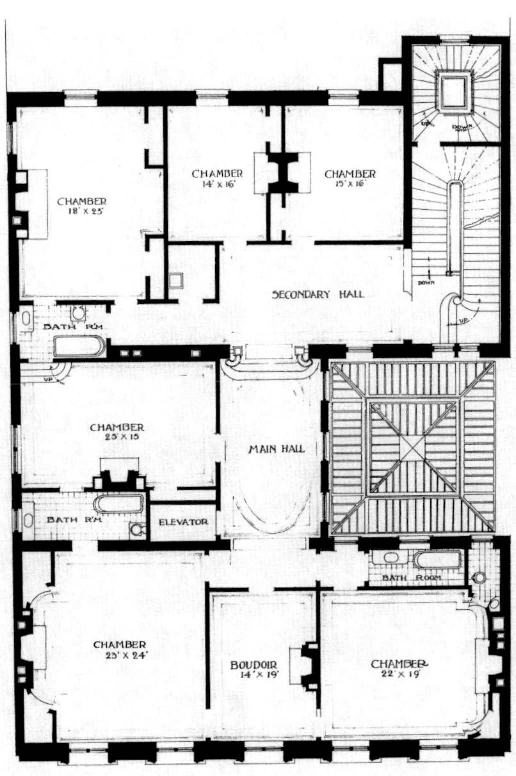

THIRD FLOOR PLAN. (Author's Collection)

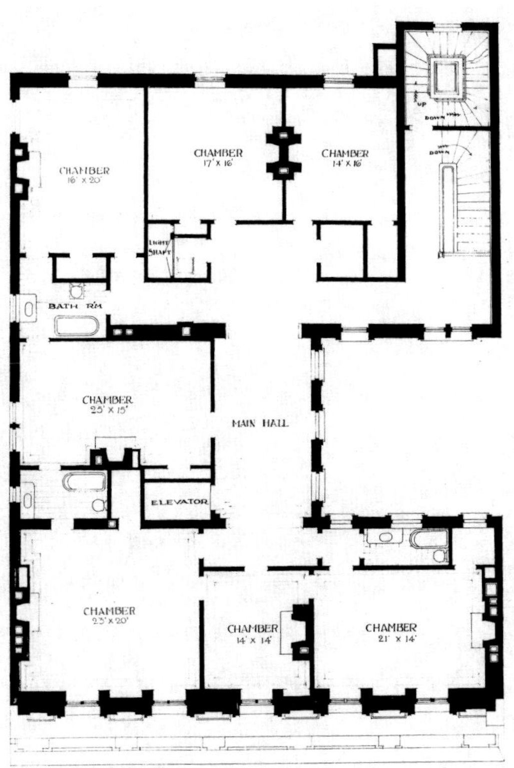

FOURTH FLOOR PLAN. (Author's Collection)

LIBRARY. (Courtesy of the New-York Historical Society)

three stories, while the two top stories are set into the mansard roof behind a balustrade.

The width of the house allows for an unusually bright interior that is rarely encountered in a mid-block house. The ground floor has a stone-sheathed main hall with a monumental staircase, and two reception rooms, each with a coat closet and lavatory. In the rear is a 27-by-38-foot Louis XVI–style paneled dining room. The second floor contains two salons, a walnut-paneled Régence library, and a 50-foot-long ballroom. The next two floors hold 12 bedrooms, a boudoir, and a sitting room. These bedroom floors are brightened by the large, light court created by the dome over the grand staircase. On the fifth floor are 13 staff rooms and 2 baths.

With a 40-room house designed for grand entertaining, the Wilsons began doing just that. A lavish party given in honor of May Goelet and her fiancé, the Scottish duke, officially opened the house. Opera singers Lillian Nordica and Enrico Caruso performed at musical soirées. The ballroom and dining room saw weekly, if not almost daily, service during the height of the New York season. In later years, the widowed Caroline Wilson opened her house for musicales and recitals for charitable purposes. Her personal philanthropies included the New York Women's League for Animals and the Beekman Street Hospital. Her younger son, Orme Jr., joined the diplomatic corps and was at one time the United States ambassador to Haiti.

In 1948, Caroline Wilson died at the Sutton Place home of her son, R. Thornton Wilson, after battling a three-year illness. She was 86 years old. Shortly after her death, 3 East 64th Street was sold to the Indian government and became the headquarters for its diplomatic representatives in the city, and remains so today.

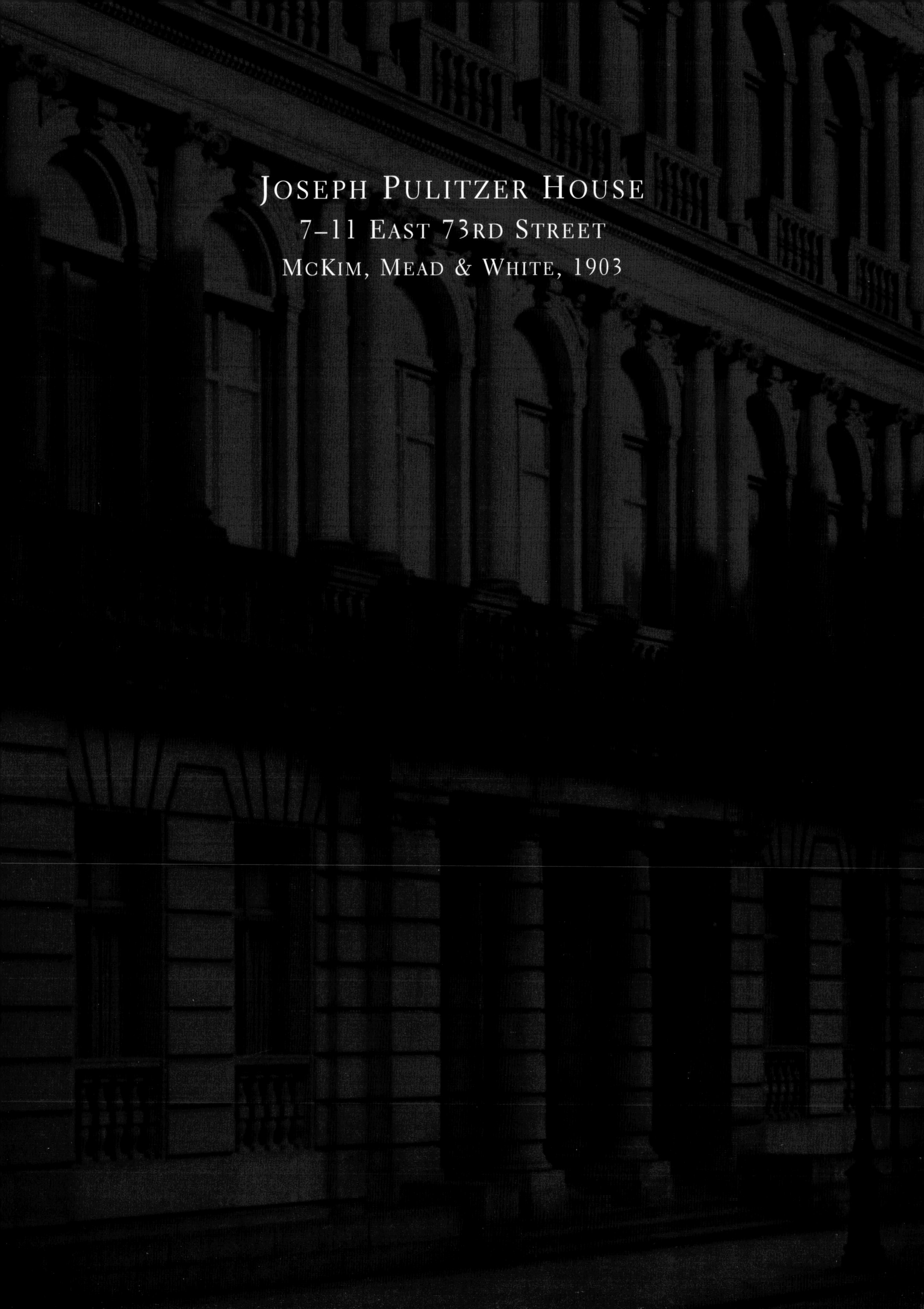

Joseph Pulitzer House

7–11 East 73rd Street

McKim, Mead & White, 1903

Joseph Pulitzer House

EXTERIOR. (Courtesy of the New-York Historical Society)

OF THE MANY prominent and influential clients of Stanford White, there probably was not anyone more difficult to work with than publisher Joseph Pulitzer. After his house and part of his art collection at 10 East 55th Street burned in 1900, Pulitzer asked White to design a fireproof house on a 74-by-100-foot plot on East 73rd Street. The owner of both the *New York World* and the *St. Louis Post-Dispatch* was by this time almost completely blind; therefore, he required White to make scale models of his architectural proposals so that he could run his hands over them. Pulitzer asked for a simple house with "no ballroom, no music room, or picture gallery under any disguise. . . no French rooms, designed or decorated to require French furniture. . . I want an American home for comfort and use and not for show or entertainment."

Following these instructions, White submitted a model of a simple Florentine palazzo to

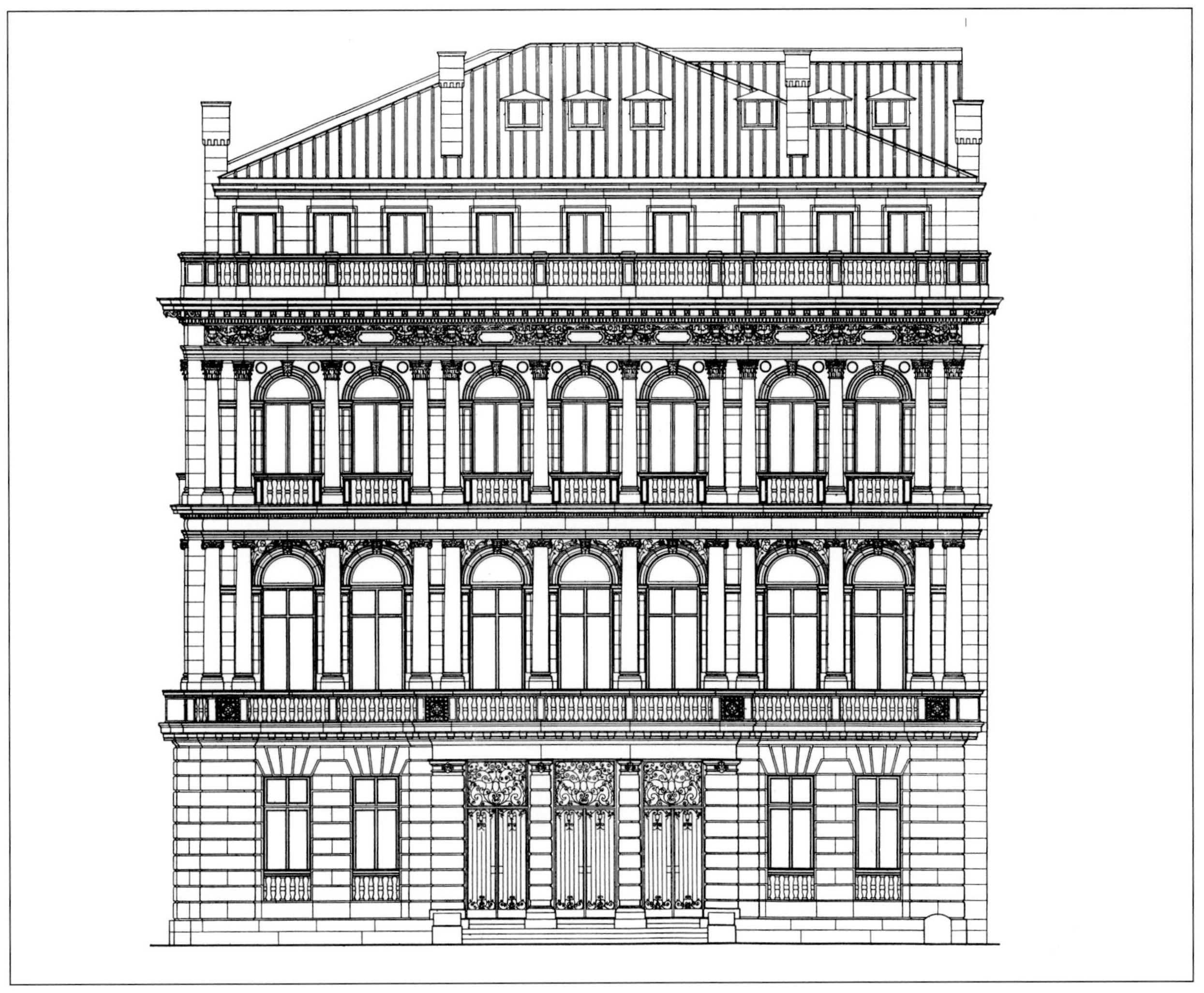

ELEVATION. (Author's Collection)

the newspaperman. This scheme was summarily rejected by the client, as were several to follow. White finally realized that Pulitzer was rejecting his proposals because the models he presented lacked the ornamental relief necessary for him to tactilely distinguish the design. White's next offering was based on the facade of the Venetian Palazzo Persaro and was wedded to the Grand Canal entrance of the Palazzo Rezzonico. This model, with its forest of engaged Doric, Ionic, and Corinthian columns, had the proper amount of movement and spatial articulation and was immediately approved by Pulitzer. Probably as a result of White's intervention, the house ended up having both a French salon and a music room. The simple American house that Pulitzer originally requested was now brimming over with fine French furniture.

As his eyesight failed, the publisher's hearing became more acute and he became almost phobic about noise. He insisted that his personal rooms in the new house be effectively soundproofed. The circular breakfast room, where he ate most of his meals, was placed in the center of the house, as far as possible from outside noises. A sealed skylight above a trellised dome lighted the area, and transparent, hollow, glass blocks filled the room's only window. Pulitzer's bedroom needed to be soundproofed as well, and a Harvard acoustics expert was

DRAWING ROOM. (Author's Collection)

SECOND FLOOR HALL. (Courtesy of the New-York Historical Society)

called in to accomplish this. The walls were stuffed with insulation, the windows were triple glazed, and the floor was put on ball bearings to prevent any vibration. When all was complete, White shut himself inside and had the workmen outside shout and pound on the walls. With no sounds penetrating, the architect was convinced the room was acoustically perfect. Unfortunately, after spending a single night in the room, Pulitzer announced that it was a failure, complaining of hearing the sounds of a pump buried far beneath the house, and accused White of trying to drive him mad. The architect's partner, William Rutherford Mead, jumped to his defense, saying, "Nerves are his trouble and that is not part of an architect's business to supply the client with a proper set of nerves." In 1904, Pulitzer hired the firm of Foster, Gade & Graham to build a

DINING ROOM. (Courtesy of the New-York Historical Society)

BREAKFAST ROOM. (Courtesy of the New-York Historical Society)

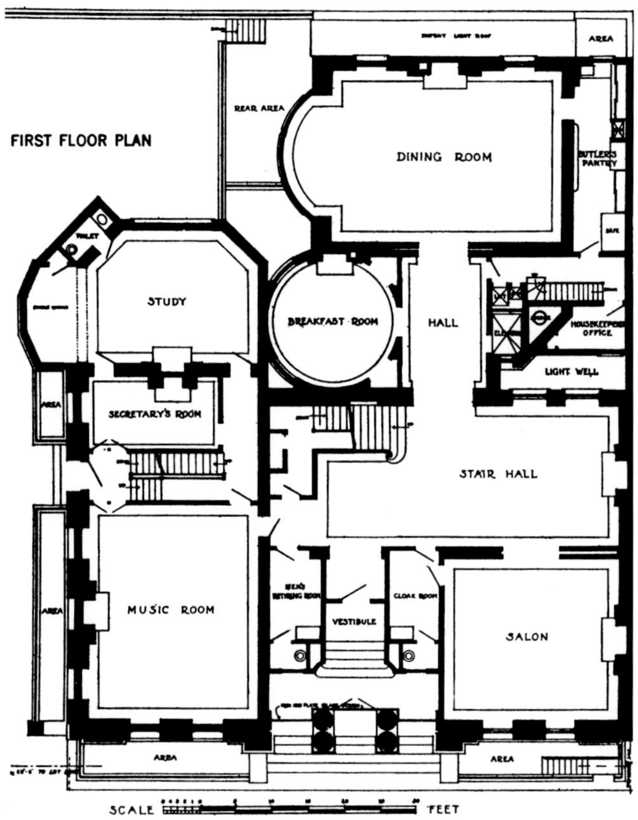

FIRST FLOOR PLAN. (Author's Collection)

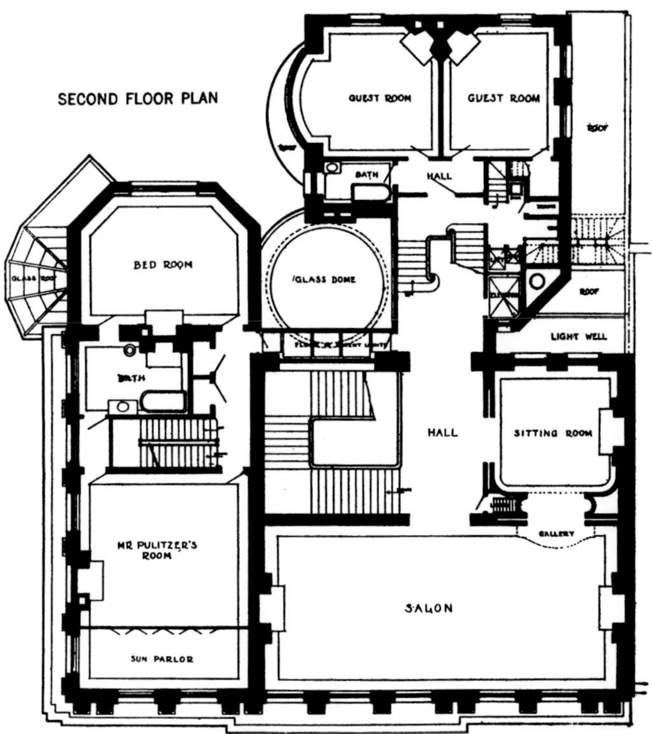

SECOND FLOOR PLAN. (Author's Collection)

new bedroom in a one-story annex located at the rear of the house, but after spending one night in it, the cranky publisher again angrily declared that he could still hear street noises and early-morning factory whistles. White came to the rescue this time by stretching thousands of silk threads across the chimney flue opening. At last, Pulitzer got a decent night's sleep.

The house, finished in 1903, had one of the most unusual residential floor plans in the city. Three sets of glazed, wrought-iron entrance doors led to a wide transverse hall with a monumental staircase. Off this hall, a reception room and a smaller hall led to the breakfast and dining rooms. Under the staircase, a door led to the music room and to Pulitzer's study with an adjoining secretary's office. On the second floor, a small sitting room was located at the top of the staircase and a 50-foot-long ballroom with five large French doors ran along the front of the house. The owner's unsuccessful first bedroom, as well as three other bedrooms, were on this floor as well. The house cost Pulitzer $369,000, exclusive of land and artwork.

Pulitzer spent only two or three months a year in his new house; he also owned homes in Bar Harbor, Maine, and Jekyll Island, Georgia, as well as a villa on the Riviera. In his later years, the publisher spent the majority of his time cruising on his 269-foot motor yacht, *Liberty*. From this boat, by telegraph, he kept firm control over his publishing empire. Joseph Pulitzer was once described by Lord Northcliffe as "the blind statesman-editor who, from his yacht in the Mediterranean, could see more than politicians in London or Washington or financiers in Wall Street." His professional life was devoted to informing and then molding public opinion for the sake of reform and social progress.

Among Pulitzer's varied philanthropic contributions was his donation of the statue of Abundance and the fountain at Grand Army Plaza, and his establishment of Columbia University's School of Journalism. Posterity will most likely remember him for the famous prize that bears his name.

After his death in 1911, the family rarely used the East 73rd Street house, and for many years it remained vacant. In 1933, after being unsuccessful in finding a buyer, the heirs decided to convert the structure into first-class apartments. This was accomplished while retaining most of Stanford White's magnificent interiors. It survives in this state today.

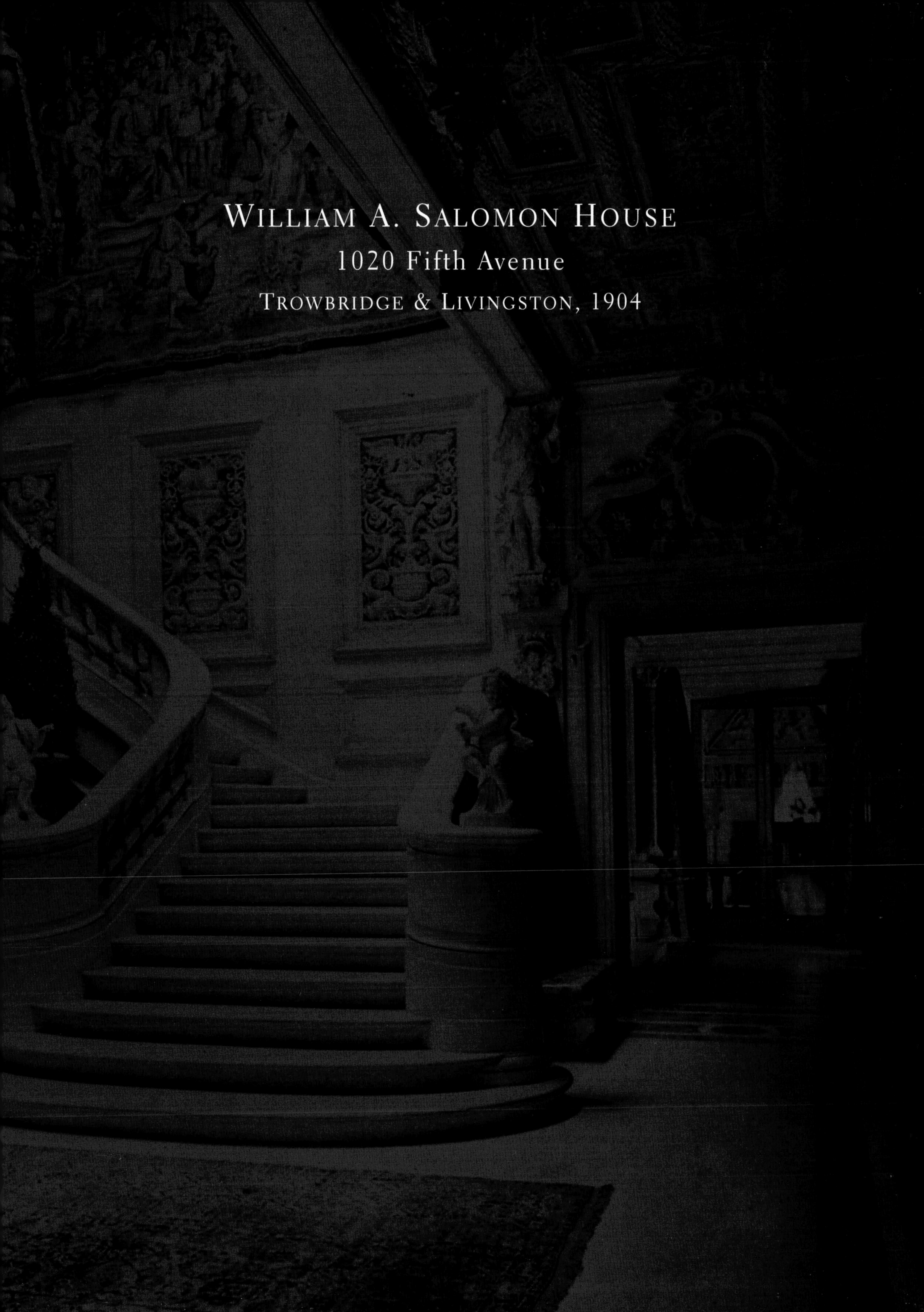

William A. Salomon House

1020 Fifth Avenue

Trowbridge & Livingston, 1904

William A. Salomon House

Exterior. (Author's Collection)

The founder of the banking house, William A. Salomon & Co., was born in Mobile, Alabama, in 1852 to a prominent local Jewish family. His mother was a great-granddaughter of Hayman Levy, who, at one time, had employed the young upstart John Jacob Astor. William Salomon began his career at the New York private banking house of Speyer & Co. He later transferred to the company's Frankfurt branch to learn European banking procedures. During the Franco-Prussian War, he moved to the London office. In 1892, the 40-year-old Salomon married Helen Forbes Lewis of Rosshire, Scotland. He and his new bride soon moved to New York, where Salomon was made a full partner in Speyer & Co. In 1902, he resigned this partnership to start his own banking house, which was soon making enormous profits by underwriting international railroad securities. Within a few years, the

HALL. (Gary Lawrance)

company established branches in Chicago, Paris, and London.

Soon after creating his company, William Salomon felt he needed an art-filled Fifth Avenue mansion to announce his financial arrival. On the northeast corner of 83rd Street, he had Trowbridge & Livingston redesign a large, if conservative, four-story brownstone mansion that had been built in the 1880s. On the renovated mansion, the first-floor windows were topped by segmental pediments, while those on the story above were triangular. In the center of the first and second floors on the Fifth Avenue facade were bay windows capped by a balustrade. To the left, a single bay-width extension housed the entrance door with a Griotte marble surround that was surmounted by a metal overhanging marquee. At the far end of the 83rd Street front was the bronze-framed bow window to the Palm Room inside.

Stepping inside past a massive pair of rosewood doors, a green marble foyer opened to a square stone vestibule with wall arches supported by Ionic columns of green and white polished

GRAND SALON. (Gary Lawrance)

PETIT SALON. (Gary Lawrance)

LIBRARY. (Gary Lawrance)

BILLIARD ROOM. (Gary Lawrance)

Dining Room. (Gary Lawrance)

marble. A square-headed door on the right opened to the large main hall that occupied the center of the building. This immense space was lined with carved white marble, most of which came from a late Renaissance villa outside of Palermo. The grand staircase rose on the innermost wall and had two large newels at its base that supported carved cherubs. From this hall, the principal reception rooms emanated. Among these was the Grand Salon, with its boiserie once thought to be from the Paris house of the Marquise de l'Hôpital. Other rooms included the Petit Salon, with delicate Louis XVI detailing, the plant-filled, stone-walled Palm Room, and a tapestried dining hall that boasted a floor-to-ceiling stone Renaissance-style mantelpiece and an ornate coffered wood ceiling.

The master suite, consisting of a large bedroom, a boudoir, and a marble-lined bathroom, occupied the Fifth Avenue front of the second floor, although William Salomon often used a separate smaller bedroom and bathroom that ran along 83rd Street. Nearby was a small family dining room where the Salomons dined when alone. The adjoining serving pantry had a dumbwaiter that brought up food from the basement kitchen. An oak-paneled inner hall contained a secondary staircase that led to the third-floor library and guest rooms. The upper part of this hall had delicately painted 18th-century panels that came from a

Dining Room Mantel. (Gary Lawrance)

Upper Hall. (Gary Lawrance)

Staircase to Third Floor. (Gary Lawrance)

MASTER BEDROOM. (Gary Lawrance)

MRS. SALOMON'S BATH. (Gary Lawrance)

CONSERVATORY. (Gary Lawrance)

house near Vienna. The library's walls were covered with red silk cut velvet, and the chimney piece held a carved stone overmantel representing a Roman naval engagement. The third-floor guest rooms were all arranged en suite around a corridor that had windows overlooking the dome of the grand staircase. On the fourth floor were 15 staff rooms and 3 bathrooms.

The civic-minded William Salomon founded the Educational Alliance to help newly arrived immigrants integrate into American life. During World War I, he donated his London house to the Red Cross as an orthopedic hospital for American officers.

Soon after his death, in 1919, his widow gave up 1020 and moved to an apartment. In 1923, the American Art Association held an auction of both the house and its treasures. Included in the sale were a Fragonard portrait of Mlle. Colombe, a 16th-century wine cooler, and an ornate Louis XVI bed from the master bedroom. The highly successful sale grossed over $1.2 million. Unfortunately, there was not a single bid for the house itself, even though the Tiepolo frescoes alone were estimated to be worth half a million dollars. It seemed that grandiose Fifth Avenue palaces were already going out of style. This one was soon to be demolished.

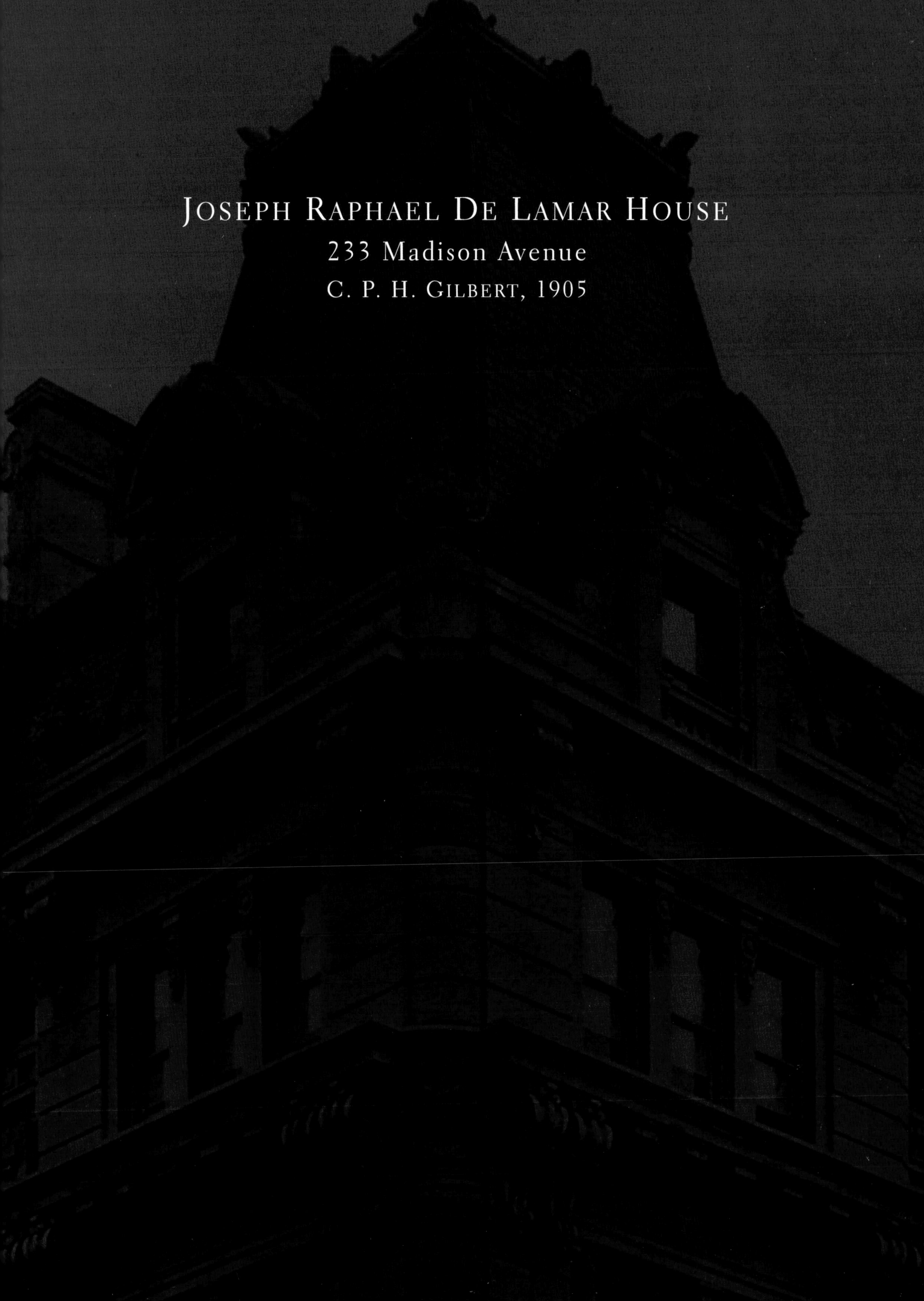

Joseph Raphael De Lamar House

233 Madison Avenue

C. P. H. Gilbert, 1905

JOSEPH RAPHAEL DE LAMAR HOUSE

EXTERIOR. (Author's Collection)

NOT EVERYONE enjoyed living in marbled magnificence. Children in particular found the large mansions of the era both oppressive and bewildering. One such afflicted youngster was Alice De Lamar, who was only eight years old when she and her father, Captain Joseph Raphael De Lamar, moved into their new Madison Avenue palace. Unlike its prim brownstone neighbors, the De Lamar house had the distinction of being the most ostentatious dwelling ever erected in Murray Hill.

The Dutch-born De Lamar went to sea as a young boy and became the captain of his own ship by the time he was 23. He later opened a successful salvage company in New England but was soon enticed to Leadville, Colorado, in search of gold. Within a few years, De Lamar was worth $20 million. In 1888, he returned to the East Coast and settled in New York, where

Staircase, c. 1928. (Author's Collection)

he invested his newfound wealth on Wall Street. On the "Street," De Lamar was always considered somewhat of a mystery man because of his taciturn ways. One newspaper called him "The American Count of Monte Cristo." He soon developed substantial interests in the Delta Beet Sugar Company, the International Nickel Company, and the American Bank Note Company. All the while, he continued to reap millions from his mining interests.

After firmly establishing himself in New York, De Lamar married Nellie Sands, the daughter of a local druggist. The couple soon went to live in Paris, where they collected paintings and decorative arts. Their daughter, Alice, was born in 1896, just a few years before the couple divorced. After the separation, De Lamar and his daughter returned to New York, where, in 1902, the captain purchased a 50-by-100-foot plot of land on the northeast corner of Madison Avenue and 37th Street. He paid $250,000

Gallery, c. 1928. (Author's Collection)

Ballroom. (Author's Collection)

Library, c. 1928. (Author's Collection)

for the site and an additional $500,000 for the new house he had erected. C. P. H. Gilbert, better known for his Gothic-style residences, such as the Felix Warburg house, was asked to design this classical Beaux Arts extravaganza. The house took almost three years to construct.

The building, constructed with steel I-beams, has fireproof interior walls made of hollow terracotta blocks. A tall mansard roof, with extensive copper cresting, caps the rusticated granite exterior walls. Flaming stone urns decorate the top of the two projecting corner towers, and large scrolled brackets support the balconies and cornice. The round-arched window above the oak double-doored entrance is set within an elaborate wooden framework. The house originally had a covered metal entrance marquee and a protective wrought-iron fence that extended around to the Madison Avenue frontage.

As elaborate as is the exterior, the lavish use of rich colors and massive amounts of gilding inside transcend it. The marble-floored entrance hall has a somewhat ill-fitting, superimposed vestibule made of glass and bronze, which seems to have been added after the structure's completion in 1905. To the left, overlooking Madison Avenue, were the library and the billiard room. The dining room and the service pantry were at the eastern end, and the kitchen was directly below in the basement. The second floor had a gold-and-white ballroom and a neo-Pompeian art gallery. The latter housed the sculpture collection that the captain chiefly acquired from the A. T. Stewart estate. This included the most famous statue of the day, Hiram Power's *The Greek Slave*. A hall between these two large rooms has a suspended musicians' gallery incorporated into the staircase. The third floor contained De Lamar's bedroom and bathroom, as well as a breakfast room and two guest rooms. Alice's bedroom, en suite with a private library and bathroom, occupied the floor above along with an additional guest bedroom. The fifth floor housed the servants' rooms, and the top floor had a laundry and a gymnasium. A dog run placed behind the mansard roof for the family canines was seldom used because of the soot that always collected there. There were two elevators: one was for the family, that went to the fifth floor, while the much smaller staff elevator went from the basement to the attic.

De Lamar almost sold the unfinished house in 1904. "His desire to be the owner of one of the finest dwellings in the city and the costliest in Murray Hill," said the *New York Times*, "is not nearly as strong as it was . . . when he bought the site." Years later, his daughter recalled, "The Ballroom never got used for that purpose. My father was in his late sixties when he moved in there, and had taken to his 'carpet slippers' pretty much of the time and did not care to entertain guests."

In 1918, at the age of 75, Captain De Lamar died of pneumonia several days after having surgery for gallstones. Of his $32 million estate, Alice De Lamar inherited one-third. Her share included her father's two yachts and Pembroke, the family's Glen Cove, Long Island, country estate. She vacated 233 Madison Avenue soon after his death. Alice later gained recognition in the art community by founding the Surrealist magazine *View*. The rest of the fortune was divided equally among the medical schools of Harvard, Columbia, and Johns Hopkins. The schools first tried to sell the mansion to a commercial enterprise but soon found out that strict Murray Hill covenants precluded this. The structure was eventually sold to The Democratic Club, which used it for many years. It was acquired in 1973 by the Polish government, and the building is still their consulate today.

Morton F. Plant House

649 Fifth Avenue

Robert W. Gibson, 1905

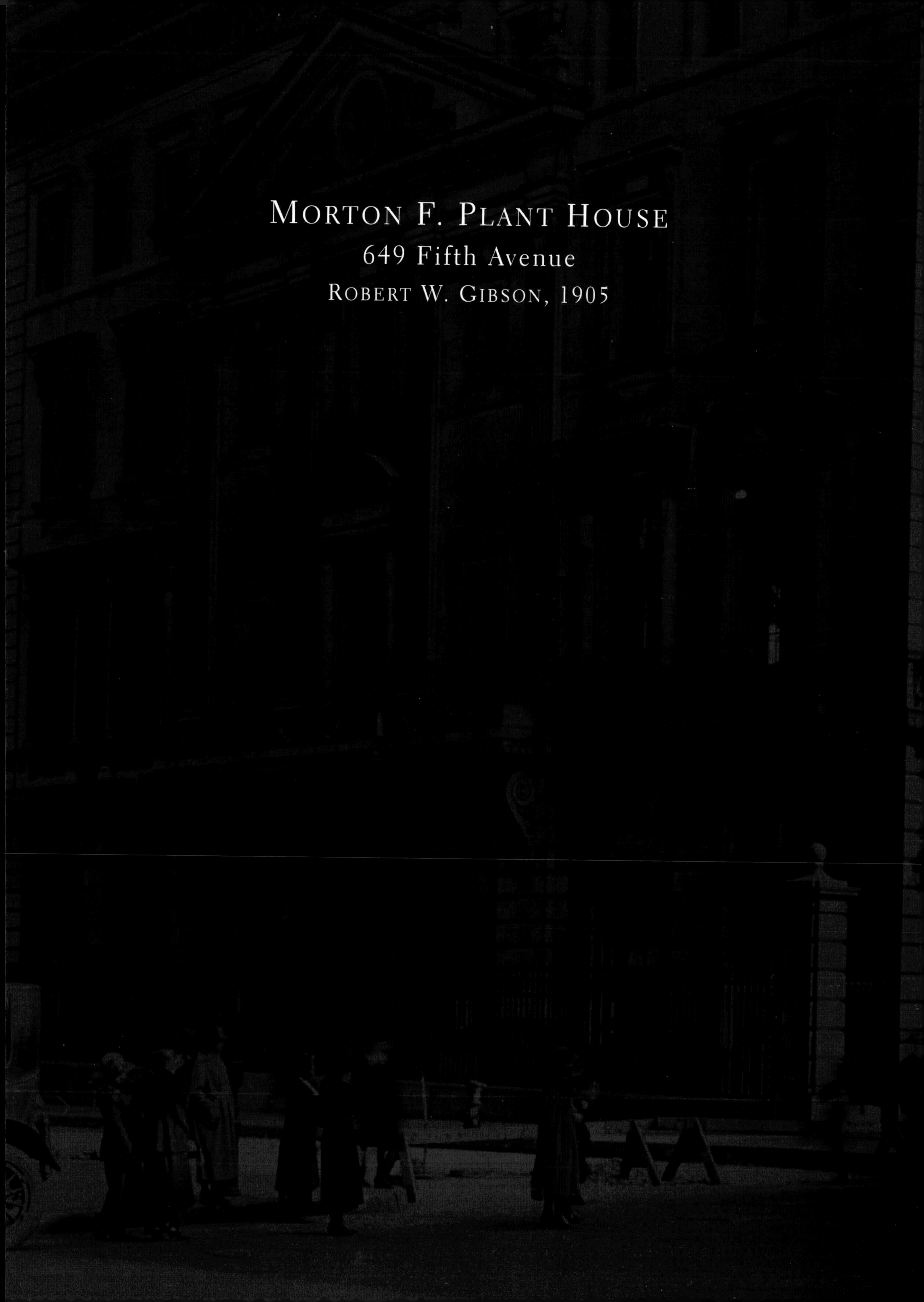

Morton F. Plant House

Exterior. (Courtesy of Cartier, New York)

In 1900, the Roman Catholic orphanage located on Fifth Avenue between 51st and 52nd streets was put up for sale by the diocese. The church undoubtedly realized that orphans could be more economically housed in less fashionable and expensive surroundings—the institution sat directly across the avenue from the late William Henry Vanderbilt's twin mansions. The Union Club purchased the southern portion of the orphanage block as the site for its new home, while William K. Vanderbilt acquired the rest of the site to protect the neighborhood from encroaching commercialization. Soon his younger brother George Vanderbilt filed plans for a pair of houses, familiarly known as the "marble twins," for the mid-block sites of 645 and 647 Fifth Avenue. This left only the 50-foot-wide lot on the corner of 52nd Street undeveloped. The choice plot remained empty until Morton

Plant, son of steamship owner H. B. Plant, paid $350,000 for it in 1902. Along with the purchase came the ironclad restrictions that only a first-class, single-family dwelling could be erected on the site, and that the house must remain exclusively residential for 25 years.

Plant hired architect Robert W. Gibson to design an English Palladian house in the style of Inigo Jones. Scamozzi Ionic capitals on the pilasters of the 52nd Street facade support a pediment decorated with two carved cornucopia. Engaged columns that support a full entablature flank the second-story windows. At the top of the building, a cornice and roof balustrade are set above a wide, intricately carved rinceaux frieze that disguises the fifth-story windows. The entrance to the house was located on 52nd Street between two stone piers that supported a decorative wrought-iron fence that wrapped around the building's two street facades. The mansion was built at a reputed cost of $400,000, exclusive of furnishings.

Inside, the center of the first floor contained a large marble-floored entrance hall with an adjoining powder room. A curved grand staircase was straight ahead, and a dining room with an adjoining butler's pantry was located on the left. A drawing room and the men's smoking room filled the Fifth Avenue end of this level. Upstairs, another large center hall gave access to the music room, library, and breakfast room. Mr. and Mrs. Plant's bedrooms and a playroom with two adjoining children's chambers occupied the third floor. The fourth floor was devoted to guest accommodations: four bedrooms, four bathrooms, and a large dressing room. At the top of the house were 12 staff rooms, a housekeeper's suite, and two enormous clothes storage rooms. Whereas most houses of the era had only one bathroom on this level, the Plant servants had the luxury of three.

Morton Plant was born in 1852 in New Haven, Connecticut, and received his education at the Russell Military School there. After his father's death, Plant expanded the family empire by branching out into railroads and banking. For pleasure, he enjoyed yachting, and his boat *Elena* won the prestigious Astor Cup race in Newport in 1913. His other passion was baseball; and he relished his ownership of the Eastern League baseball team in New London, whose yearly deficit he gladly paid. After the death of his first wife, Nellie, in 1913, Plant married the beautiful Mrs. Mae Cadwell Manwaring of Waterford, Connecticut, the following year. Soon after the marriage, he legally adopted her son, Philip, who later had the dubious distinction of being the first young man ever to be labeled a playboy by the third estate. By all accounts, he amply lived up to this title. Morton Plant and his new family principally resided at 649 Fifth Avenue but also spent time at Branford House, their country place near Groton, Connecticut.

Even with the precautions taken by the Vanderbilt family to keep their stretch of Fifth Avenue exclusively residential, commercial encroachment continued to invade the area. By 1916, Plant had had his fill of the traffic and noise that surrounded his mansion, so he went back to William K. Vanderbilt to ask him to remove the restrictions that had been placed on the property. Vanderbilt was then not quite ready to give up on the residential aspect of the neighborhood, but he did agree to buy the house from Plant for $1 million. Plant promptly removed himself to the upper reaches of Fifth Avenue and settled in a princely new dwelling that faced Central Park at 86th Street.

Vanderbilt unsuccessfully tried to sell or even lease the building as a residence. He finally allowed the French jeweler, Cartier, to lease the building for an annual rent of $50,000. The famous jeweler eventually purchased the property outright and today still occupies the building. Even though missing its decorative wrought-iron fence, and with the ground-floor fenestration altered to allow for showcase windows, the structure still retains much of its original dignity. Along with the adjoining half of the "marble twins," 649 is all that remains of the magnificent private palaces that once lined Vanderbilt row.

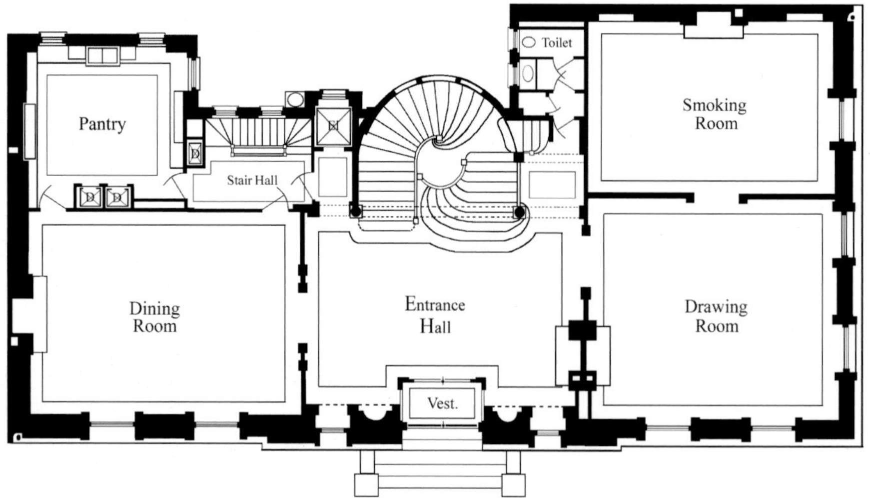

FIRST FLOOR PLAN. (Richard Marchand)

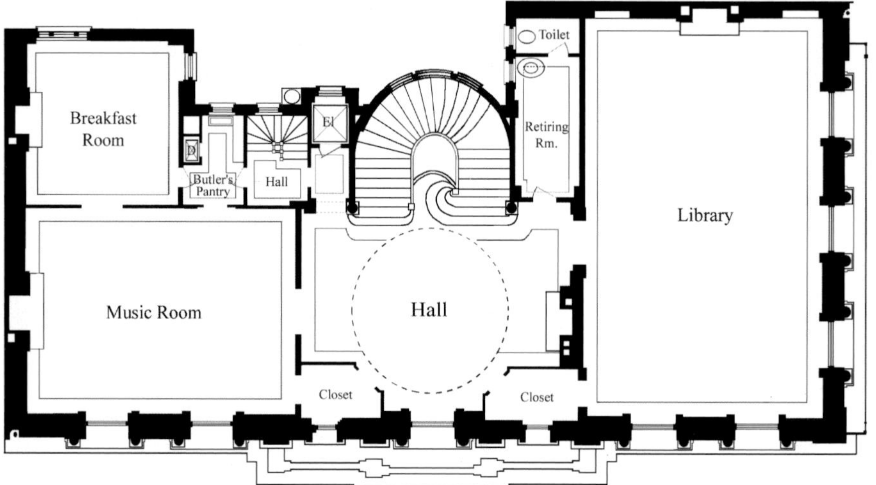

SECOND FLOOR PLAN. (Richard Marchand)

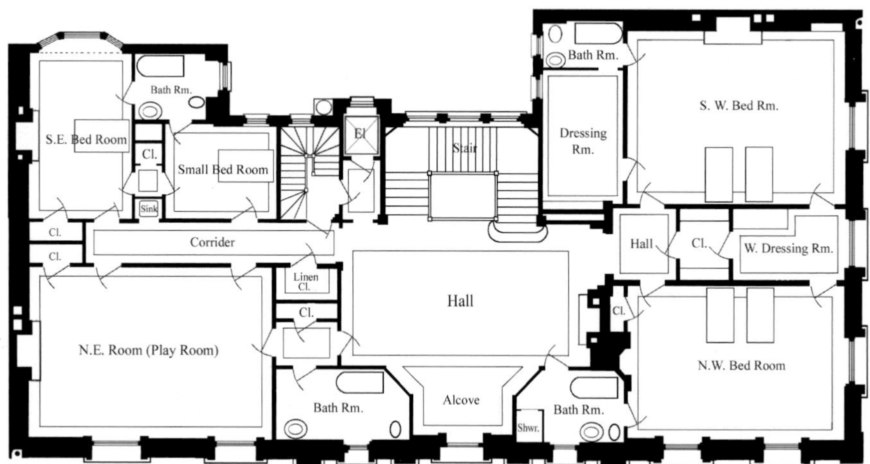

THIRD FLOOR PLAN. (Richard Marchand)

Henry Phipps House

1063 Fifth Avenue

Trowbridge & Livingston, 1905

Henry Phipps House

Exterior. (Courtesy of the Museum of the City of New York)

Born in Philadelphia, the third child of English immigrants, Henry Phipps moved at the age of six to Allegheny, Pennsylvania, where his father opened up shop as a cobbler. A boy living in the neighborhood was Scottish-born Andrew Carnegie; he and young Phipps became lifelong friends as well as eventual business partners. Henry, who was always called Harry, was shy and retiring by nature but possessed a keen financial genius that led him in 1862 to borrow $800 to become a partner in the fledgling ironworks company of Kloman Brothers. This company later merged with Carnegie's Cyclops Iron Company, which eventually became the nucleus of the giant Carnegie Steel Corporation.

Next to Carnegie, Harry Phipps was the largest stockholder in the corporation when it was sold in 1901 to a J. P. Morgan–led syndicate; his share was of the sale was worth $40 million.

ENTRANCE HALL. (Courtesy of the New-York Historical Society)

With this windfall, Phipps, like Carnegie, donated large amounts to different institutions for the betterment of mankind. He gave $3 million to found the Phipps Institute for the Study, Treatment, and Cure of Tuberculosis at the University of Pennsylvania. He also founded the allied Phipps Tuberculosis Dispensary at Johns Hopkins Hospital in Baltimore. In New York, he built the Phipps Houses, which set the standard for functional lower-income housing in the United States. Before his death, the beneficent Phipps gave away over $10 million.

In 1872, when he was still only moderately well-to-do, Phipps married 22-year-old Annie Childs Shaffer. Of German-French descent, she bore him four children: Amy, Jay, Henry, and Howard. Harry, who liked to travel, took them abroad so often that they acquired an international polish at a very young age. In addition, the family often leased an estate in the English countryside and stayed there for extended periods. By 1891, they had given up their house in America completely and opted for a life of continual travel. As the boys grew older, however, they were sent back to the United States to be educated.

In 1901, the same year that Carnegie Steel was sold, Harry and Annie thought it time to settle down and build a house in New York in order to be near their children and grandchildren. They purchased a large lot on the northeast corner of 87th Street and Fifth Avenue and hired the prominent New York architectural firm of Trowbridge & Livingston to

RECEPTION ROOM. (Courtesy of the New-York Historical Society)

DINING ROOM. (Courtesy of the New-York Historical Society)

MUSIC ROOM. (Courtesy of the New-York Historical Society)

Second Floor Hall. (Courtesy of the Museum of the City of New York)

design a white marble mansion for the site. The structure was set behind a drive-through terrace that contained a large, low fountain on axis with the front door. The architects designed a single-story orangerie at the east end of this terrace to block out the view of neighboring buildings.

Even though 1063 was one of the more dignified houses on Fifth Avenue, Mr. and Mrs. Phipps were not completely satisfied with it. Annie thought the interiors were overtly cold and formal. The formation of these disputed rooms began on a trip to Europe in 1903, when the Phippses met an architect named George Crawley, whom their eldest son, Jay, had just hired to design a country house in Old Westbury, Long Island. Crawley told Harry and Annie that he would be happy to see what he could do for them when he came to the United States to supervise the construction of Jay's house.

Initially, they must have been pleased with the Englishman's suggestions, because Phipps hired Crawley to do the principal interiors of the house. Harry, writing to his brother-in-law, said, "The new house looks first rate. . . Crawley is really able in the line that Jay selected him for, and that is decoration." Annie, however, was still not pleased, because she did not wish to live with Crawley's "expensive taste." He, on the other hand, was more than just a little put out because of the intransigence of his client. He neatly explained the problem in a letter to Jay:

> Your mother has decided not to have
> the bronze work done for the Library

> mantelpiece, I regret to say. You saw and approved the design but she did not like it—the 2 tables for the breakfast room she saw & called them awful—she dislikes them so much that she will not have them sent over—which is most unfortunate. Her own taste is for simple & inexpensive things & the thought of what the cost of my various work has been preys upon her mind to such a degree that she simply loathes the sight of everything I have done great & small. She means to be very kind about it—but that is the plain fact. It seems a terrible pity that her wishes were not consulted more at the start—or in fact that I ever undertook the work but it can't be helped now. The total cost of all the work and furniture & plate. . . has amounted to under $400,000. . . I don't really think that very excessive for a white marble palace which cost with its ground near 3 times that amount. Many people both in England & America have spent far larger sums in similar cases, I trust you will see this & later endeavor to defend my work and reputation with your mother and father & tell them that I am not the awful monster of wasteful extravagance that they suppose & that many men of far less wealth have spent infinitely greater sums on their homes—which is the simple truth.

Even though it was a great source of disappointment for Annie, the house was finally completed in 1905. It largely became an empty stage because Harry and Annie preferred to travel and spend time with their children rather than stay in 1063. The unsocial couple chose to follow fashion and build a Great House without fully

BREAKFAST ROOM. (Courtesy of the New-York Historical Society)

comprehending the purpose behind it. This may have been urged on them by their socially ambitious offspring. Jay's Westbury House was a great success and would be used by his branch of the family until the mid-1950s. The only grand functions ever held at 1063 were those given by Harry's children, none of whom seemed to have any problem dwelling in "Crawley's expensive taste."

The largest room in the house was the music room on the ground floor overlooking Fifth Avenue. Its chief glory was the magnificent collection of tapestries that hung in it, and most of the accompanying furniture was 17th- and 18th-century English. Also on this floor, connected by a long stone traverse hall, was a reception room with Watteau–style panels and a Queen Anne–style paneled breakfast room. But the building's most acclaimed room was

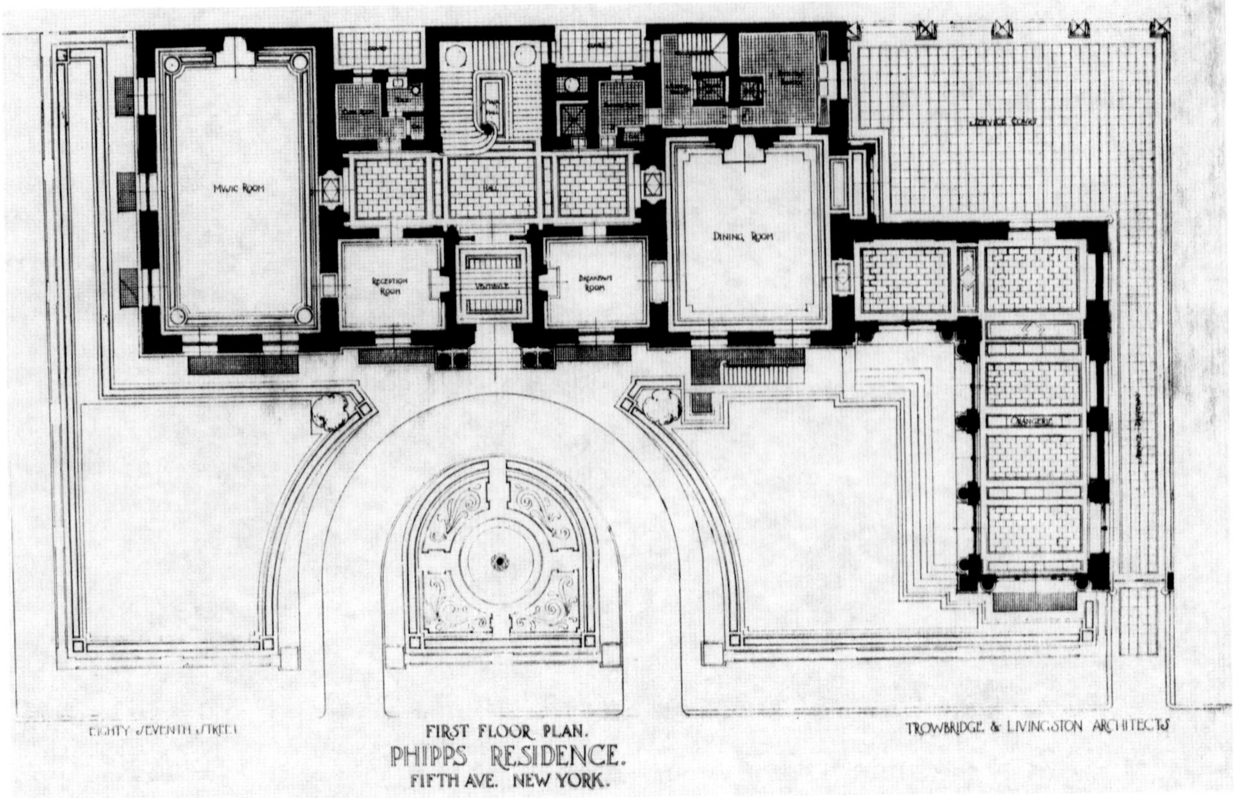

FIRST FLOOR PLAN. (Author's Collection)

the paneled dining room with its two overmantel pendants carved by Grinling Gibbons. Off this room was the plant-filled, L-shaped orangerie. The second floor had a library that overlooked the park, as well as suites for Mr. and Mrs. Phipps. Guest rooms, nurseries for grandchildren, and staff rooms filled the third floor.

In 1914, Phipps and Andrew Carnegie went to Thomas Alva Edison's studio in New Jersey to have their voices and images recorded on his kinetoscope. The following year, Harry became very ill and retired from public life. He spent the last 15 years of his existence as a semi-invalid. Soon after her husband's illness began, Annie hired Horace Trumbauer to build Bonnie Blink, a Georgian Revival country house in Great Neck, Long Island. This house was much simpler in scope and considerably more to her taste. It also had the advantage of being close to the estates of her children and grandchildren. Just before Harry's death in 1930, his wife sold 1063 to developers. Before the building was demolished, the white marble veneer was stripped from the facade and taken to daughter Amy's Long Island estate, where it lay until quite recently in an empty field. The only intact remnant of the mansion, the Gibbons dining room, was taken by Jay to Westbury House and housed there in a new wing especially designed for it.

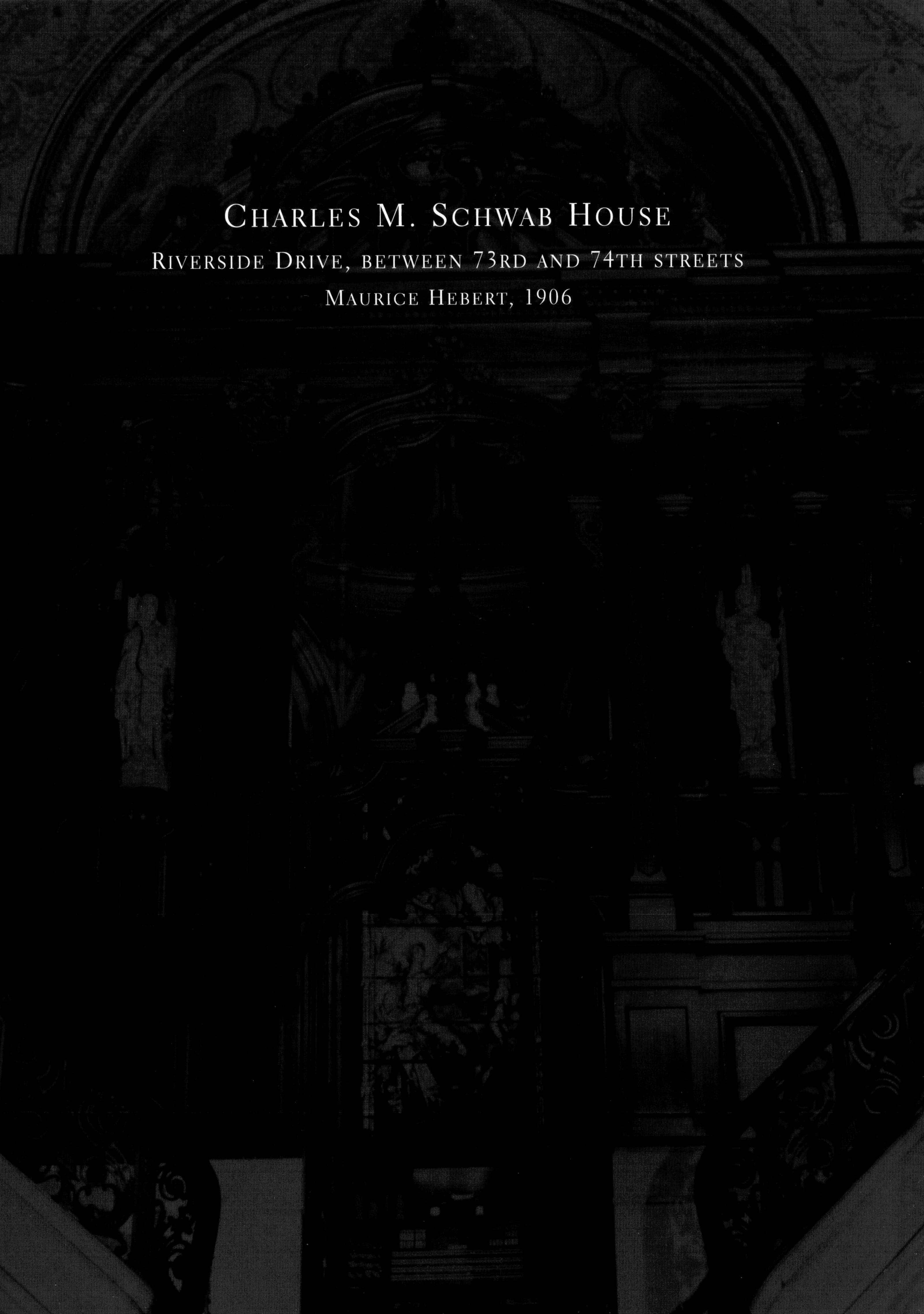
CHARLES M. SCHWAB HOUSE
RIVERSIDE DRIVE, BETWEEN 73RD AND 74TH STREETS
MAURICE HEBERT, 1906

Charles M. Schwab House

Exterior. (Author's Collection)

Charles Schwab was radically different from most of his fellow plutocrats in that he was personable, friendly, and approachable. He was also egalitarian: he once introduced his servant to the king of Sweden by saying, "King, this is my valet—he's a Swede, too!" Schwab was as comfortable with a sweaty steel mill worker as he was with captains of industry. Born in Williamsburg, Pennsylvania, he was educated at a Franciscan college where he studied mathematics, Latin, and his special favorite, music. At 16, he moved to nearby Braddock, Pennsylvania, to work in a Carnegie-owned steel mill.

Schwab began his career by driving stakes for one dollar a day, but within two years, the industrious Schwab had become the plant's chief engineer. He soon married the daughter of a local chemist, and to make extra money, he gave music lessons for 60 cents an hour.

WEST END AVENUE FACADE, C. 1940S. (Courtesy of the New-York Historical Society)

RIVERSIDE DRIVE GATES, C. 1940S. (Courtesy of the New-York Historical Society)

Entrance Hall, c. 1940s. (Courtesy of the New-York Historical Society)

The man who once said, "I expect every man to do a little more than he's paid for. I do!" became the head of Carnegie Steel at the age of 35. When it was incorporated into U.S. Steel in 1900, the J. P. Morgan–controlled board elected him president with an annual salary of $2 million and a percentage of the profits. A few years later, after having a difference of opinion with its board of directors, Schwab left U.S. Steel to found and develop Bethlehem Steel into one of its major competitors. He also began to buy shipyards in anticipation of war in Europe.

With an annual income in excess of $2 million, Charles Schwab could afford an imposing city dwelling. After a futile search of upper Fifth Avenue, for a plot large enough for his architectural ambitions, the steel czar purchased the entire block between Riverside Drive and West End Avenue from 73rd to 74th Street, as the site for his new house. He paid $865,000 for the former Orphans Asylum Society property and became the only modern New Yorker whose exclusive residential site had four street frontages. In 1901, after clearing the area of the asylum buildings, construction started on a 75-room, 30-bath house that Schwab called "On The Hudson." Designed by Maurice Hébert, the structure took over four years to erect.

Set in the midst of extensive gardens, the four-story granite house had a facade adapted from the French Renaissance chateau Chenonceaux, with details from other Loire Valley chateaux. The 116-foot corner towers had incomparable views of the

STAIRCASE, C. 1940S. (Courtesy of the New-York Historical Society)

Hudson River and the Palisades. Schwab, being athletic by nature, equipped the basement with a swimming pool, bowling alley, gymnasium, and steam room. Because of the site grading, the principal rooms were placed on a first floor that was some 20 feet higher than Riverside Drive. This floor was centered on a two-and-a-half-story Francis I–style great hall that had a vaulted ceiling and stained-glass windows by John La Farge. A gallery ran around the second level of the great hall and looked down on an elaborate white marble staircase. A Louis XVI music room held a pipe organ that, unlike his peers, Schwab actually enjoyed playing. The library was patterned after the 16th-century rooms at Fontainebleau, and the drawing room was inspired by the salon at the Petit Trianon. Four Gobelin tapestries, hanging from the walls in the dining room, represented the seasons. There was also a Louis XII breakfast room and a Henri II billiard room. The art gallery, located in a separate wing at the rear of the building, featured important paintings by Corot, Hals, Rembrandt, Titian, and Velázquez. One of Schwab's favorites, Turner's *Rockets and Blue Lights*, was among many art objects he purchased from the renowned art dealer Joseph Duveen.

On the second floor was a consecrated chapel where the devout Schwabs had a local priest come and say daily Mass. Extensive individual suites for Mr. and Mrs. Schwab adjoined chapel; each contained a sitting room, bedroom, dressing room, and bath. On the third floor were guest accommodations,

LIBRARY, C. 1940S. (Courtesy of the New-York Historical Society)

ART GALLERY, C. 1940S. (Courtesy of the New-York Historical Society)

Drawing of Louis XVI Parlor. (Author's Collection)

Drawing of Louis XVI Bedroom. (Author's Collection)

Bedroom Suite, c. 1940s. (Courtesy of the New-York Historical Society)

MASTER BATH, C. 1940S. (Courtesy of the New-York Historical Society)

and the top floor was reserved for the staff. The total cost for this baronial magnificence came to over $4 million, along with an additional annual maintenance cost of close to half a million dollars.

With all of its antique-inspired atmosphere, On the Hudson was also, mechanically speaking, in the vanguard of new construction. As with Carnegie's mansion, Schwab had one of the first installations of central air-conditioning in the country. In the subbasement, the mansion had its own power plant and an enormous heating system that required six tons of coal a day in the winter. The building was also equipped with its own telephone switchboard and three electrically powered elevators.

The Schwabs moved into the mansion two weeks before Christmas in 1905, although the interior finish was not completed for another year. Charles Schwab often entertained his many musical and theatrical friends at parties at the new house, he once paid Enrico Caruso $10,000 to sing at a soirée. For the next quarter of a century, notables from the worlds of business, society, and entertainment filled the mansion.

After his wife's death in 1932, Schwab seemed to lose his rare zest for life. Suffering financial setbacks, he tried to sell the Riverside Drive house, but in the midst of the Great Depression, no one wanted a block-size Loire Valley–style chateau. He remained the owner of On the Hudson until his death in 1939.

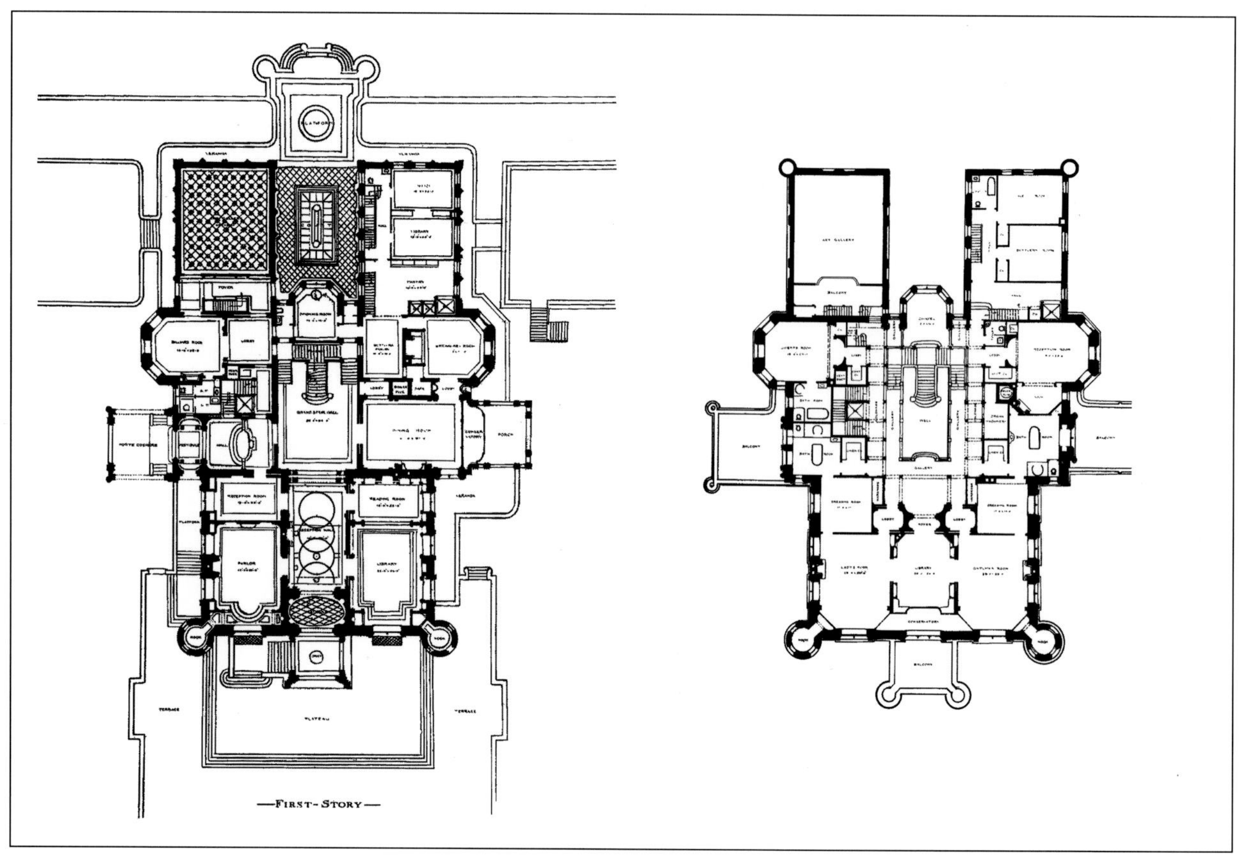

First (left) and Second Floor Plans. (Richard Marchand)

At that time, the financial world was stunned to learn that he was almost $2 million in debt. There was some talk during the 1940s of the city buying the Schwab house as an official residence for the mayor, but Fiorello LaGuardia took one look at it and said, "What, me in THAT?"

After an auction of its contents, the house remained vacant and decaying for eight years. It was finally torn down in 1948 to make way for a large brick apartment complex of unsurpassed banality.

(Author's note: All interior photographs were taken just prior to demolition.)

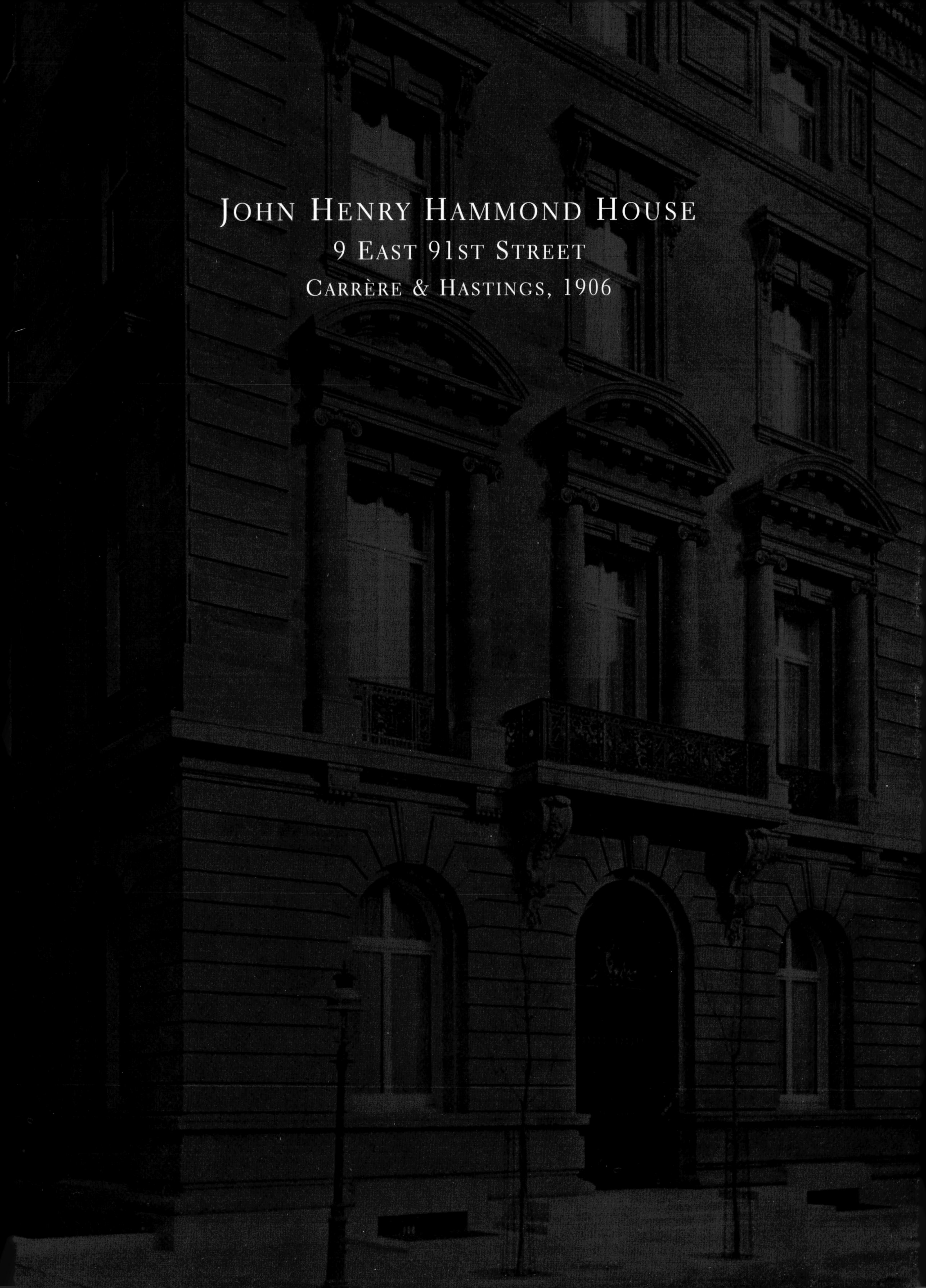

John Henry Hammond House

9 East 91st Street

Carrère & Hastings, 1906

John Henry Hammond House

Exterior. (Author's Collection)

In 1899, Mr. and Mrs. William Douglas Sloane's daughter Emily married lawyer John Henry Hammond. Hammond, who had attended both Yale and Columbia Law School, was the son of General William Tecumseh Sherman's chief of staff. The Sloane-Hammond nuptials took place at St. Bartholomew's Church, followed by a wedding breakfast for 300 of the "Oh-So-Social" at the home of the bride's uncle, George Washington Vanderbilt. After the wedding trip, the couple returned to live in a house on East 72nd Street. They resided there until Emily's mother decided to give the quickly expanding family a new home on a far more sumptuous scale. This house was constructed on the eastern portion of the East 91st Street property that the Sloanes had purchased from Andrew Carnegie in 1901. The western half of this site was already occupied by the house of Emily's sister, Mrs. James A. Burden Jr. At the

First Floor Gallery. (Courtesy of the New-York Historical Society)

unveiling of the plans for the 65-by-100-foot house, Hammond was heard to utter, "Emily, I'm going to be considered a kept man."

The couple and their five children moved into the new East 91st Street house in 1906. One individual who was definitely not put off by the immensity of the place was the owner's son, musicologist John Hammond, who found he could easily slip in and out without being noticed by his parents. The limestone structure designed by Carrère & Hastings is less original than the adjacent Burden house, but it does convey a massive dignity. The five-story mansion has a rusticated ground floor with arched window and door openings. On the second floor, the windows have engaged Ionic columns that support a complete entablature and pediment. A heavy cornice hides the fifth floor from view.

This very large house required a full-time staff of 16, with the male servants' rooms relegated to the basement, far from the female staff on the top floor. The latter shared their floor with an infirmary that was used whenever any of the Hammond children were ill. The fourth floor held children's bedrooms plus a large playroom with a piano. The floor below contained Mr. and Mrs. Hammond's private suite as well as guest bedrooms.

Dining Room. (Courtesy of the New-York Historical Society)

The second floor, which had 18-foot-high ceilings, had a Louis XVI–style ballroom and an adjoining music room. The doors between these rooms could be opened to create an immense space for the musical evenings the family loved. Two children, John and Emily, together gave violin-piano recitals for family and friends. In 1935, after John had discovered Benny Goodman, his mother allowed the clarinetist to play in the music room as long as he played the Mozart clarinet quintet. The boy's sister later shocked society by marrying the King of Swing.

Emily Hammond was a deeply religious woman who suffered from the "conflict between living in opulence and the always nagging sin of ostentation." Her answer, as her son relates, "was to furnish it as she accoutred herself, in a subdued and often tasteless fashion." Most of the furnishings came from "the undistinguished but expensive stock of the family store," W. & J. Sloane, which sold works of carpets, art, antiques, and new furniture. In later years, John Hammond Jr. could not remember a single piece of important art or a rare antique anywhere in the house. But the mid-1940s auction catalogue of the home's furnishings speaks differently, as it abounds with antiques, tapestries, porcelain, and paintings that many would consider rare works of art.

SALON. (Courtesy of the New-York Historical Society)

BALLROOM. (Courtesy of the New-York Historical Society)

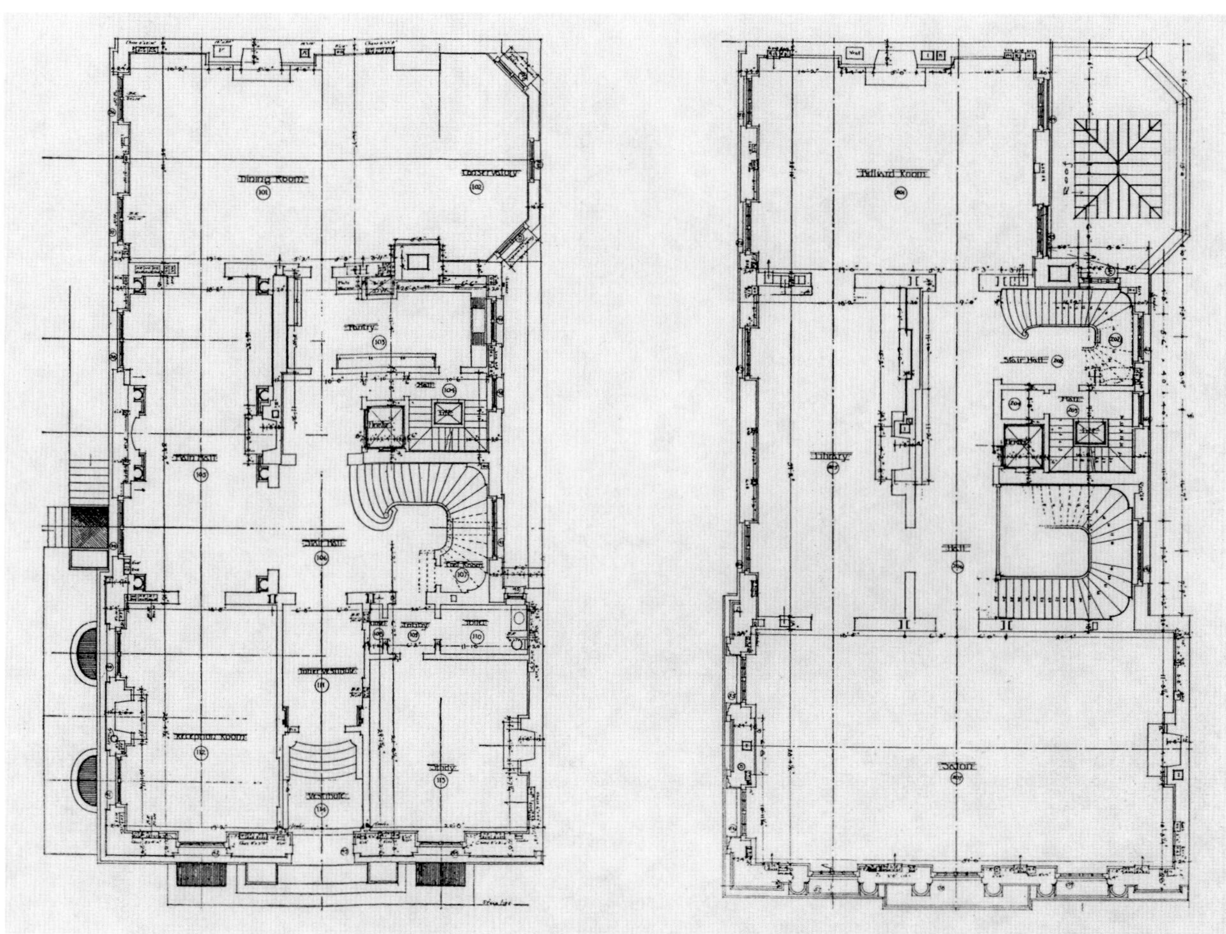

First and Second Floor Plans. (Author's Collection)

In the early 1940s, the Hammonds tired of the responsibilities of maintaining their elaborate residence and decided to move to an apartment at 778 Park Avenue; they also acquired an estate, Dellwood Farm, in Mount Kisco, New York. The house was sold in 1946 to Dr. Ramon Castroviejo, a prominent Spanish-born ophthalmologist, who used it as a combined private eye hospital and residence. In 1975, the landmarked building was bought by the Soviet government and is now the Consulate General of the Russian Federation.

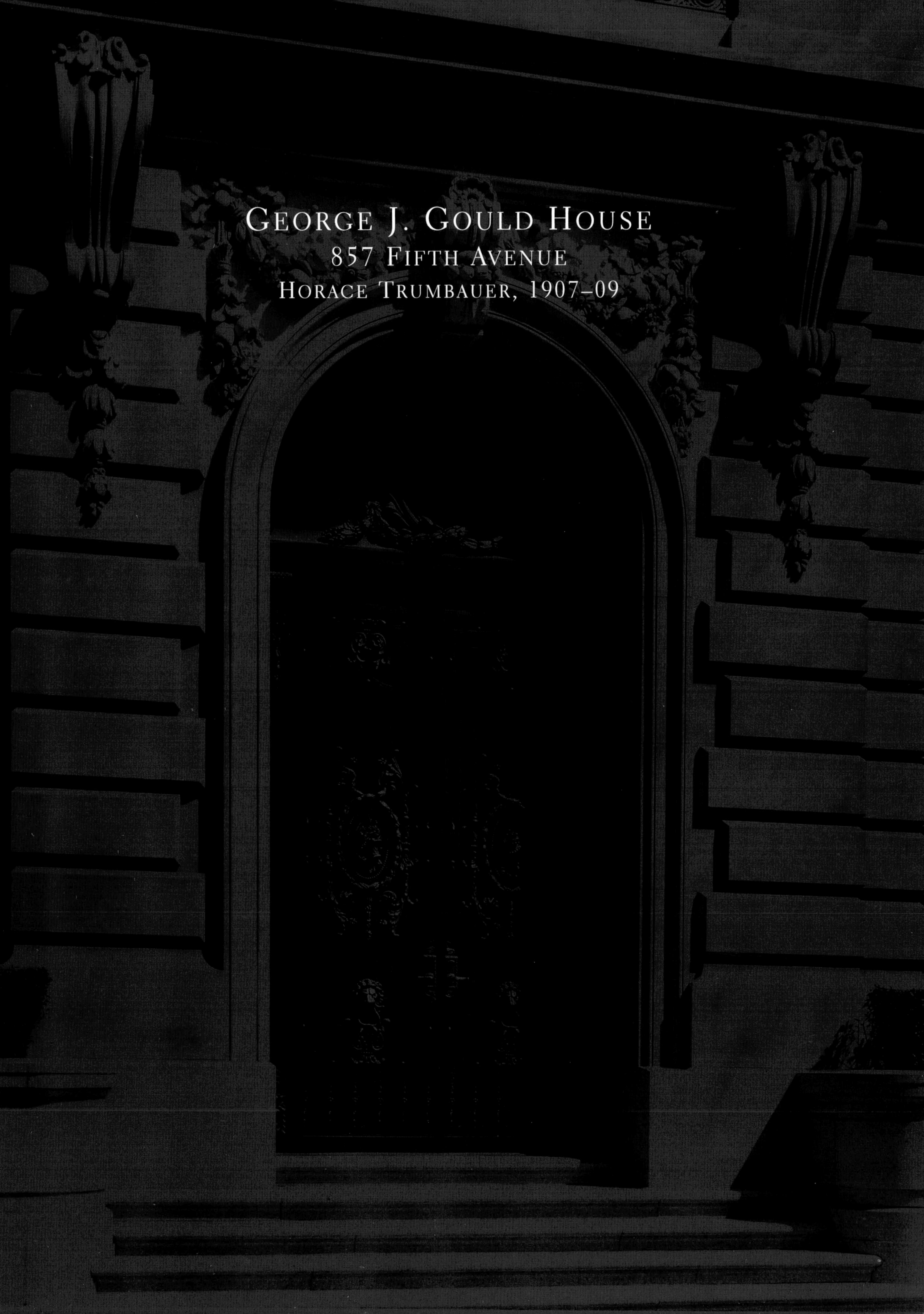

George J. Gould House

857 Fifth Avenue

Horace Trumbauer, 1907–09

George J. Gould House

Exterior. (Courtesy of the Museum of the City of New York)

The Gould family's association with 857 Fifth Avenue began just before the death in 1892 of financier and railroad tycoon Jay Gould. His eldest son, George J. Gould, in 1886 married the beautiful New York actress Edith Kingdon, and as a wedding gift, the groom's father gave the couple a comfortable brownstone at 1 East 47th Street. Though the senior Gould had never been accepted into the "400," George and Edith began making headway into the social fabric of the city. With a growing family—they eventually had seven children—and a hectic social schedule, the couple was soon in need of larger quarters. Jay presented George with a Victorian mansion at 857 Fifth Avenue, on the northeast corner of East 67th Street.

Within half a decade, this commodious residence was overflowing with family and the large staff of servants required to maintain it. In

ENTRANCE DETAIL. (Courtesy of the Museum of the City of New York)

ORIGINAL GOULD HOUSE. (Byron Collection, courtesy of the Museum of the City of New York)

Entrance Hall. (Author's Collection)

Reception Room. (Moss Collection)

Dining Room. (Author's Collection)

Ballroom. (Moss Collection)

Drawing Room. (Moss Collection)

1906, Horace Trumbauer was called in to replace the Victorian house with something larger and in a more fashionable Modern Renaissance style—an amalgam of devices culled from Italian and French architectural philosophies of the 16th through the 18th centuries. Had all the decorative, and decidedly French, detailing of the Gould house been removed, a rather stark, but completely recognizable, Florentine palazzo fenestration would have been left. During the two-year construction period, the Gould family primarily resided at Georgian Court, their Lakewood, New Jersey, estate.

Trumbauer's finished work represented an inventive reinterpretation of the French classical decorative idiom. The limestone-finished mansion had four visible stories that rested on a raised basement set behind a protective street-level balustrade. Set within a roof-level parapet, which was interspersed with balustraded sections, a copper-crested, slate-covered mansard roof enclosed the fifth floor. Sitting on a robust rusticated base, the main entrance was placed in the center of the long East 67th Street facade. The principal body of the house was defined by heavy quoining at each corner and was crowned by a fleur-de-lis-embellished frieze. Each level of the house received a unique, but related, window treatment. The first-floor windows had gently arched openings that were centered by carved facial voussoirs; the

Second Floor Hall. (Moss Collection)

floor above had balustraded windows, each capped by a full entablature supported by scrolled brackets. Supporting brackets and carved floral festoons adorned the third-floor sills, and the lintels bore floral carvings centered by a decorative keystone. A guilloche band divided the third and fourth floors, where the latter's windows were separated by projecting rectangular panels.

Trumbauer designed the mansion's period rooms to celebrate and enhance the lifestyle of the Gould family. The principal reception room, predominantly French in style, often accommodated over 500 people. A marble-lined vestibule led into a French Caen stone–sheathed entrance hall that at its center had a skylighted staircase with an ornate wrought-iron railing. Overlooking the park was a reception room in the Louis XV style; at the other end of the house, the dining room was finished in a Louis XVI style.

On the second floor, a large hall separated the drawing room and the ballroom. These spaces were finished in an authentic French 18th-century idiom. The exceptional architectural decoration here was compromised by the furnishings. Photographs of these rooms give the impression that Edith Gould simply did not know when to stop adding objects. Much of the furniture and objects were of high quality but seemed to get lost in the generally cluttered and overstuffed rooms.

In the private family quarters located on the next two floors were bedrooms for each of the seven Gould children, as well as master suites for George and Edith. His bedroom was French Renaissance in style, whereas her chamber used a Louis XVI

ADAM SITTING ROOM. (Moss Collection)

vocabulary, with her royal-sized canopy bed placed upon a cushioned dais. As a respite from the over-poweringly French atmosphere of the house, an Adam-style sitting room was part of the decorative scheme here.

When it was completed in 1909, the Gould family made 857 their base for the New York seasons until Edith's death in 1921, when she died while playing golf on the private family course at Georgian Court. Doctors examining her body discovered something curious: she was completely encased in rubber from ankle to wrist in an attempt to regain her once-famous hourglass figure. Her funeral, unusually private for a family of this standing, was held at 857. A cortege consisting of some of the most important people in New York society escorted the body to Woodlawn Cemetery in the Bronx, where she was laid to rest next to her father-in-law in a family mausoleum that resembles the Parthenon.

At the time of his wife's death, Gould was experiencing the additional burden of dissension from his siblings over his stewardship of the family fortune. He turned increasingly to his mistress of 11 years, Guinevere Sinclair, marrying her the following year and legitimizing the three young children they had had. They sailed for Europe to escape scandal, and Gould purchased a house in the Scottish Highlands, intending it to become his principal residence. His

Mr. Gould's Room. (Moss Collection)

Mrs. Gould's Room. (Moss Collection)

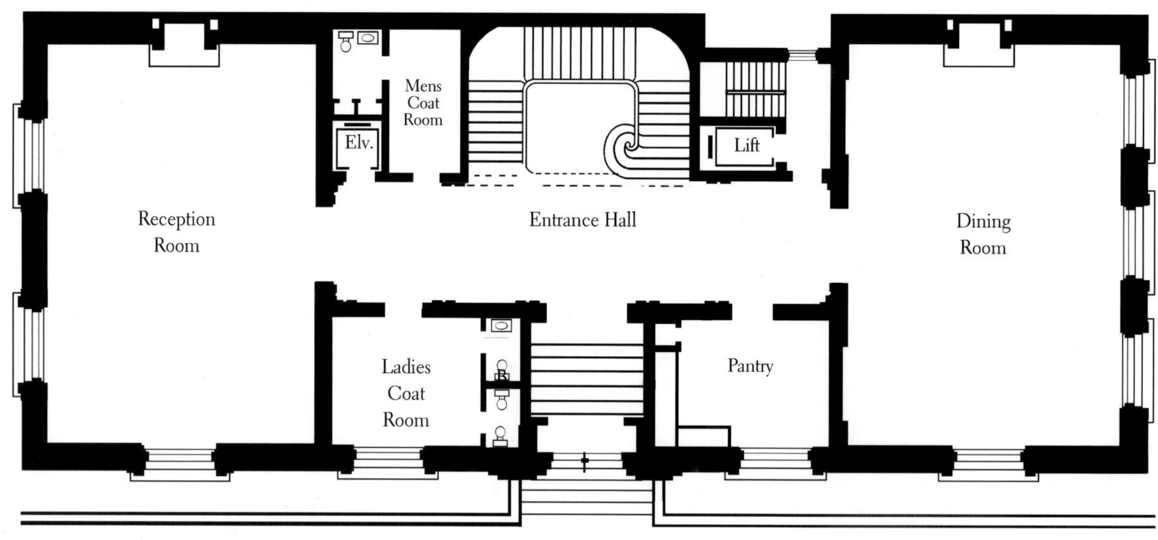

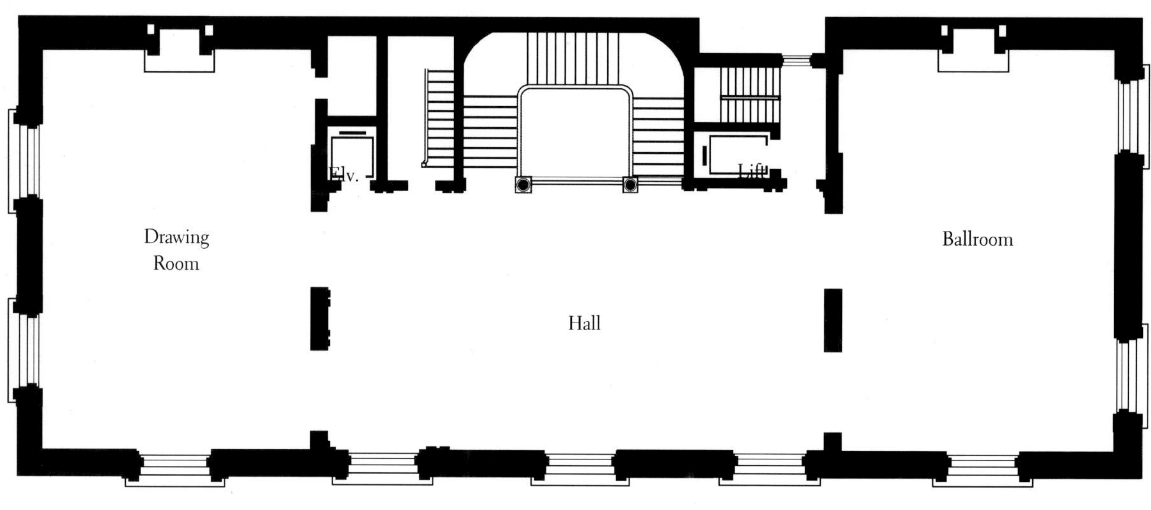

B

FIRST (TOP) AND SECOND FLOOR PLANS. (RICHARD MARCHAND)

health took a turn for the worse, though, so the family moved to the French Riviera, where he died of pneumonia on May 16, 1923. His body was returned to the United States, where it was interred next to Edith's.

In the mid-1920s, 857 was purchased by Mrs. Cornelius Vanderbilt II. At her death, the house passed to her youngest daughter, Countess Szechenyi, who sold the property to the Institute of International Education. A decade later, 857 was demolished to make way for an apartment building whose designer used Trumbauer's decorative wrought-iron balconies as a central decorative device on every other floor.

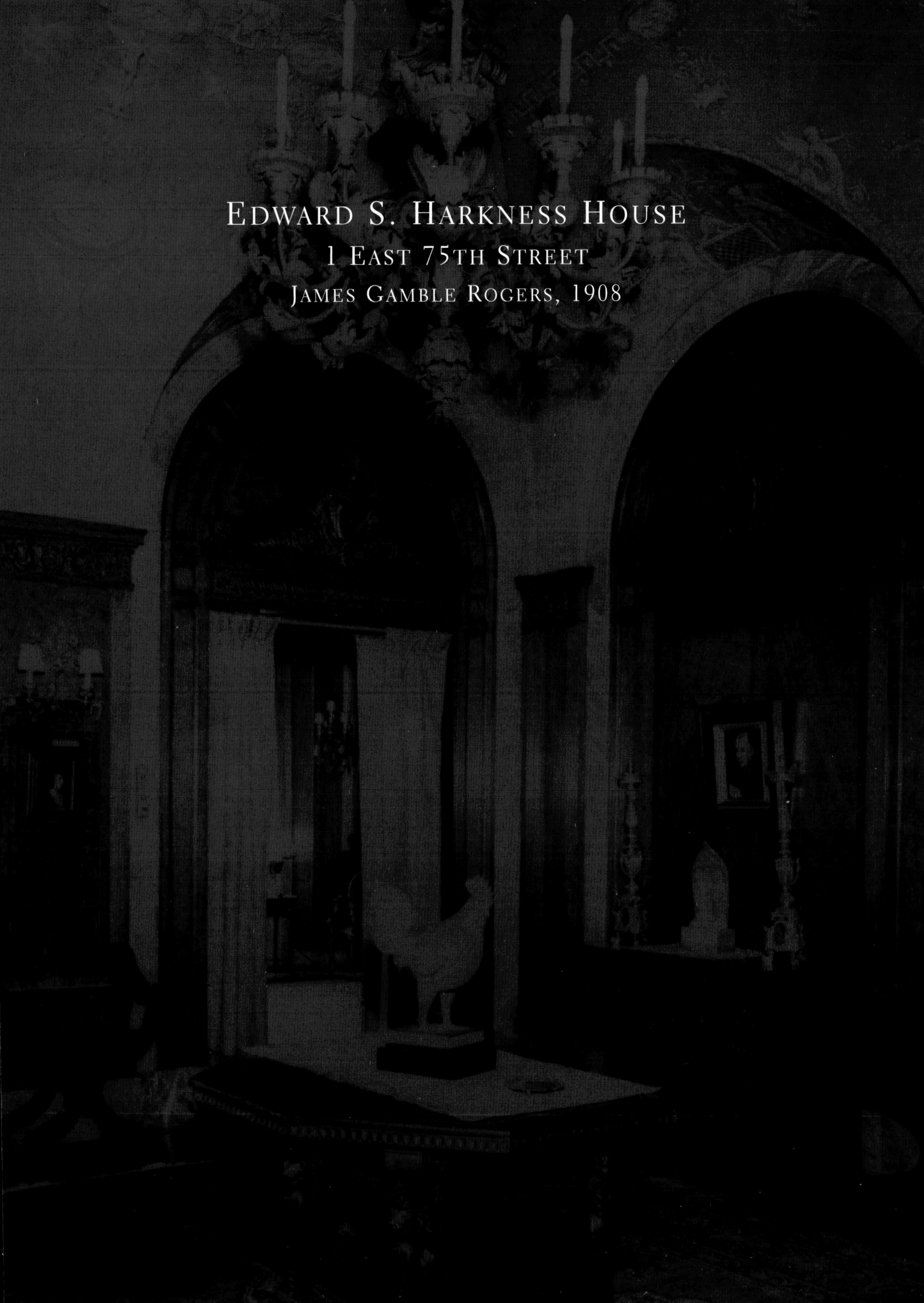

Edward S. Harkness House

1 East 75th Street

James Gamble Rogers, 1908

Edward S. Harkness House

Exterior. (Courtesy of the Museum of the City of New York)

Edward S. Harkness, the son of Stephen V. Harkness—an early partner of John D. Rockefeller in Standard Oil—was born in 1874 and graduated from Yale in 1892. He had received a sizable inheritance by the time he married Mary Stillman in 1904. Soon after his wedding, Harkness decided to live in New York City in order to be close to family investments and business interests.

His mother, Anna M. Harkness, gave her son and his wife a new home in the city as a wedding present. Anna purchased a 35-by-100-foot lot on the northeast corner of 75th Street and Fifth Avenue, and Harkness chose his Yale classmate James Gamble Rogers as architect. The building, completed in 1908, has an exterior of blush-colored Tennessee marble in a restrained Italian Renaissance design and is surrounded by an iron fence

Entrance Detail. (Courtesy of the Museum of the City of New York)

ENTRANCE HALL.
(Courtesy of the Museum of the City of New York)

RECEPTION ROOM.
(Courtesy of the Museum of the City Of New York)

adapted from the Scalegari tombs in Verona, Italy. Rogers' talent for subtlety gave the building a clean, elegant look with little extraneous ornamentation. The architect cleverly implied ground-floor pilasters, accomplished by using capitals and bases without shafts, that deemphasized the structure's vertical thrust.

As was typical on large corner lots, the entrance was placed in the center of the long side street facade rather than on the avenue frontage in order to improve spatial flow inside the house. Although a Fifth Avenue address identified the previous house on the site, Harkness wanted his address to be 1 East 75th Street. To accomplish this, he first, by legal recourse, had to convince Stuart Duncan, who lived in a house designed by C. P. H. Gilbert to the east, to relinquish the address and settle for the number three. These realignments were not unusual because by 1910, the 1 and 2 East numbers were considered more fashionable than a Fifth Avenue address.

The first floor held a paneled Louis XVI–style reception room and a velvet-lined Renaissance revival dining room. These were separated by a limestone-and-wood-paneled entrance hall that was capped by a vaulted ceiling with delicate plaster reliefs. Adjacent to the hall was a Cassis marble staircase, with a fine wrought-iron rinceau-style balustrade. The stairs curved up to the piano nobile and its walnut-paneled gallery, which was architecturally divided by composite pilasters and covered by a barrel-vaulted ceiling painted in a classical Italian

STAIRCASE. (Courtesy of the Museum of the City of New York)

Dining Room.
(Courtesy of the Museum of the City of New York)

Second Floor Gallery.
(Courtesy of the Museum of the City of New York)

Renaissance manner. A book-lined library, with a massive stone fireplace and a deeply coffered Brazilian rosewood ceiling, was accessed from one end of the gallery, and the music room was entered from the other. The latter was originally finished in a heavy decorative program of brocaded silk wall coverings, heavily carved window and door surrounds, and a monumental wooden overmantel. Four bronze chandeliers hung from the ceiling. Around 1920, this treatment was removed except for the beamed ceiling and was replaced with a much more subdued finish. The upper floors held seven bedrooms and adjoining bathrooms, Mary Harkness' boudoir, a linen room, and numerous staff rooms. To save on electricity, Rogers designed a refrigerator room in the basement, whose outer wall could open onto the exterior moat when the outside temperature dipped. As the house was detached to the east, the rooms on that side were fitted with Kenyon Cox–designed decorative leaded-glass windows.

A 1910 issue of *Architectural Record*, effusive with praise for the house, stated, "If there is any facade on upper Fifth Avenue which gives an effect of quiet elegance by worthier architectural means it has not been our good fortune to come across it." The Harkness family was pleased with their new home and especially with the architect who designed it. They later commissioned Rogers to design family benefactions such as Columbia

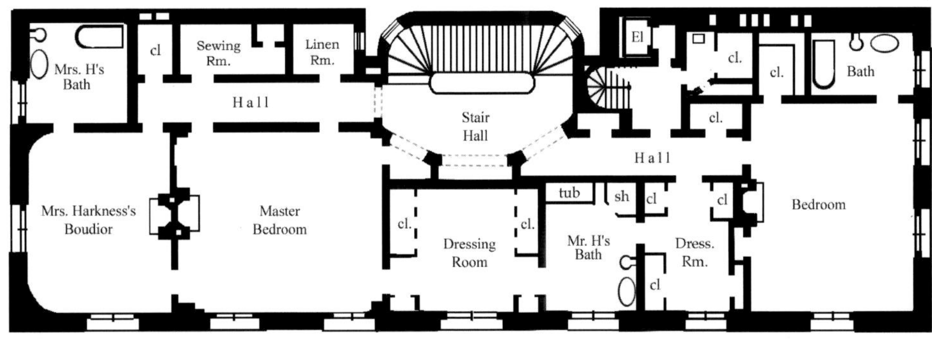

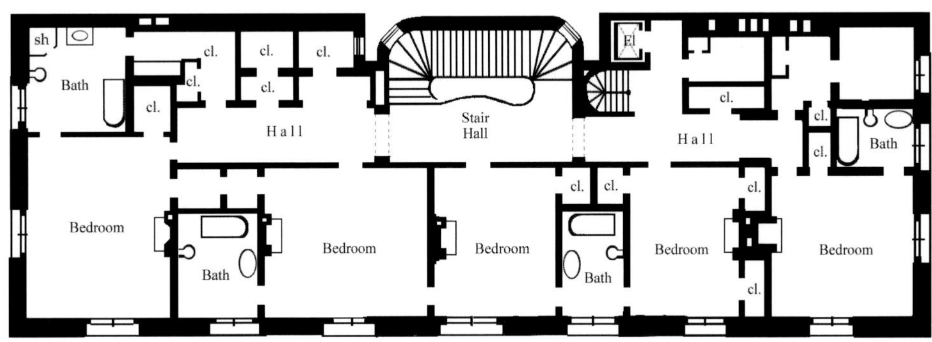

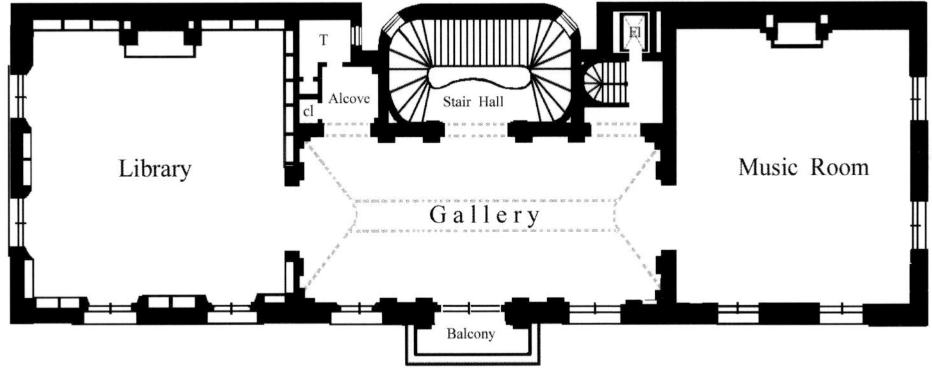

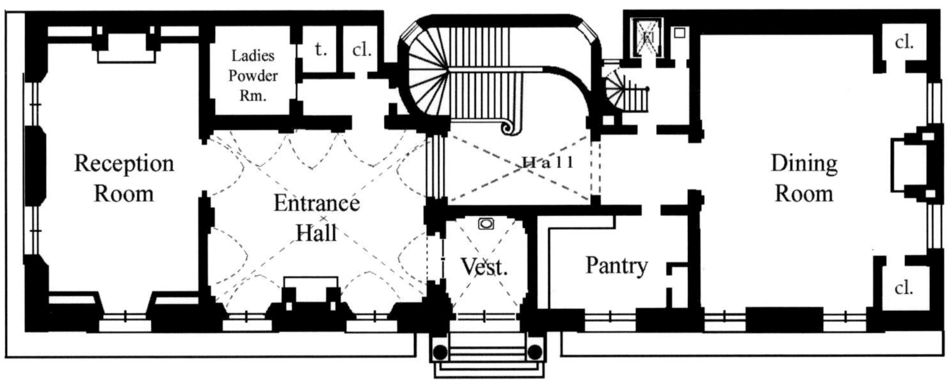

First through Fourth Floor Plans (bottom to top). (Richard Marchand)

University's Butler Library, the Yale University quadrangle, and Columbia-Presbyterian Hospital.

Edward Harkness, a quiet man, was a philanthropist on a grand scale, and he eventually gave away most of the immense fortune that his father had left him. Some of the more notable recipients of his largesse included Harvard University ($11 million); Phillips Exeter Academy ($7 million); Yale University ($6 million); Columbia University ($4 million); Columbia-Presbyterian Hospital ($4 million); and the New York Public Library ($1 million). In 1918, the creation of The Commonwealth Fund marked the family's greatest gift. Initially endowed with $30 million by Edward's mother, it was chartered "to do something for the good of mankind." Anna's son subsequently bequeathed an additional $8 million to this fund.

The childless philanthropist died in 1940, leaving life tenancy of 1 East 75th Street to his wife. At her death 10 years later, the artworks in the house, by artists including Gainsborough, Holbein, and Stuart, were given to The Metropolitan Museum of Art. The building itself is, in a matter of speaking, still in the family: it currently houses the headquarters of The Commonwealth Fund, which meticulously maintains it.

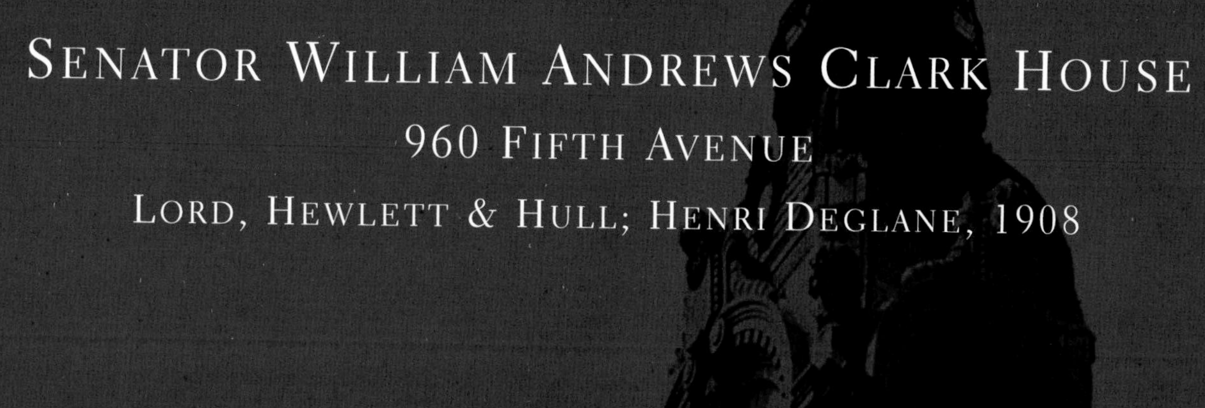

Senator William Andrews Clark House

960 Fifth Avenue

Lord, Hewlett & Hull; Henri Deglane, 1908

Senator William Andrews Clark House

Exterior. (Author's Collection)

What kind of house would a copper king from Montana dream of building on Fifth Avenue to proclaim his arrival? The answer, in Senator William Andrews Clark's case: a 100-plus-room Beaux Arts–baroque pile of lavishness unparalleled in the history of New York. In 1862, Clark left the Pennsylvania farm where he was born for Montana to look for gold. Although he made some money on gold and somewhat more on silver, he reaped a fortune mining copper. He later branched out into coffee, tea, tobacco, sugar, rubber plantations, newspapers, smelters, and railroads. Clark felt comfortable only when he owned 100 percent of his business ventures. Allen Churchill's *The Splendor Seekers* states: "Of all the great undertakings with which he was connected, not one share of stock nor bond issue by any of them was either listed or quoted or could be bought on any stock exchange in the United States or

77th Street Elevation. (Author's Collection)

DORMER DETAIL. (Author's Collection)

elsewhere." By the late 1890s, he reportedly had an annual income of $10 million.

Clark surprised everyone by taking an extended trip to France to study the language and art history. The reason: Clark wanted to collect paintings, but was afraid of being taken advantage of.

With his vast wealth, Clark became the most powerful man in Montana and led the fight for its statehood. He also aspired to be the state's first senator and eventually paid out hundreds of thousands of dollars in bribes to accomplish this. During the campaign, the most frequently asked question was, "How much are they paying for votes today?" Clark's first attempt failed, but in the 1893 election he was victorious. However, the day he was to take his seat in Washington, the Senate Committee on Elections was handed evidence that the senator-elect had paid 45 legislators $430,000 for votes. Clark indignantly resigned, saying, "I have never in my life been charged with a dishonorable act, and I prefer to leave to my children a legacy worth more than gold—an unblemished name." He eventually did serve a term as senator when he was elected by the state legislature of Montana to fill a vacant seat.

While Clark was served in Washington, he was also vigorously adding to his art collection. His first major acquisition was Mariano Fortuny's *The Choice of a Model*, which he purchased in 1898, to which he added Corot's *Dance Under the Trees*, Raeburn's *Portrait of the Artist's Daughter*, and

GRAND STAIRCASE. (Courtesy of the Museum of the City of New York)

GRAND STAIRCASE DRAWING. (Author's Collection)

GRAND SALON–SALON DORE. (Courtesy of the Museum of the City of New York.

PETIT SALON. (Courtesy of the Museum of the City of New York)

Rembrandt's *Portrait of a Young Man*. His collection eventually included works by masters such as Cazin, Daubigny, Gainsborough, Hogarth, Raffaelli, Reynolds, Rubens, Titian, and Van Dyck. His 22 Monticellis were said to rival those in the Louvre. He also collected Sèvres porcelain, museum-quality antique furniture, paneling from French chateaux, ornate nine-foot birdcages, and a $120,000 gold dinner service. This orgy of spending was directly related to the senator's decision to build a new house.

After deciding to move his business headquarters to New York, he purchased a 200-foot-deep lot on the northeast corner of Fifth Avenue and 77th Street, upon which Clark wanted to erect the finest house in the city. Lord, Hewlett & Hull was hired to design it, but finding their proposal to be lacking in sufficient scope and grandeur, Clark had the drawings sent to Henri Deglane in Paris for further embellishment. Deglane had just completed Grand Palais on the Champs Elysées.

The mass that rose on 77th Street was six stories of the most opulent architectural repast that New York ever had been asked to digest. The main body of the house overflowed with consoles, balconies, Ionic columns, and carved floral swags. However, the limestone mansion's most vigorous decoration was reserved for areas above the cornice line. The massive copper-crested mansard roof was full of fantastically carved dormers, which were watched over by a pinnacled tower. Even in Paris, this kind of ornamentation was usually found on only the grandest public buildings, and never on private houses.

The critics began to swarm long before the $7 million building was completed. One individual thought it would make a perfect home for P. T. Barnum. Someone else pontificated, "If, as Schelling said, architecture is frozen music, this edifice is frozen ragtime discord." *Architectural Record* called it an aberration, and *The American Architect* wanted to know more about the tower: "Is this a steeple, belvedere, crowning lantern, belfry, or what?" Another critic declared that "a more meaningless or fatuous feature than this steeple would be impossible to find in the wildest vagaries of art." *Collier's* magazine's Will Irwin iced the cake with the following ditty:

Senator Copper of Tonopah Ditch
Made a clean billion in minin and sich
Hiked for Noo York, where his money he
    blew
Buildin' a palace on Fift' Avenoo.
"How," sez the Senator, "Can I look the
    proudest?"
Build me a house that'll holler the
    loudest—"

Forty-eight architects came to consult,
Drawin' up plans for a splendid result;
If the old Senator wanted to pay,
They'd give him Art with a capital A.

Pillars Ionic
Eaves Babylonic,
Doors cut in scallops, resembin' a shell;
Roof wuz Egyption.
Gables caniption,
Whole grand effect, when completed,
    wuz—Hell!

In dismissing the senator as a tasteless parvenue, his accusers showed little knowledge of the man himself. Clark was far more cultured and knowledgeable in artistic matters than were most of his fellow Americans, as well as most of his fellow plutocrats. Had his house been completed in the early 1890s when it had been originally

PRINCIPAL ART GALLERY, (Courtesy of the Museum of the City of New York)

planned, the structure would have been in the vanguard of good taste. Because it took 13 years to finish, it was already old-fashioned on the day of its completion. Clark weathered the storm well because, like most self-made men, he truly did not care what anyone else thought of him or his new home. Within a few years, public opinion swayed in his favor. A later critic described the mansion as "the nearest thing to an imperial palace. . . in this hemisphere."

The interior of the 120-room edifice was, if possible, even more extravagant than the facade. One writer felt, "The coldness, the stoniness, the marbleness of the halls and staircase grope timidly toward what the (21) bathrooms alone achieve." After passing through bronze entrance doors and a small stone vestibule, visitors found themselves in a large marble entrance hall facing a monumental curved staircase. Off this hall was a reception room, Clark's suite of offices, a billiard room, and a paneled smoking room. The rest of the ground floor was devoted to service areas.

Up the grand staircase of Maryland marble were the large public rooms. The grand salon had antique paneling and a painted ceiling taken from the Hôtel de Clermont in the Faubourg Saint-Germain in Paris, while the oval petit salon was adapted from Germain Boffrand's famous salon at

FAIENCE GALLERY. (Courtesy of the City of New York)

the Hôtel de Soubise in Paris. The morning room had oak paneling with gold leaf trim and walls that were hung with French tapestries. Next door was a plant-filled conservatory. The main dining room had upper walls of intricately carved white marble, and a wood ceiling made from 2,000-year-old oak trees taken from Sherwood Forest. In addition, each floor had its own smaller dining room and kitchen so members of the Clark family never had to experience hunger anywhere in the house. The round sculpture hall led to four large art galleries and a music room that contained a $100,000 pipe organ. The general impression was one of unsurpassed American imperial splendor.

Numerous family and guest suites were on the third and fourth floors. Mrs. Clark's bedroom had a floor and carved paneling made of sandalwood, which gave off a delicate scent. The house also contained secret doors and staircases, a wine cellar, a cold storage plant, and a furnace that devoured 14 tons of coal a day during the winter. In the basement was a colonnaded swimming pool, and a garage that could accommodate a dozen automobiles. Even with unlimited private transportation options available, Clark always took the subway on the daily trips to his Wall Street office.

Clark died in 1925 and the mansion was the setting for his spectacular funeral. Wesley Towner wrote,

Dining Room. (Courtesy of the Museum of the City of New York)

Bedroom. (Courtesy of the Museum of the City of New York)

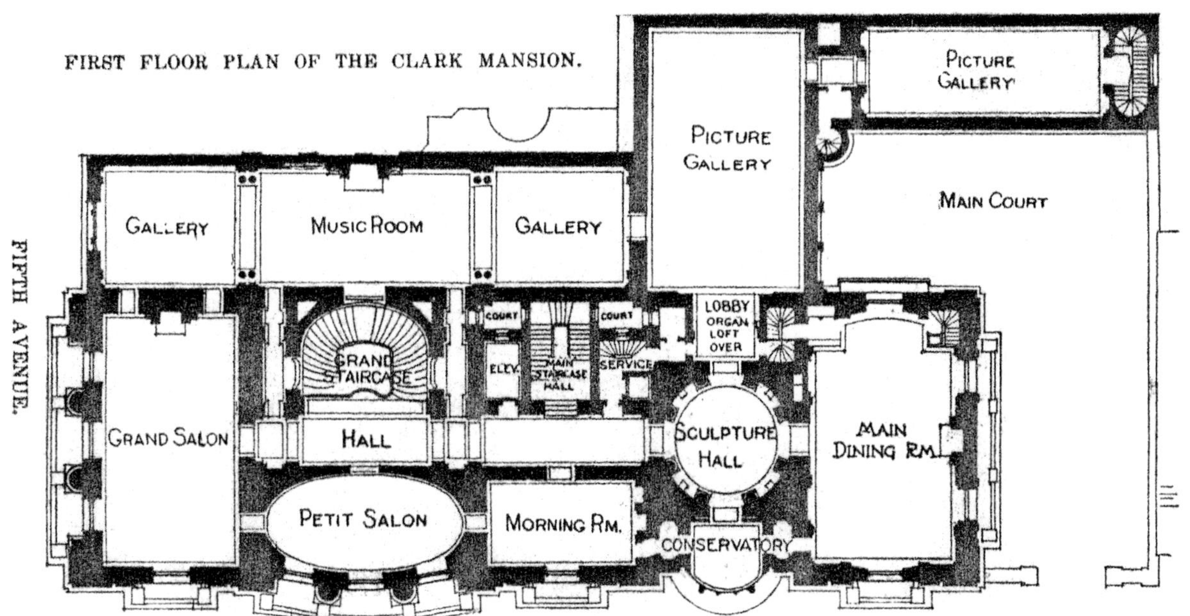

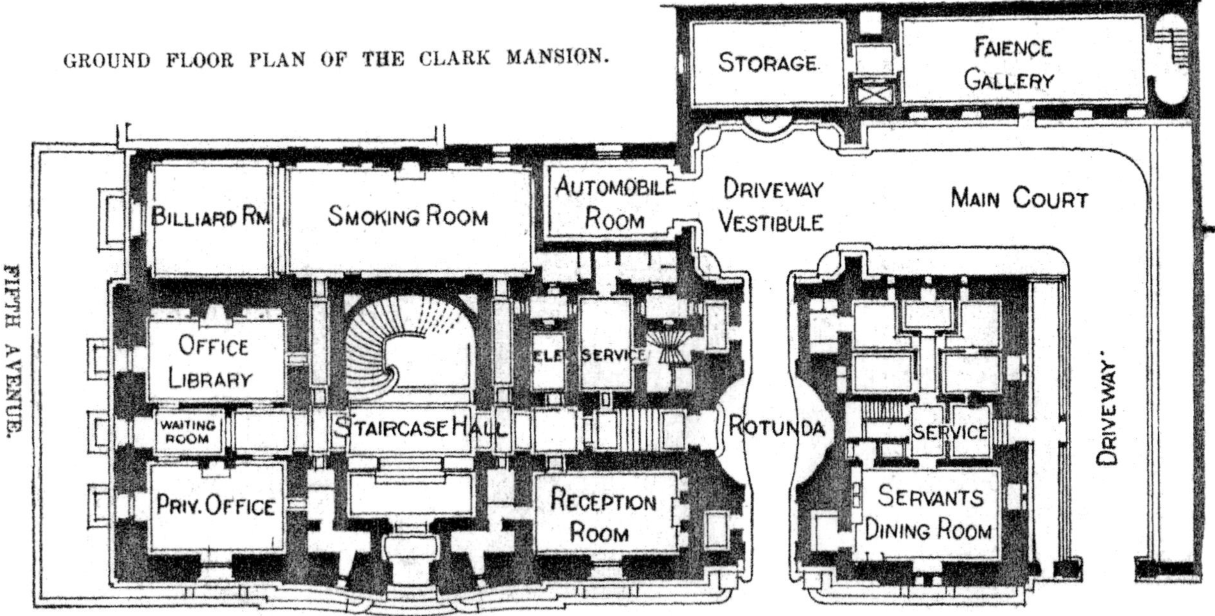

First and second floor plans. (Author's Collection)

"Thirty thrush-voiced choirboys trilled his $77-million soul to rest...From the bowels of the 121-room mansion, that was to outdo all other mansions, the colossal organ wailed and sang and whined. Its 65 stops all lent their syrupy voices to the wild-haired, brazen copper king's send-off. The great organ bawled and brayed. . . the 23 couplers brought the manuals together in a peal of lamentation that may well have given God-fearing residents of Fifth Avenue the impression that the Day of Judgment was at hand."

Soon after, the family agreed to dispose of the mansion as quickly as possible. Clark had willed 125 of his best paintings to The Metropolitan Museum of Art, which promptly turned them down because there were no funds attached to the bequest for housing them. The family then offered the collection to the Corcoran Gallery in Washington, this time with the funds to pay for a new wing. President Coolidge presided over the opening of the W. A. Clark Collection at the Corcoran three years later. The rest of the furnishings were auctioned and the building was sold to an apartment developer for $3 million. Clark's ornate palace for the ages lasted only 25 years.

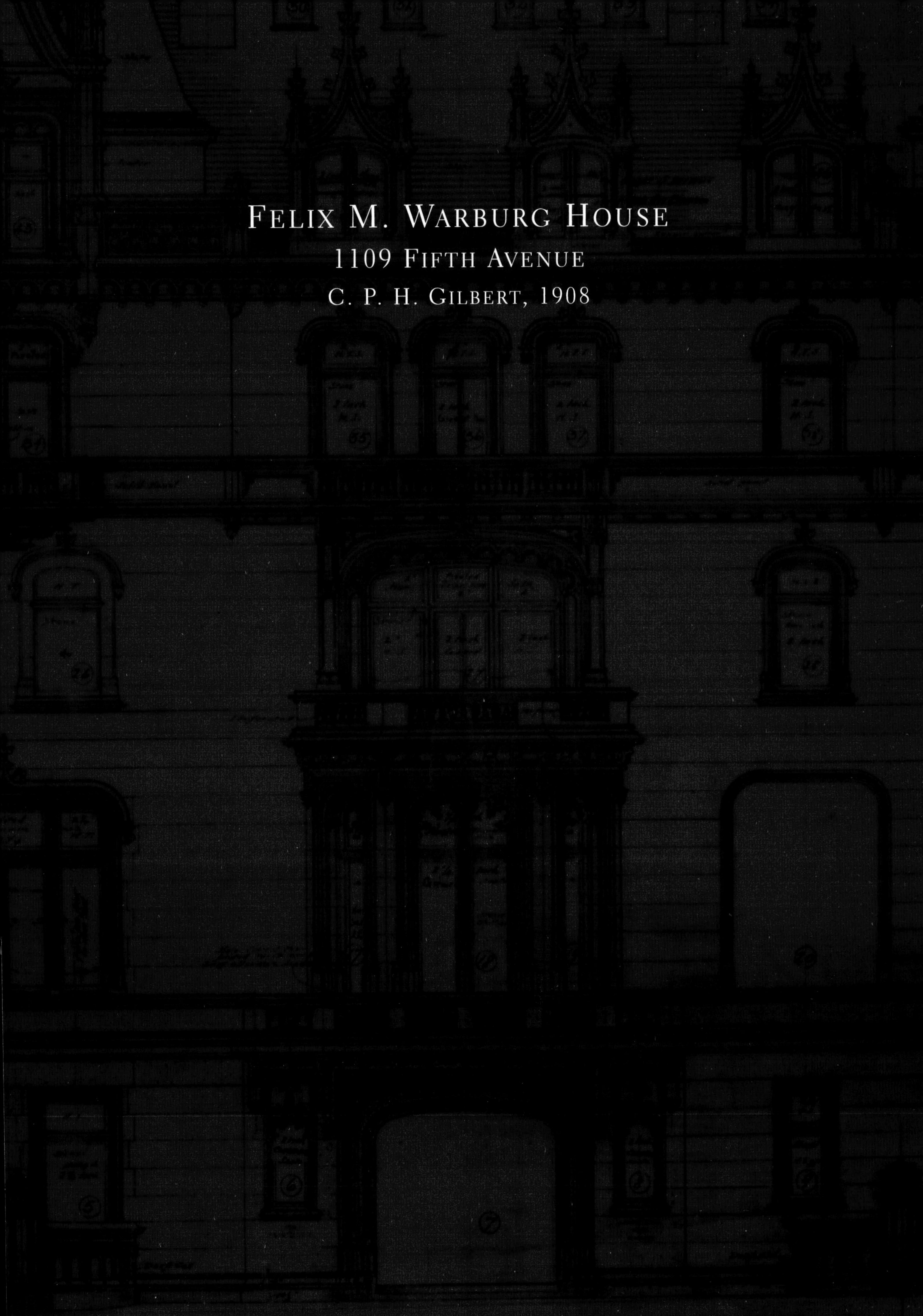

Felix M. Warburg House

1109 Fifth Avenue

C. P. H. Gilbert, 1908

Felix M. Warburg House

Drawing of 92nd Street Facade. (Courtesy of the Jewish Museum)

Felix Warburg was born into a family of Jewish bankers long prominent in Hamburg, Germany. The family firm, M. M. Warburg & Co., was founded in 1798, making it one of the oldest banking houses in Germany. In 1894, at the age of 23, while working at a relative's precious-stone business in Frankfurt, Felix met Frieda Schiff. Her father was banker Jacob Schiff, a senior partner of New York's powerful Kuhn, Loeb & Company.

In 1895, Felix Warburg immigrated to New York to marry Frieda, and two years later he became a junior partner at Kuhn, Loeb. By 1907, the Warburg family, with four children and a fifth on the way, had outgrown their five-story town house at 18 East 72nd Street. The couple had long admired the Isaac Fletcher house at 79th Street and Fifth Avenue, so they asked its architect, C. P. H. Gilbert, to design a house for them in a similar Gothic style. For this

DRAWING OF FIFTH AVENUE FACADE. (Courtesy of the Jewish Museum)

ENTRANCE HALL. (Courtesy of the Jewish Museum)

Music Room. (Courtesy of the Jewish Museum)

purpose, the Warburgs had purchased from Perry Belmont a 100-by-100-foot plot of land at 92nd Street and Fifth Avenue. The stylistic decision to use the French Gothic vernacular went against the then-current trend for sleek classical houses. Having been thoroughly explored since its advent with the William K. Vanderbilt mansion a quarter of a century earlier, the architectural community had moved away from the once-fashionable Gothic revival style, finding it both ponderous and old-fashioned for residential commissions.

Frieda's father also objected to the style, but for quite a different reason. While viewing the plans, Schiff told his daughter, "That's rather conspicuous and will add to the social anti-Semitism in New York if a young couple builds such an ornate house right on Fifth Avenue." He felt so strongly about this that his daughter consulted with the architect about having the facade altered to a less robust style. This could not be done without incurring prohibitive additional expense, so the house was completed according to its original plan. Schiff refused to visit the newly completed house for many months. Relenting, he came to see his daughter and her family in their palatial abode without commenting on or seeming to notice any detail about it. But the house must have made a good impression because he

Second Floor Parlor. (Courtesy of the Jewish Museum)

immediately sent Frieda a check for $25,000 as a housewarming gift.

The limestone-finished house did have features similar to the Fletcher house. The facade bristled with ogee-arched windows, filigreed balconies, and crocketed gables. Pinnacled, carved-stone dormers and tall chimneys punctuated the copper-crested roof. The building filled only the southern half of the property, while leaving plenty of room for an adjacent garden.

The Warburgs' youngest child, Edward, recalled how the entrance hall was "terrifying in its formality, especially when a footman in livery answered the doorbell." All the children made it a point to be at the door when any of their friends came to call. The hall had a large stone fireplace and an ornately carved wooden Gothic staircase. On the left were two connecting rooms where Felix kept a group of etchings by Cranach, Durer, and Rembrandt. This collection, eventually bequeathed to The Metropolitan Museum of Art, was displayed on ingeniously designed rotating pedestals that held double-faced frames. Elsewhere on the ground floor were the servants' dining room, the housekeeper's office, and a large kitchen.

On the second floor, facing the park, was the music room where Felix Warburg's musician friends often gave concerts and recitals, frequently using

DINING ROOM. (Courtesy of the Jewish Museum)

the four Stradivarius instruments that he owned. This spacious area was also used for balls and dances. Next door was the Red Room, so named because of the ruby velvet on the walls. Here hung four panels painted by the early Renaissance painter Francesco di Stefano, known as Pesellino. A dining room on the other side of an adjoining conservatory could accommodate 60 for dinner. Tapestries hung on the upper part of its paneled walls, and complementary gros point needlework covered the high-backed dining chairs.

The third floor comprised comfortable rooms for daily use by Mr. and Mrs. Warburg. Family portraits hung in the sitting room, and a small table near the fireplace held Sabbath candles. Frieda served tea here every afternoon, and her husband's desk overlooked the Central Park reservoir. Next door was a small dining room where the family generally took their meals. The senior Warburgs each had a dressing room and bath adjacent to a shared bedroom. The floor above contained the children's bedrooms, plus a sitting room where they were given music lessons on an upright piano. On the fifth floor was the squash court, which was later converted into an art gallery for son Edward's collection of modern works by Calder, Lachaise, and

CONSERVATORY. (Courtesy of the Jewish Museum)

Picasso. The sixth floor held numerous staff rooms and the laundry.

Although large and formal, the house was remembered by those who grew up there as a place full of fun and children's pranks. In fact, Felix Warburg once told his children that if he had known what kind of family he was going to have, he never would have built so formal a house.

In 1916, 1109 Fifth Avenue was the setting for the wedding of the Warburgs' only daughter, Carola, to Walter Rothschild. Nine hundred people were invited to toast the young couple. One of their wedding gifts was a house and 30 acres carved from the 500-acre Warburg estate, Woodlands, in White Plains, New York.

Felix Warburg died on October 20, 1937, at the age of 66, with his wife and children in attendance. The cause of death was a heart attack brought on by stress related to his attempts to save family and friends in Nazi Germany. The benevolent banker had, with his wife, given away over $13 million to worthy causes. Warburg's *New York Times* obituary stated, "Never has there been shown in our time a finer sense of the obligations of wealth than he put into his daily deeds of human sympathy." The 35 house servants at Woodlands and 1109 Fifth Avenue received bequests of between $100 and $10,000, and all of the 125 Kuhn, Loeb employees received amounts between $200 and $2,000, depending on their length of service. The rest of his considerable fortune was divided among his children.

After Felix's death, Frieda continued to live in the mansion, sharing it with her eldest son, Freddy, and refugee German relations. The last major social event to take place in the house was Edward Warburg's 1939 wedding to Mary Whelan Currier. Five years later, Frieda decided to give up the house and moved to a duplex apartment at 1 East 88th Street. Not wishing to see the home demolished, she generously donated it to the Jewish Theological Seminary, which used it as the Jewish Museum, an institution that Felix Warburg helped to found some four decades earlier.

The museum, which opened in 1947, seemed a perfect inhabitant for a house whose former occupants had always been deeply involved with Jewish causes in America and around the world. In 1993, the museum completed an addition designed by Kevin Roche, John Dinkeloo & Associates that perfectly matches the original fenestration of the Gilbert-designed chateau.

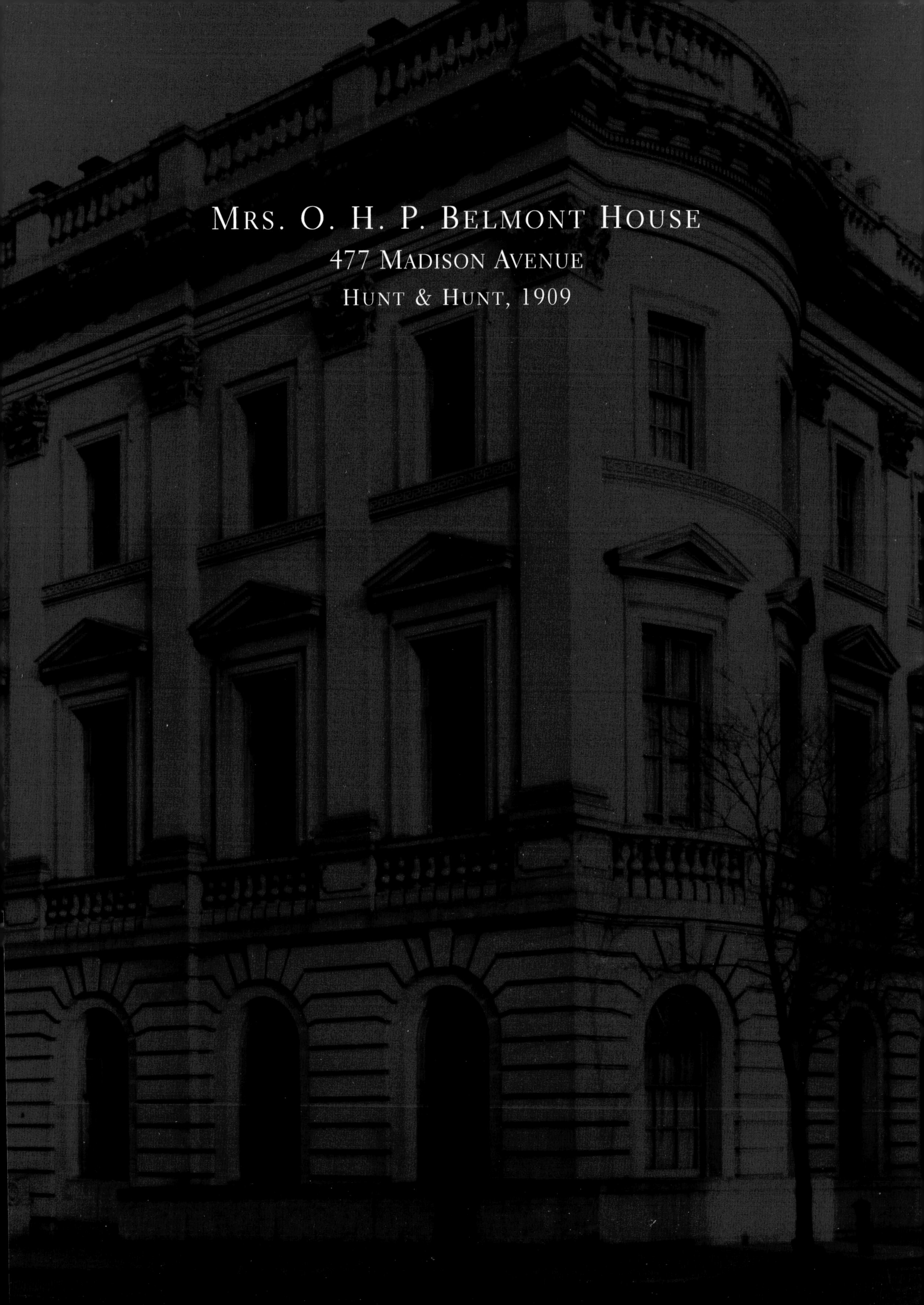

MRS. O. H. P. BELMONT HOUSE

477 MADISON AVENUE

HUNT & HUNT, 1909

MRS. O. H. P. BELMONT HOUSE

EXTERIOR. (Courtesy of the Museum of the City of New York)

WITHIN A YEAR of her sensational 1895 divorce from William K. Vanderbilt, Alva Vanderbilt married Oliver Hazard Perry Belmont. He was the son of banker August Belmont, the American representative of the Rothschild family, and the former Caroline Slidell Perry, the daughter of Commodore Mathew Perry, who opened Japanese trade to the West. Oliver Belmont had also been one of William K. Vanderbilt's best friends and had spent much time cruising on the Vanderbilt yachts. It was on one of these excursions that Alva, tired of her husband's numerous infidelities, fell in love with the handsome Oliver Belmont. Soon after her divorce, and immediately following her daughter Consuelo's marriage to the ninth Duke of Marlborough, Alva and Oliver decided to marry. She was the first important society matron to divorce and remarry without

DRAWING OF FACADE. (Author's Collection)

losing caste. Soon many other unhappily married socialites followed suit.

In 1899, Oliver Belmont purchased a large corner lot on 51st Street and Madison Avenue. He required a house large enough to hold his growing collections and to accommodate his wife's large-scale social functions. He entrusted its design to the two sons of Richard Morris Hunt, Alva's favored architect. Unfortunately, Oliver Belmont died from complications following an appendectomy a year before the home was finished.

Alva completed the house, and she and her youngest son, Harold Sterling Vanderbilt, took possession of it in the fall of 1909. With its pilastered facade over a rusticated base, the limestone exterior clearly represents Inigo Jones' interpretation of Andrea Palladio in the finely articulated facade of London's Lindsey House, which was designed by Jones in 1641 for Sir David Cunningham.

The most interesting interior aspect of the house was the armory on the second floor, designed to display Oliver Belmont's extensive collection of medieval and early Renaissance armor. Taking up half of this level's square footage, it was the largest room in the house and was connected by a ceremonial stone staircase to a library located directly beneath it. The library's rare volumes had been studiously collected by Belmont, and both it and the armory were kept as a loving wife's memorial to her deceased husband.

The rest of the interiors were an eclectic mix of styles executed by the most fashionable decorating firms of the day. These rooms included a Gothic reception room with linenfold paneling, a dining room based on Inigo Jones' famous double-cube room at Wilton, and a marble-walled neoclassical entrance hall.

By the end of the first decade of the century, Alva galvanized her resources, both physical and financial,

Entrance Hall. (Author's Collection)

Gothic Room. (Author's Collection)

Reception Room. (Author's Collection)

Dining Room. (Author's Collection)

Armory. (Author's Collection)

Library. (Author's Collection)

in support of the women's suffrage movement—she even led a women's rights parade down Fifth Avenue. During the 1914 season, she shocked her Newport neighbors by hosting a suffrage event on the grounds of Marble House, her summer villa. All was forgiven when, later in that same season, Alva gave a splendid costume ball to inaugurate her newly completed Chinese teahouse that sat directly on the cliffs overlooking the Atlantic. The always-thorough Alva had sent her architect to China to assure accuracy of detail. The guest of honor, her daughter Consuelo, the Duchess of Marlborough, came beautifully attired in an antique costume of a lady of the imperial Chinese court. Although still a duchess, she was by then officially separated from the duke.

By 1923, Alva was spending a large percentage of her time in France to be near Consuelo and her French husband, Colonel Jacques Balsan. By the end of the decade, Alva had almost completely abandoned the United States. The Madison Avenue house had been sold to publisher Arthur Brisbane, and her Sands Point, Long Island, estate was now the home of William Randolph Hearst. However, Alva's interest in houses never waned. She soon purchased in France near Fontainebleau a chateau that needed extensive restoration. Alva,who liked nothing better than to be "knee deep in mortar," was in her element. Not liking the width of the river that wound past the chateau, she had it doubled in size.

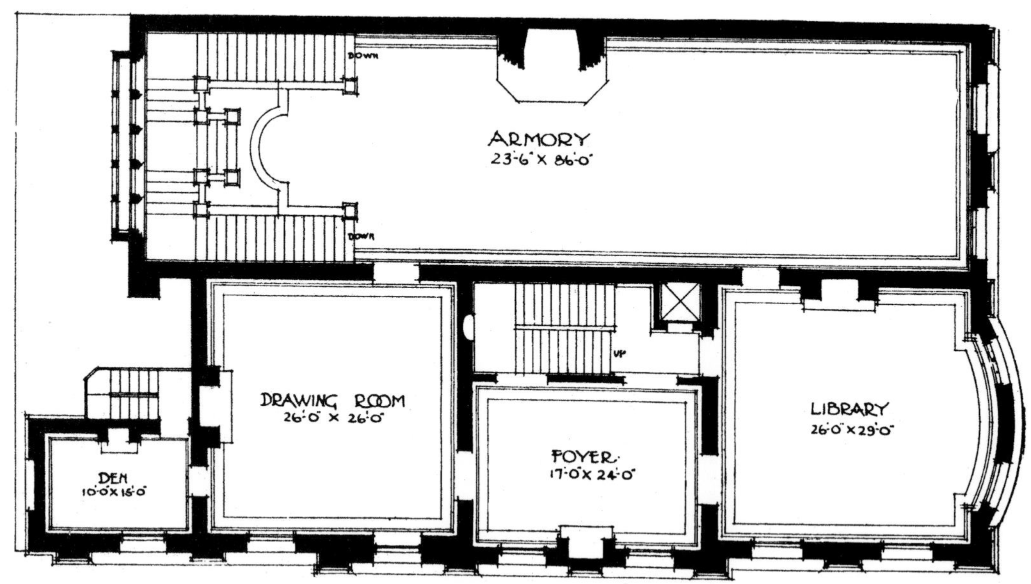

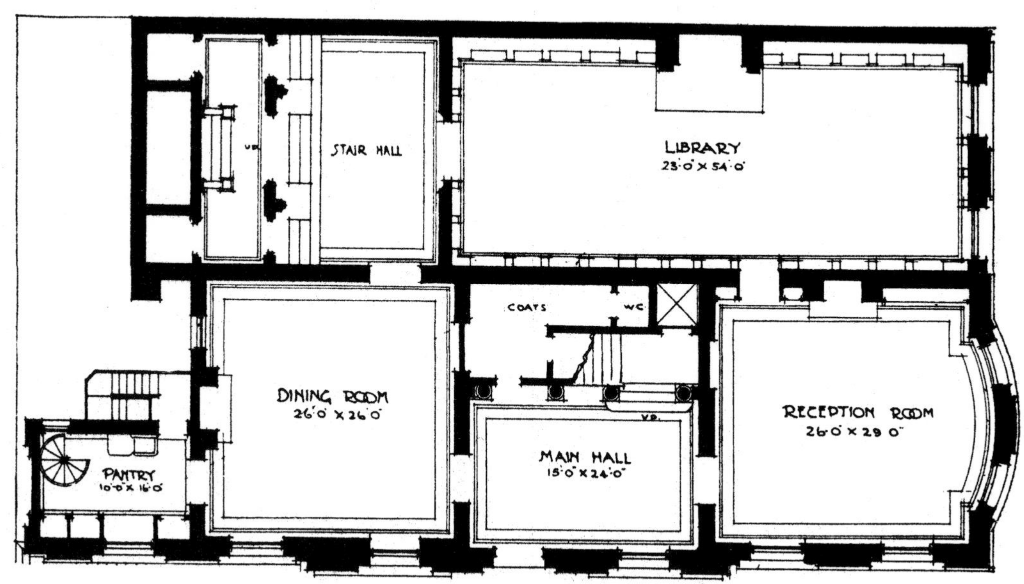

FIRST (BOTTOM) AND SECOND FLOOR PLANS. (Author's Collection)

On January 26, 1933, Alva died in her Paris home at the age of 80. Her body was brought back to the United States, and she was laid to rest at Woodlawn Cemetery in the Bronx, next to Oliver in the mausoleum she had commissioned from Hunt & Hunt in 1908. A magnificent adaptation of St. Hubert's chapel at Amboise, France, the Belmont mausoleum was complete with gargoyles, stained-glass windows, and a copper-pinnacled roof. In death, as in life, Alva Erskine Smith Vanderbilt Belmont was extremely well housed.

James B. Duke House

1 East 78th St

Horace Trumbauer, 1912

James B. Duke House

Exterior. (Collection of the New York Public Library)

Perhaps the most elegant house ever erected in New York, this completely detached structure has received rave reviews since its 1912 completion. Even the confirmed modernist Phillip Johnson declared it the most successful of all the revival houses. Its elevated patrician facade exudes an aloofness that seems to separate it from the surrounding houses.

In 1908, James Buchanan Duke, the tobacco and utilities magnate, purchased a 72-by-140-foot piece of property on the northeast corner of Fifth Avenue and 78th Street for $1.2 million. The Renaissance revival–style mansion of Henry H. Cook, from whose estate he had purchased the land, then occupied the site. That large, if somewhat cumbersome-looking, house had been designed by architect W. Wheeler Smith and was completed in 1884. Originally, Duke was interested only in having a stylish C. P. H. Gilbert renovation

Exterior of the Henry H. Cook House. (Author's Collection)

of the Cook house. Early in the proceedings, perhaps persuaded by his socially ambitious wife, Naneline, he changed his mind and instead hired Horace Trumbauer to design an entirely new house for the property. At that time, the Philadelphia architect was working on plans for a grand chateau that was never completed for the family's country estate, Duke Farms, in Somerville, New Jersey. Later, Trumbauer drew up plans for a substantial renovation and enlargement of Rough Point, the Duke summer house in Newport, Rhode Island, as well as a design for the extensive campus of Duke University.

Trumbauer found inspiration for the New York house in Étienne Lacotte's 1770 design of the Maison Labottèire in Bordeaux, France. As was typical for this talented American architect, Trumbauer improved upon the source. The Duke house is much larger than the original and the proportions are better. The elegantly swagged window surrounds are nearly identical to Lacotte's, but the projecting panels between them are larger, giving the facade an smoother, less cluttered appearance. The handsome and well-articulated pedimented entrance pavilion, the principal focus of the entrance facade, is entirely a Trumbauer design. Also, the siting was vastly improved by placing the entire composition on a raised basement framed by a balustrade. Lastly, the veneer of the structure, a

Vestibule Detail. (Author's Collection)

Entrance Hall. (Collection of the New York Public Library)

Entrance Hall Detail. (Author's Collection)

STAIRCASE DETAIL. (Author's Collection)

SALON. (Author's Collection)

DINING ROOM. (Collection of the New York Public Library)

high-quality limestone that resembles finely tooled white marble, enhanced the building's overall appearance.

Lucien Alavoine et Cie created authentically detailed, 18th-century-inspired interiors for the house. Beautiful modeled paneling and appropriate flooring finishes were designed and executed in the Parisian workrooms of Alavoine, then crated and shipped across the Atlantic with the workmen to install them. It is rumored that Duke paid substantial overtime wages because he wanted the house completed in time for the birth of his first, and ultimately only, child, Doris. The total cost for the entire project—architect, fine art dealers, and antiquaries—came very close to $2 million.

Crossing through a marble-floored vestibule, one entered a large French Caen stone–lined entrance hall. At one end was a mantlepiece with a decorative overmantel inspired by one found in

MUSIC ROOM. (Author's Collection)

l'appartement du Comte d'Artois at the Château de Maisons-Laffitte. Straight ahead, the grand staircase's marble treads made a noble sweep to the second level. Overhead a decorative bronze-framed skylight flooded the areas with light. Dovetailed in and around the staircase were a butler's pantry, silver safe, elevator, and service stairs. Across the hall, on either side of the entrance, was a reception room with its accompanying lavatory.

Entrances to the library and dining room were at either end of the western wall of the room, while on the opposite wall were entrances to both the drawing and music rooms. These room were both sheathed in boiserie in the Louis XVI style with gilded decorative detailing. The music room had a musicians' gallery located above the mirrored central opening of its long interior elevation; on the opposite side of the room, the mirrored shutters on the three windows could be closed on gala nights to reflect the magnificently accoutered belle époque guests of the Dukes. The handsome oak-paneled library in the French Régence style filled the 78th Street and Fifth Avenue corner of the house, with four large windows, two of which overlook the park. Completing the first floor was the polychrome, marble-walled dining room with its 18th-century tapestries and gilded bronze neoclassical appliqués.

On the second floor, the Dukes' master suite filled the Fifth Avenue end of the house; it consisted of two bedrooms, each with an en suite bath divided by a common sitting room. These rooms were all finished with luxurious Louis XVI–style detailing,

BOUDOIR. (Collection of the New York Public Library)

LIBRARY DETAIL. (Collection of the New York Public Library)

including carved marble mantelpieces. Adjacent to Duke's bedroom was a serving pantry replete with a dumbwaiter that delivered food from the basement kitchen. His wife had a balconied, two-story dressing room that was fitted on both levels by specially designed cabinets and drawers to house all aspects of her extensive wardrobe. Next door was a bedroom and sitting room for their daughter, also furnished in the Louis XVI vernacular. The sitting room was designated as a bedroom on the original plans and may have been used as such by Doris' governess. Filling the eastern end of this floor were three guest bedrooms, each with its own bath.

Female staff members were housed on the third floor, behind the parapet roof balustrade. This level had 12 servants' bedrooms and two baths, plus a sewing room and a linen room. The service areas were in the basement. Along with the kitchen, there were also a large service pantry, laundry, wine cellar, servants' dining room, and

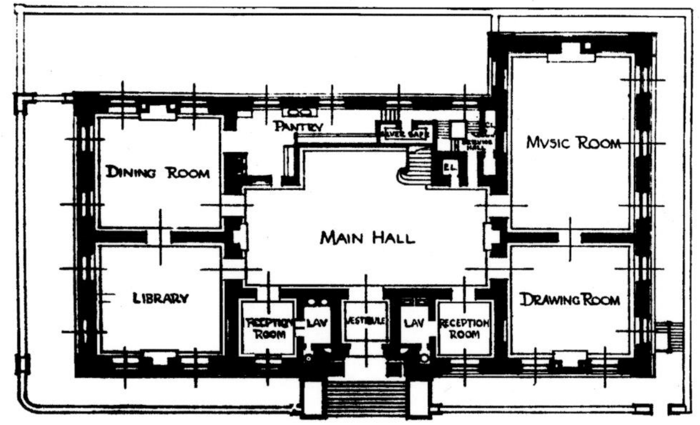

FIRST FLOOR PLAN.

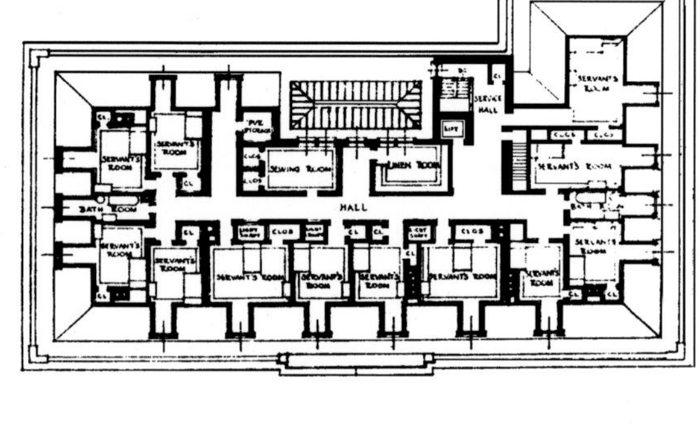

THIRD FLOOR PLAN.

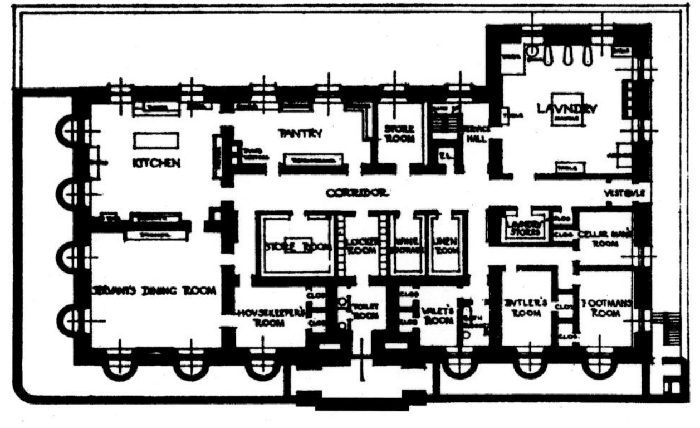

BASEMENT PLAN.

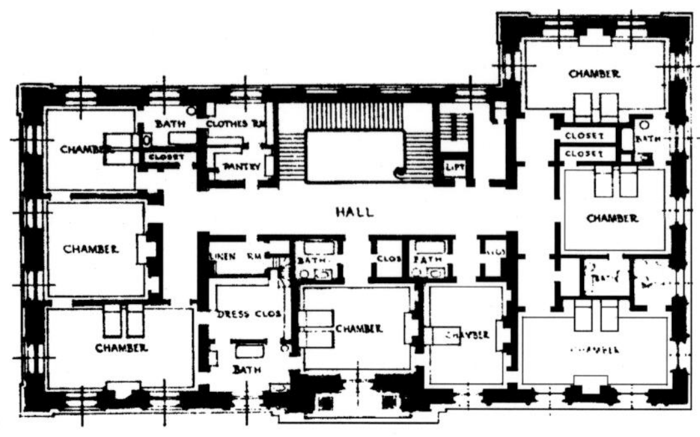

SECOND FLOOR PLAN. (All Author's Collection)

assorted storage and trunk rooms. This level also contained sleeping rooms for the housekeeper, butler, and Duke's valet, as well as rooms for other male members of the staff. The mechanicals, such as the boiler and hot water systems, were placed in the sub-basement.

Duke died in 1925, leaving an estate valued in excess of $150 million, most of which was left in trusts for his wife and daughter. Of his many charitable bequests, the largest was one for $7 million to Duke University to enable it to complete its Trumbauer-designed campus. This benevolence brought the Duke gift to the university to near $50 million. Duke's widow continued to live at 1 East 78th Street until 1957, when she and her daughter jointly donated the house to New York University to be used as the headquarters for its Institute of Fine Arts. Trading the sumptuousness of Trumbauer's stately palace for a simple suite of rooms up the avenue at the Stanhope Hotel, Mrs. Duke lived four more years. She was interred next to her husband in the family crypt under the chapel at Duke University in Durham, North Carolina.

Ogden Codman Jr. House

7 East 96th Street

Ogden Codman Jr., 1913

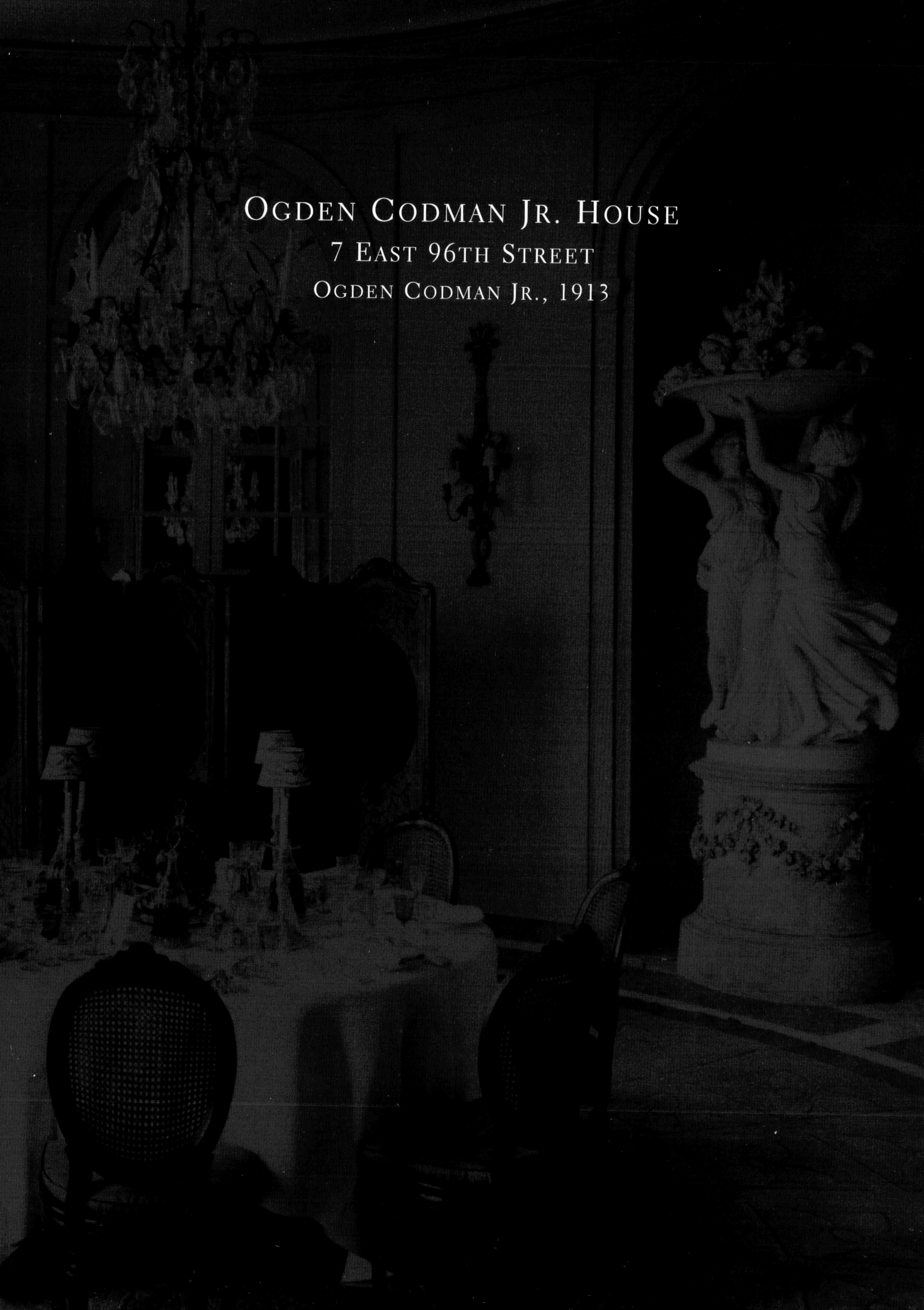

Ogden Codman Jr. House

Exterior. (Courtesy of the Metropolitan Museum of Art)

Coming from an old and well-connected New England family, Ogden Codman was considered a "gentleman architect" who received most of his commissions through the drawing room rather than the office. He also differed from most of his professional contemporaries in that he learned his trade by exposure and intuition without the benefit of a formal education. His commissions were almost exclusively residential, many of them for interior work alone. Codman was considered one of the great decorators of his time, with a sure and authoritative eye for the 18th-century styles of England, Italy, and especially France. The modern use of the term "interior decorator" usually denotes someone who selects carpets and drapery and arranges furniture while working with extant architectural features. Codman's work certainly encompassed this, but only as augmentations to his fully developed architectural interiors.

ENTRANCE HALL. (Courtesy of the Metropolitan Museum of Art)

Walls, floors, and ceilings were all carefully detailed to create functional yet beautiful rooms. With the exception of Horace Trumbauer, for whose work alone he had any real regard, Codman felt no one else in this country had a sure grasp of 18th-century European proportion and scale. American connoisseurs who demanded the finest in correct French neoclassicism generally found their way to Codman.

Born in Boston on January 19, 1863, in the Beacon Hill home of his maternal grandfather, Jones Bowdoin Bradlee, Codman was the first of five children born to Ogden and Sarah Codman. A childhood of comfort ended in 1872 when a great fire that swept through Boston destroyed much of the Codman family property. With considerable loss of their annual income, the family moved to France while waiting for their fortune to rebound. Living there during his formative years, the young Codman was instilled with a keen understanding of French 18th-century classical architecture, as well as a deep appreciation for its decorative arts. When the family returned to the United States in the early 1880s, Codman enrolled in the School of Technology—later MIT—in Cambridge but chafed under its rigid instruction and left. His uncle, Richard Codman, the head of a successful decorating firm in Boston's then-developing Back Bay, encouraged him in his architectural pursuits.

Dining Room. (Courtesy of the Metropolitan Museum of Art)

Although he began receiving commissions from 1884—most of them from relatives—Codman did not officially open his own office until six years later. At the same time he started spending his summers in Newport, Rhode Island, which was becoming the most fashionable resort in the country. With discriminating and wealthy summer residents, it was just the place for a young architect with proper social credentials to develop a lucrative trade. In Newport he met Edith Wharton, who asked him to redecorate her recently acquired summer cottage, Land's End. Their close collaboration on the project inspired them to write *The Decoration Of Houses* (1897), a treatise on interior decoration using their shared aesthetic values. "The clever young Boston architect," though often difficult to work with, by the end of the 19th century became one of the foremost practitioners of his profession in the country.

In 1904, at the height of his career, he married Leila Griswald Webb. She had been left a considerable fortune on the death of her first husband, H. Walter Webb, a vice president of the New York Central Railroad. In 1908, they purchased a 40-foot lot from Andrew Carnegie on East 96th Street, on which Codman wanted to construct a house that

Sitting Room. (Courtesy of the Metropolitan Museum of Art)

would exemplify his own design philosophy. Construction on the new house was delayed until the Codmans sold the house they owned on East 51st Street. Leila died in 1910 following emergency surgery and never saw the completed house.

In 1913, Codman moved into the finished town house, whose beautifully articulated limestone facade was the embodiment of understated French elegance. Its floor plan was adapted from houses Codman had seen in Bordeaux, since the sizes of lots there very closely resembled those in New York. A large pair of wooden carriage doors that faced the street gave access to a covered porte cochere, which in turn led to the front door. This type of entry had been used before in the city, most notably by architect Whitney Warren in the James A. Burden Jr. house on East 91st Street. Beyond the entrance was a garage with a turntable that allowed Codman's automobile to be turned around, alleviating the need to ever have to back out into traffic.

The first thing seen upon entering the house is the sweep of the elegant stone staircase in the hall. The walls here are coursed faux limestone inset with arched French doors. The only formal reception room on this floor is a Louis XVI living room with two large windows that face the street. As in almost

LIBRARY. (Courtesy of the Metropolitan Museum of Art)

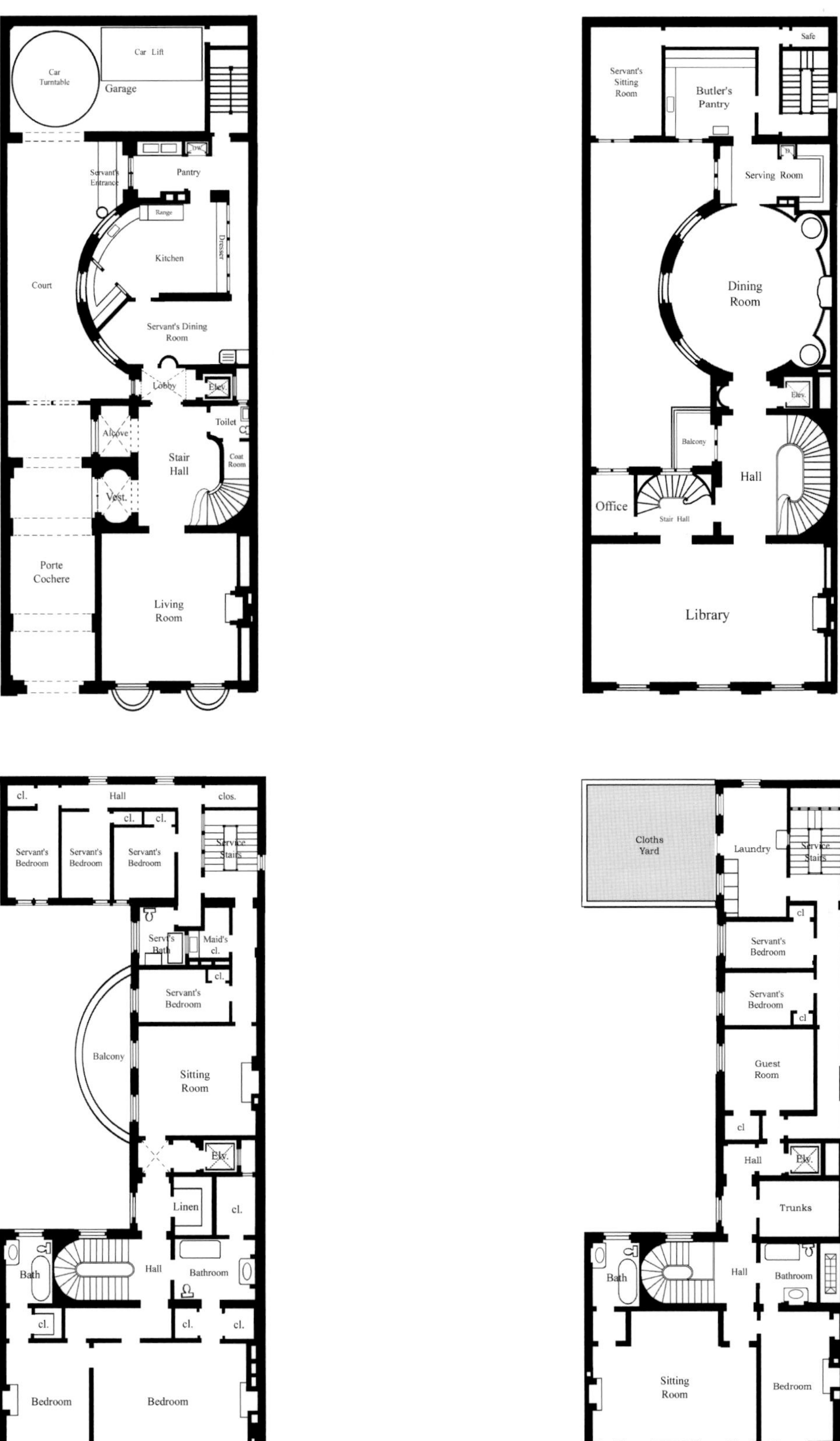

First through Fourth Floor Plans, upper left to lower right. (Richard Marchand)

all Codman town houses, the main rooms for entertaining were located on the second floor. A large paneled library ran the full width of the front of the house; behind it was the oval dining room with its three large windows overlooking the courtyard and two arched wall niches holding a pair of massive sculptural groupings adapted from Clodion. The third floor had two bedrooms and baths, plus a sitting room. At the top of the house, Codman's private suite consisted of a sitting room with an adjoining bedroom, both lit by deep dormer windows. Service areas were located at the rear of all levels.

The house was very well received by the architectural community, and Codman received several commissions because of it. The start of the World War I in Europe, though, soon brought his practice to a veritable standstill, as he relied almost entirely on Continental workshops for his furniture and interior finishes. After the war, Codman, perhaps sensing that an era had passed, closed his office and moved permanently to his beloved France. There he occasionally worked on projects for friends, but mainly he was immersed in his plans for La Leopolda, his estate at Villefranche-sur-Mer on the Riviera, finished in 1931. He lived to be 88, dying at his other home, Château de Gregy, in 1951.

The architect had originally conceived of an entire block of houses such as his, but only two others were built: one was for Lucy Drexel Dahlgren, built in 1915, and the other for Susan de Peyster Livingston, in 1916. Today the block is almost completely lined with apartment buildings, the three Codman houses still survive. For many years, 7 East 96th Street was the home of the Nippon Club, but since 1966 it has been occupied by the Manhattan Country School.

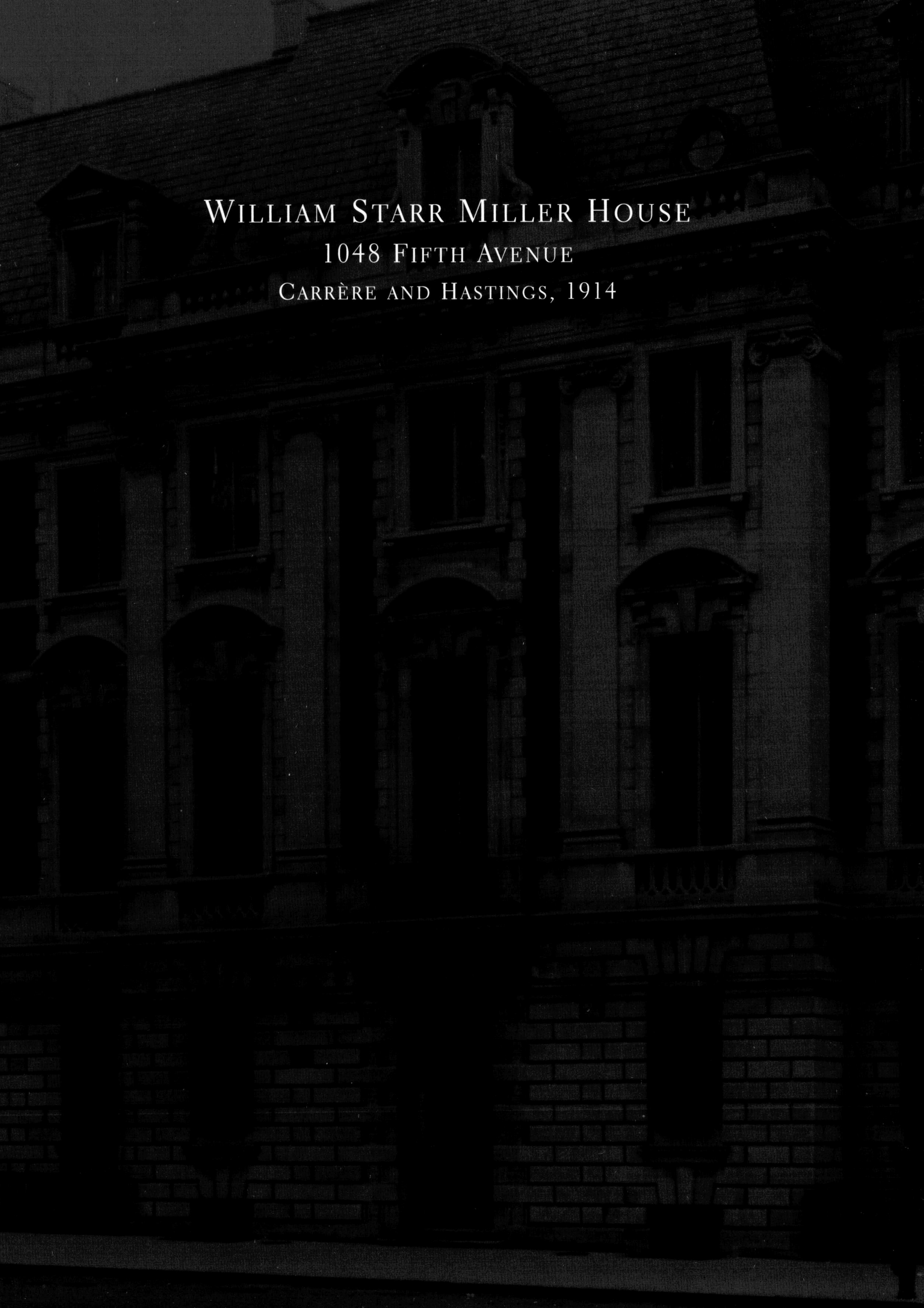

William Starr Miller House

1048 Fifth Avenue

Carrère and Hastings, 1914

William Starr Miller House

Exterior. (Courtesy of the Museum of the City of New York)

William Starr Miller, a Harvard graduate, was an industrialist and venture capitalist with large holdings in the Chase National Bank and the United New Jersey Railroad & Canal Company. He married Edith Warren in 1886, and their only child, Edith Starr Miller, was born five years later. The socially active Millers alternated between their Newport villa, High Tide, and their Louis XIII-style town house located at 86th Street and Fifth Avenue. Modeled on elements found in the houses on the 17th-century Place des Vosges in Paris, the 28-room brick and limestone mansion sits on a 47fi-by-100-foot site. Its chief designer may have been Richard H. Shreve, for at the time of the Miller commission, Shreve had assumed many of the Carrère and Hastings design responsibilities, after the death of John Carrère in 1911. (With partner William Lamb, Shreve later opened his own

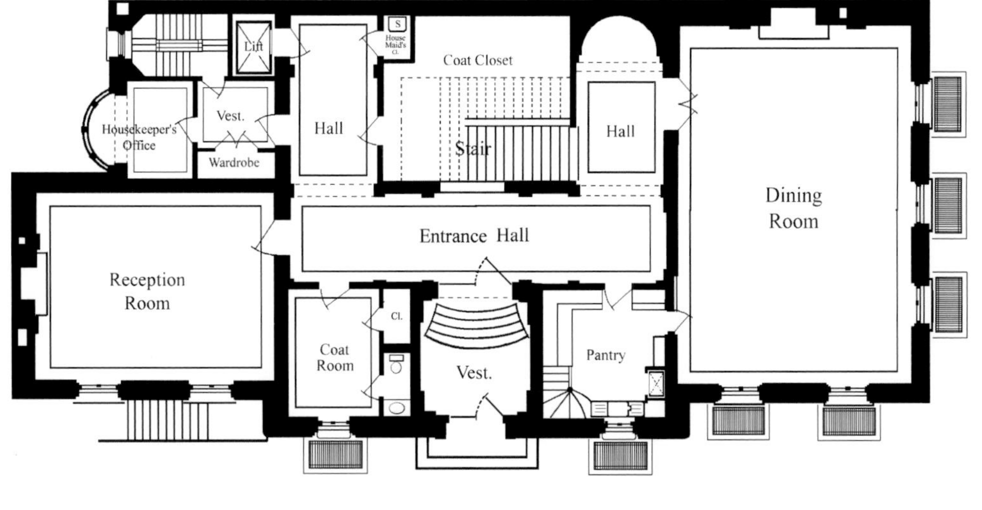

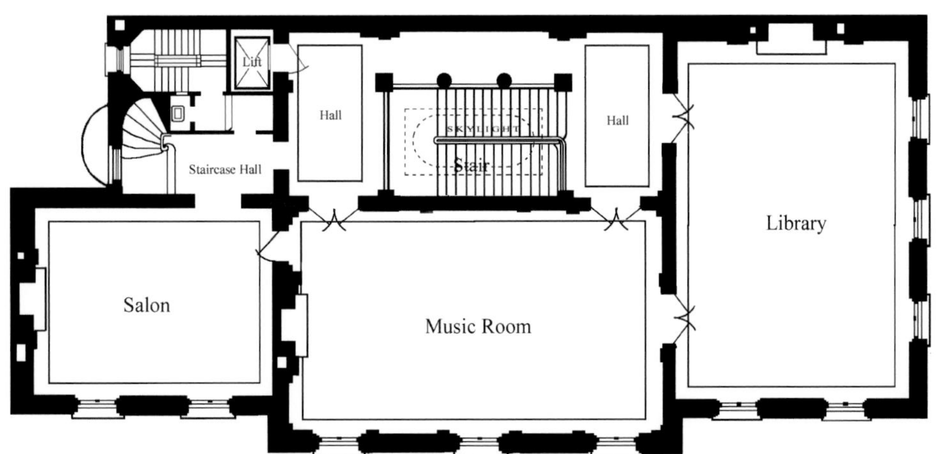

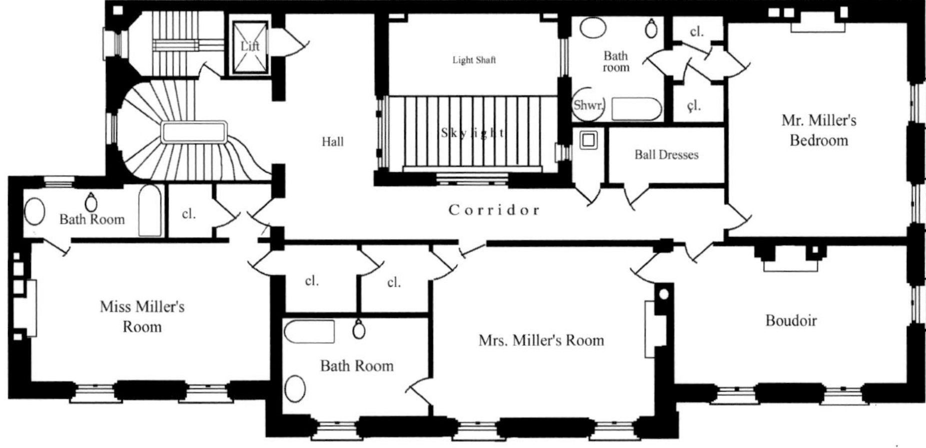

First, second, and third floor plans (top to bottom). (Richard Marchand)

office, which eventually received the Empire State Building commission.)

The 86th Street facade of the Miller house has a three-bay-wide center entrance pavilion defined by four applied Ionic pilasters. The rusticated first floor has square-headed windows that support a small cornice. Scrolled brackets with decorative pendants support the pediments located above the second-story windows. The roof cornice sits on a rosette-embellished frieze, and a balustraded roof parapet anchors a high slate mansard roof, punctuated by alternating decorative stone dormers and smaller bull's-eye windows. The basement held a spacious kitchen, scullery, and service pantry as well as a walk-in safe, wine cellar, and servants' hall. The simply treated entrance vestibule on the first floor led to a transverse hall of similar style, behind which was a domed grand staircase. A richly paneled Louis XVI reception room filled the eastern end of this floor; a paneled dining room comprised the western end. The principal entertaining rooms were located on the second floor: a Louis XV salon in green and gold, a Louis XVI marble-walled salon, and a classically designed library overlooking Fifth Avenue and Central Park. A secondary, family staircase led up to William and Edith's third-floor bedrooms—her spacious bathroom was over 15 feet long—their daughter's room, and a boudoir. On the fourth floor were two guest rooms, as well as the housekeeper's suite and three staff bedrooms. A fifth floor, which was completely hidden from view behind the mansard roof, had additional staff accommodations with their windows facing an interior court.

On July 19, 1921, the Millers' daughter, at the age of 30, married Almeric Hugh Paget, Baron Queenborough. This titled Englishman seemed particularly enamored of American heiresses, as previously he had been married to Pauline Whitney, the late elder daughter of William Collins Whitney. In her book *Common Sense in the Kitchen*, published in 1918, Edith described herself as responsible for the running of 1048, a household that consisted of "12 servants and 3 masters." The four male and eight women servants included a butler, two footmen, and a lady's maid.

After Miller's death in 1936, 1048 was his widow's principal residence until she died eight years later. After the auction of 1048's contents, in November 1944 Grace Wilson Vanderbilt, the wife of the late Cornelius Vanderbilt III, reluctantly moved in, regally bringing her butler and her bathroom. She had been compelled to vacate the 70-room Vanderbilt palace at 640 Fifth Avenue after its sale. In the late 1940s the *New York Times* described "Her Grace" as "one of the last remaining links between regal pre-World War I and American society with a capital S and the larger more democratic, post World War II society." Mrs. Vanderbilt died in the 86th Street house in January 1953. Later that year the mansion was acquired by the Yivo Institute for Jewish Research, which maintained the original interior decoration on the first two floors, while gutting the third and fourth floors to create needed book and manuscript stacks.

In 1992 the house was put on the market for $5 million. Two years later it was sold to Ronald S. Lauder and Serge Sabarsky who, after an extensive renovation, opened the Neue Gallery New York. Annabelle Selldorf sensitively renovated the building, keeping most of the remaining original residential interior finishes.

JAMES SPEYER HOUSE
1058 FIFTH AVENUE
HORACE TRUMBAUER, 1914

JAMES SPEYER HOUSE

EXTERIOR. (Author's Collection)

MANY PROSPEROUS German-Jewish families who lived in New York City in the 19th century were involved in the world of banking. One of the most prominent was the Speyer family, with its eponymously named private banking house. James Speyer was born in New York on July 22, 1861. His parents moved to Frankfurt, where his father took a position at the German headquarters of the family firm. At the age of 19, James joined the firm and began honing his craft. After working in the London and Paris branches, he returned to the city of his birth as a senior partner in the New York office of Speyer & Co.

Shortly thereafter, Speyer met and fell in love with the socially prominent Ellin "Nellie" Dyneley Prince. Ten years older than Speyer, she had recently been widowed and left nearly pennyless. To remedy her precarious financial situation, the formerly well-to-do Nellie opened

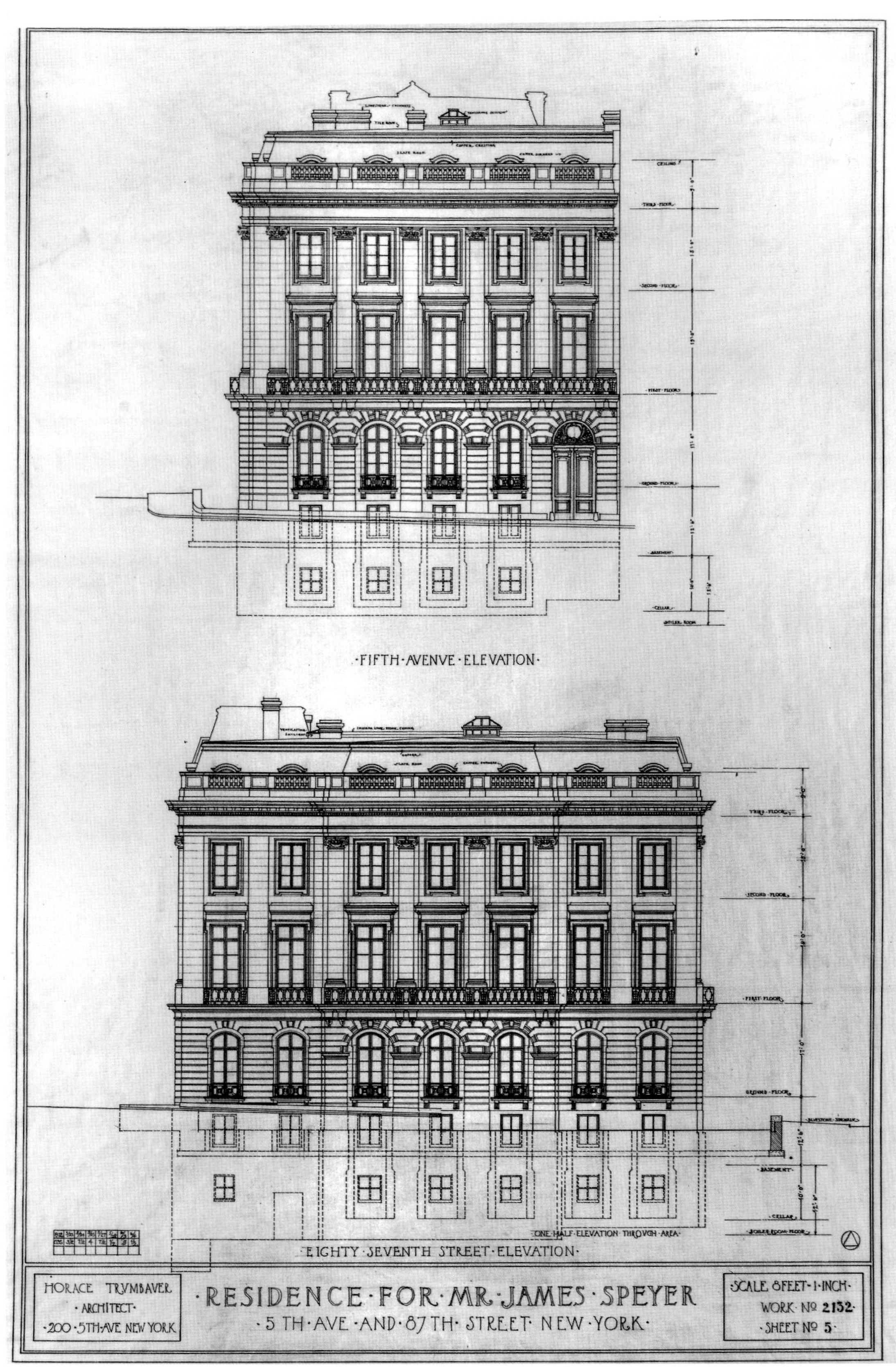

ELEVATION DRAWINGS. (Author's Collection)

Main Hall. (Courtesy of the Museum of the City of New York)

RECEPTION ROOM. (Courtesy of the Museum of the City of New York)

the Afternoon Tea Room in the Knickerbocker Hotel. The "400" flocked there en masse to witness the novelty of a socialite actually working. Speyer soon became a devotee of the establishment. In a short time he proposed, and the couple married in 1897.

Around 1910, Speyer purchased a choice Fifth Avenue lot on the southeast corner of East 87th Street and hired the noted Philadelphia architect Horace Trumbauer to design a palatial home for the site. The architect, who had just completed the James B. Duke residence, was chosen because of his keen ability to interpret 18th-century French neoclassicism—a style the Speyers preferred. As inspiration Trumbauer used the Hôtel de Tessé on quai Voltaire, overlooking the Louvre. Constructed between 1766 and 1768, the dignified *hôtel particulier* was the work of architect Pierre-Noel Rousset.

The tooled limestone facade of the completed Speyer house was set behind a protective stone balustrade that helped separate the unusually low first-floor windows from the sidewalk. With a five-bay width on Fifth Avenue, the structure had a rusticated ground floor that contained slightly inset round-arched French windows. Ionic pilasters, with carved swags elegantly draped from their capitals, defined the next two floors, and a delicate wrought-iron balcony anchored each pair of glazed French doors on the second story. The longer 87th Street facade repeated this fenestration.

GRAND SALON. (Courtesy of the Museum of City of New York)

A service floor at the top of the house was partially hidden behind a balustraded roof parapet. The reserved architectural composition made it a welcome foil to much of the residential exuberance lining the avenue.

The simple exterior disguised a complex and well-defined internal plan. The property was entered through a set of detailed wooden carriage doors located on the southern end of the Fifth Avenue frontage. The driveway proceeded past the entrance door for the length of the building and out the back, where an exterior driveway along the rear of the house proceeded to 87th Street.

A set of steps leading to a pair of decorative wrought-iron-and-glass entrance doors were located immediately to the left upon entering the driveway. Inside, the house was set around a two-story French Caen stone–sheathed main hall, classically detailed with Ionic columns and bas-relief decorative panels over the doorways. Through a screen of columns

SECOND FLOOR STAIRCASE. (Courtesy of the Museum of the City of New York)

Dining Room. (Courtesy of the Museum of the City of New York)

located at the eastern end of the room rose a graceful divided staircase leading to the principal rooms for entertaining, located on the floor above. On the northern side of the great hall was a reception room executed in the Louis XVI style, although it held a rather incongruous Adam–style mantelpiece. The adjacent dining room had curved corners and walls that were punctuated by bronze-capped marble Corinthian pilasters. A marble mantel embellished with bronze rams' heads highlighted the eastern end of the room, and an allegorical painting was mounted on the ceiling.

On the second floor, a skylighted solarium, decorated with intricately detailed wooden treillage, overlooked the south side of the great hall. The large salon, with a view of Fifth Avenue, had naturally finished wooden walls adorned with 17th-century tapestries, a François I–style polychromed beamed ceiling, and a large Renaissance fireplace in the center of the long inside wall. Next door, filling the angle between Fifth Avenue and 87th Street, was a *petit salon* paneled in the Louis XVI style. The Speyers used the adjoining ballroom for large-scale entertaining, such as balls and recitals. In this space, also finished in the Louis XVI style, 18th-century tapestries were the decorative focus. A set of mirrored doors in the center of the southern wall opened to create a balcony from which one could look down upon arriving guests in the hall below. An exclusively male preserve, the smoking room at the rear of the house completed the assortment of rooms on this level.

CONSERVATORY. (Courtesy of the Museum of the City of New York)

To access the next floor, Trumbauer implemented a traditional French solution. The treads of the graceful staircase rose in an arc with a landing at its midpoint, which created a balcony whose gentle curve extended out into the hall. The master suite on the third floor included a bedroom for Nellie with paneled walls inset with striped silk that matched the draperies hanging from her sumptuous bed *à la Polonaise*. In contrast, her husband's bedroom had sparsely detailed paneling and simple English Georgian furniture. Also on this level were Nellie's boudoir and a sitting room shared by both Speyers. Completing the master suite were a small bedroom and bath for Nellie's personal maid. The floor also had two guest rooms, each with an en suite bath.

Trumbauer collaborated on the rooms with the noted Boston-bred architect and decorator Ogden Codman, who is probably best remembered as the coauthor with Edith Wharton of their treatise on taste, *The Decoration of Houses*, which is still in print today. Codman continued to refine the Speyer interiors until as late as 1917.

BOUDOIR. (Courtesy of the Museum of the City of New York)

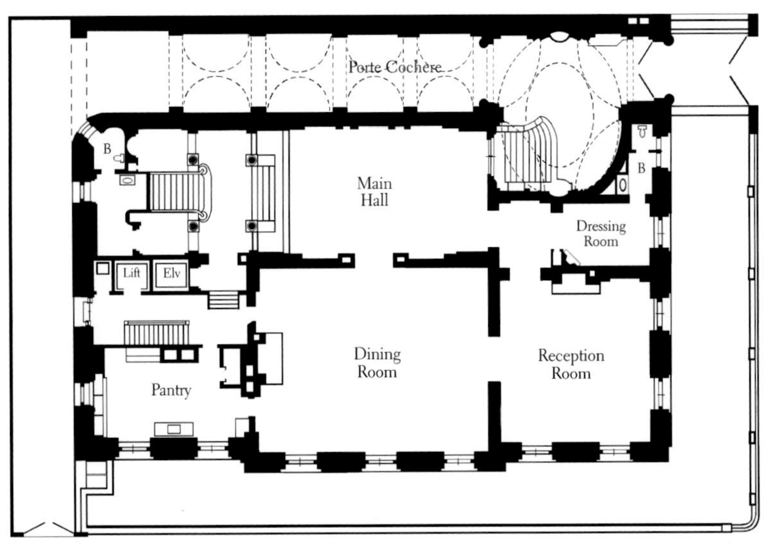

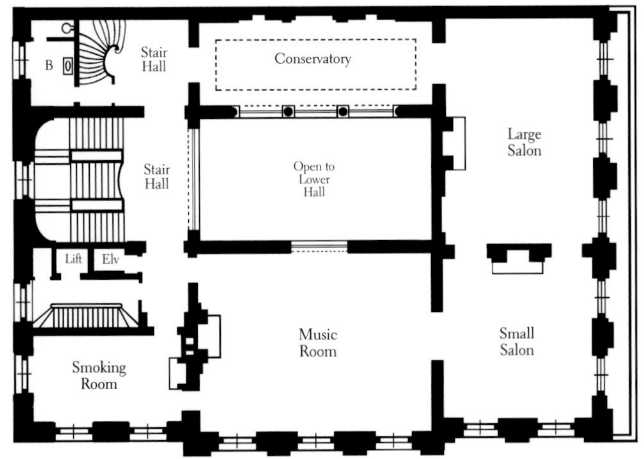

Mezzanine
Level

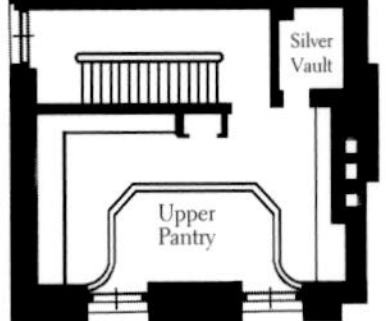

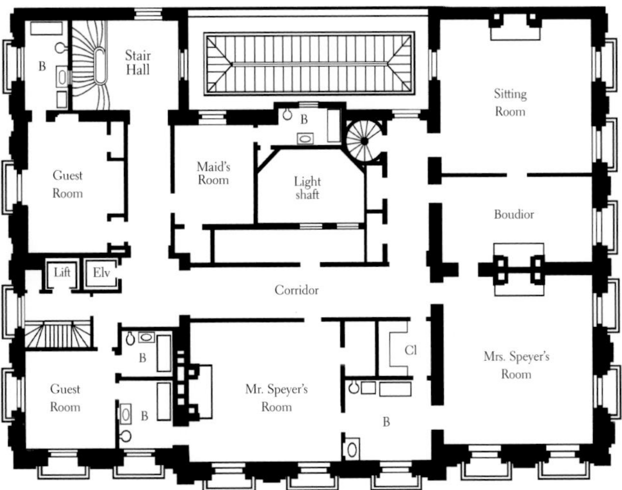

FIRST, SECOND, AND THIRD FLOOR PLANS. (Richard Marchand)

In 1914, Matilda Gay, the wife of artist Walter Gay and a cousin of Nellie, wrote after her first visit to the mostly completed structure: "The house is very large, beautifully built, planned with great care and intelligence and special attention paid to harmony and color. The pictures, tapestries, and bibelots are not of the first quality, but their setting is so perfect that they have a reflected value." She went on to say that her cousin seemed to be overwhelmed by the project. When viewing the kitchen, Nellie was "over-strained, nervous, fatigued, looked a wreck as she showed me the wonderful appliances which have taxed her beyond her strength. At sixty-four, with no children, was the gigantic effort worth while?" But William Reider, in his insightful book on the Gays, relates that the childless Matilda was herself then 59 years old and at the time living in the infinitely larger Château du Breau in France.

As the couple aged they became less concerned with the social aspects of their lives and more involved with their charitable and philanthropic works, which included the University Settlement Society, the Provident Loan Society, Mt. Sinai Hospital, and the Salvation Army. Speyer was also instrumental in founding The Museum of the City of New York, and his wife established the New York Women's League for Animals and the Ellin Prince Speyer Hospital for Animals (the Animal Medical Center).

Nellie Speyer died in 1920, fewer than six years after 1058's completion. Her husband outlived her by 21 years, devoting his retirement almost exclusively to his philanthropic causes. He was buried next to her at the Sleepy Hollow Cemetery in Westchester County. Lasting nearly 40 years, 1058 was demolished in the 1950s to make way for yet another banal buff brick apartment building.

Henry Clay Frick House

1 East 70th Street

Carrère & Hastings, 1914–16

HENRY CLAY FRICK HOUSE

EXTERIOR. (Courtesy of the Museum of the City of New York)

ON A MILD, early spring evening in the mid-1880s, two Pittsburgh business associates, Henry Clay Frick and Andrew Mellon, were strolling down Fifth Avenue admiring the newly completed Vanderbilt houses. Stopping at 51st Street, in front of the site of William Henry Vanderbilt's neo-Grec palace, the two began to discuss the expenditure required to live in such splendor. Doing some quick mental calculations, they both agreed that it would cost in the neighborhood of $1,000 a day to maintain such ducal magnificence. Each gentleman went away nursing his own private thoughts on the matter. Two decades later Frick would be living in the Vanderbilt mansion, having leased it from Vanderbilt's youngest son, George, who had inherited it in 1896. Frick did not intend to stay there long; both he and Andrew Mellon were soon to embark on ambitious construction

Construction View. (Author's Collection)

projects pivotal to the ultimate destinations of their respective art collections. While Mellon was just beginning to formulate ideas on establishing the National Gallery of Art in Washington, D.C., Frick took more concrete steps when he hired the firm of Carrère & Hastings to build his block-long Fifth Avenue mansion. According to Thomas Hastings, the house, from its inception, was designed to be eventually presented to the city as a museum.

Henry Clay Frick was born on December 19, 1849, in a two-room springhouse in West Overton, Pennsylvania. His mother, Elizabeth Overholt, was a member of the prosperous Overholt distillery family. When she married John Frick, a distillery worker, against her parents' wishes, she was three months' pregnant. Ostracized, she received little of the family fortune. Poverty made it necessary for her son to leave school after only three years and take a job with a local grocer. Somehow the ambitious young man managed to take a business school course in accounting, which enabled him to attain a $1,000-a-year position at the family distillery. A few years later, he convinced Judge Thomas Mellon, Andrew Mellon's father, of the importance of coke (coal residue) in fueling the steel ovens of Pittsburgh. With a $10,000 investment from the judge, he built his first 50 coke ovens. By the time he was in his early 30s, Frick was worth over $1 million.

In 1889, he accepted a partnership in Carnegie Steel while retaining his lucrative coke interests.

CARRIAGEWAY ENTRANCE. (Courtesy of Martha Frick Symington Sanger)

COURTYARD. (Collection of the Smithsonian Institution)

The efficiencies he instituted soon made production and profits soar. However, public opinion was vigorously against him after the ruthless way he had handled the famous Homestead Strike. Suddenly it turned in his favor in 1892 after a young anarchist broke into his office, shot him twice, then stabbed him seven times. Miraculously surviving the attack, he continued on his rapacious way. The growing friction between Carnegie and Frick from their fundamental differences regarding the operation of the company came to a head in 1900. Carnegie asked his partner to sell his stock back to the company at the book value of $4.5 million instead of at its real value of $15 million. Frick got up from his desk, eyes flashing, to chase the tiny Scotsman from his office. By standing his ground, the Pittsburgh coke-and-steel magnate realized $60 million when Carnegie Steel was later sold to the J. P. Morgan interests, which wanted to make it the nucleus of the giant United States Steel Corporation. This, along with his other assets, brought Frick's personal wealth to somewhere near $100 million.

STAIRCASE. (Courtesy of Martha Frick Symington Sanger)

To be near his fortune, now predominantly invested on Wall Street, Frick made New York City his principal residence, although he retained Clayton, his Victorian mansion in Pittsburgh. In 1905 he signed a 10-year lease at $100,000 a year for the old Vanderbilt mansion from Vanderbilt's youngest son, George, who had inherited it in 1896. Frick was content to hang his growing art collection on its velvet-lined walls until the day he took a drive through Central Park and decided to exit the park on East 90th Street. There, so the story goes, he noticed a large brick mansion surrounded by a garden. "Whose place is that?" inquired the multimillionaire. "That's Mr. Carnegie's new home," answered his secretary. "Carnegie's, eh?" he snarled. "New home, eh? Why, I'll build a place that'll make his look like a miner's shack!"

In the summer of 1906, Frick purchased, for $2.47 million, the Fifth Avenue block front between 70th and 71st streets. This was the last complete residential block front on the avenue, and Frick was able to buy it only because the Lenox Library, then occupying the site, was merging with the Astor Library and the Tilden Trust to create the New York Public Library system. The three institutions were soon going to be consolidated in a new building at 42nd Street and Fifth Avenue. He had to wait over five years for the completion of the new library building before he could take possession of his property, all the while fuming that the workmen were purposely working slowly to get back at him for his union-busting past. He was afraid that he might not live long enough to see his house built.

During this period Frick was choosing among several architectural versions for his new residence. One design that he rejected was for an 18th-century Italian palazzo submitted by a family friend,

Chicago architect Daniel H. Burnham. The winning proposal, offered by Thomas Hastings of Carrère and Hastings, was what Hastings called "a free treatment of eighteenth-century English architecture, with something of the spirit of the Italians." Throughout the waiting period, Frick continued to buy important works of art from Knoedler, Duveen, and other prominent dealers. From the J. P. Morgan estate, he acquired the famous Fragonard panels that were originally commissioned for Madame du Barry for her pavilion at Louveciennes.

Sir Charles Carrick Allom, of the London firm of White, Allom & Company, was then hired to supervise the decoration of the first-floor state rooms. Local society decorator Elsie de Wolfe was commissioned to design the second-floor bedrooms, sitting rooms, and marble-lined hallways. During a buying trip to France, de Wolfe asked Frick to cancel a golf engagement to view the important 18th-century French decorative objects that were going to be sold from the Wallace Collection. She had gone to considerable trouble to secure a preview of the highly important collection so Frick could see the exquisite items before anyone else. He agreed to postpone his golf game for only half an hour and only because de Wolfe assured him the selection was of the very first order. According to de Wolfe, "He went through the gallery like a streak, while I followed at his heels, aghast, as his purchases mounted up into millions of francs and I realized"—because of her 10 percent commission—"that in one very short half-hour I had become tantamount to a rich woman."

Frick finally took possession of his Fifth Avenue site in 1912, and because the project had already been so well considered, it took only two years to complete the fabric of the house. With war raging in Europe, though, Allom's interior work took an additional two years to complete. The not-always-patient Frick, after living in an unfinished house for over two years, was by 1916 rewarded with a home whose dignified classical limestone facade, many felt, was the finest on the avenue. Based on the tradition of the Parisian *hôtel particulier*, the residence had a garden on one side and a large formal entrance court on the other, which gave it, by New York standards, the almost unheard-of luxury of having breathing space all around it.

The building's interiors were even more distinguished than its elegant facade. The marble-lined entrance hall has stone walls and a ceiling exquisitely carved by the Piccirilli brothers. On the right is a marble staircase with an intricate wrought metal balustrade. On the landing, the pipes for an Aeolian organ are partially concealed behind an ornate marble and metal screen designed by Eugene W. Mason. At the far end of the entrance hall, on the left, is the 18th-century English-paneled dining room, where on the walls were 18th-century portraits by Gainsborough, Romney, Hoppner, and Reynolds. Along the Fifth Avenue front of the house is the Fragonard room with the famous du Barry panels. Next to it, the warm-toned living room holds portraits by Titian, an image of Sir Thomas More by Hans Holbein the Younger, and El Greco's powerful portrait of St. Jerome. Opposite the El Greco hangs one of Frick's favorite paintings, *St. Francis in the Desert* by Giovanni Bellini. This room is followed by a paneled Georgian library whose paintings include *Lady Peel* by Thomas Lawrence, *George Washington* by Gilbert Stuart, and John Constable's *Salisbury Cathedral from the Bishop's Garden*. Above the simple bolection chimney piece, with its beautifully carved overmantel in the style of Grinling Gibbons, hangs a handsome portrait of Frick painted posthumously by John C. Johansen. During Frick's lifetime, this space was filled by a portrait of Miss Mary Edwards by William Hogarth.

The most important room of the house is the 100-foot-long west gallery. Here hang works such as

DINING ROOM. (Courtesy of Martha Frick Symington Sanger)

Rembrandt's *The Polish Rider*, Velázquez's *King Philip IV of Spain*, and Turner's *The Harbor of Dieppe*. The tables and ornately carved Renaissance chests that furnish this vast space are topped with superlative Italian bronzes. Frick enjoyed coming to this room late at night, when everyone else was in bed, to move from one velvet sofa to the next, quietly contemplating the room's artworks. After his death, his daughter, Helen Clay Frick, commissioned Walter Gay to paint interior views of the living hall and the Fragonard room. The painter's wife, Matilda, related in her diary that after dinner one evening, Helen invited the couple into the west gallery. "All the light was extinguished, with the exception of the special lights over the pictures; so that the pictures stared out of the gloom at us. This gave the effect of projections on the screen; the masterpieces therefore lost the quality of painting and looked like ghosts."

On the second floor facing the park were the extensive personal suites of Frick, his wife, and his daughter. They are accessed from a marble-lined hallway that has a painted decorative barreled ceiling. Artistically, the most important room on this floor was Frick's wife's boudoir, which held eight François Boucher panels depicting the arts and sciences. The room has subsequently been relocated to what was formerly the ladies' dressing room on the first floor.

The enormous basement was devoted to kitchen and service areas except for a wing that contained Frick's billiard room and bowling alley. These masculine spaces were handsomely decorated in Jacobean style with ornate strapwork ceilings. During the 1920s and early 1930s, Helen Frick used them to house the fledgling Frick Art Reference Library, which is now ensconced next door at 10 East 71st Street in a structure specifically designed for it.

After Frick's death in 1919, his family continued to live at 1 East 70th Street until his wife died in 1931. John Russell Pope was called in to create a new public entrance, enclose the courtyard, and

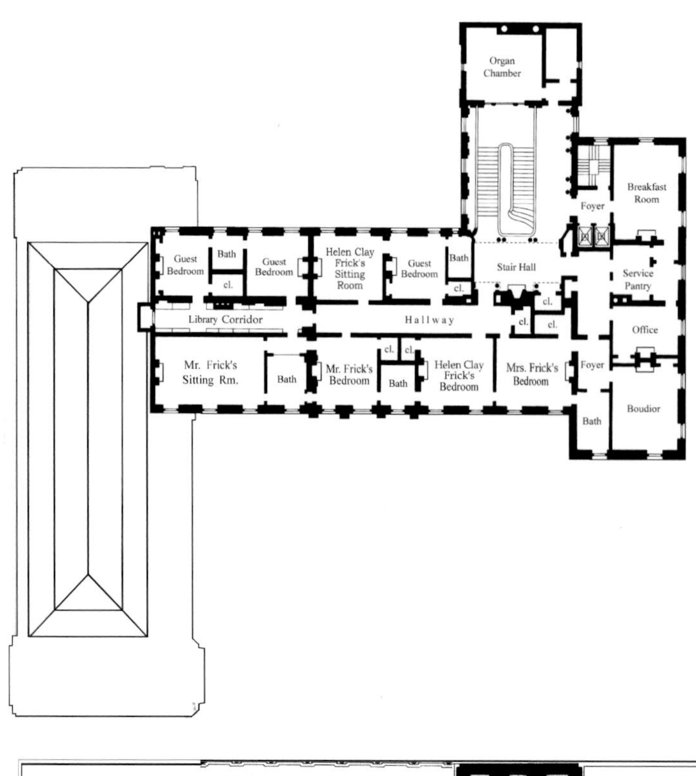

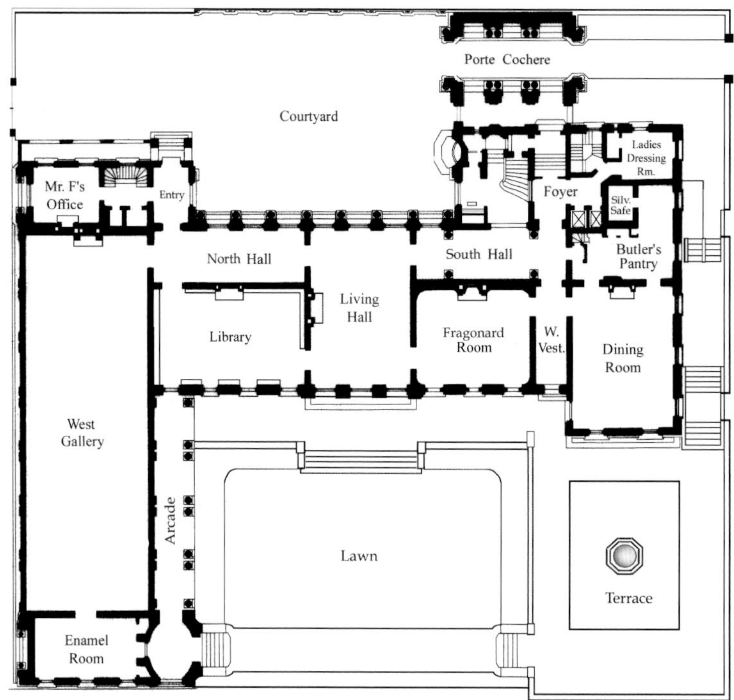

FIRST (BOTTOM) AND SECOND FLOOR PLANS. (Richard Marchand)

add several new galleries and a lecture hall to the north and east sides of the house. The Frick Collection formally opened to the public on December 16, 1935. Filled with his remarkable collection of paintings, sculptures, and decorative arts, the building still retains the hushed feeling of a luxurious private house and stands as an enduring cultural monument for the city of New York.

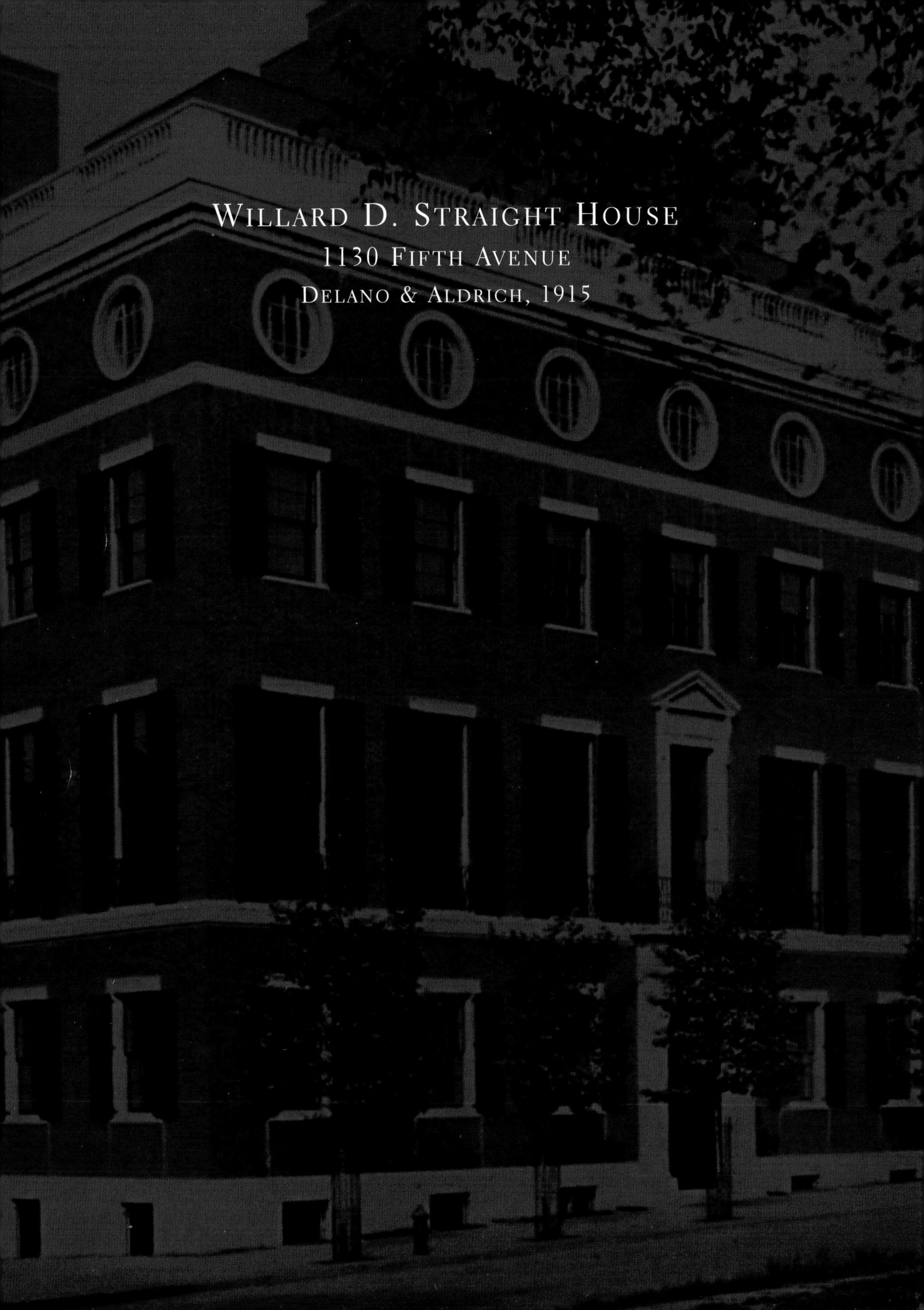

Willard D. Straight House

1130 Fifth Avenue

Delano & Aldrich, 1915

Willard D. Straight House

Exterior. (Collection of the American Academy of Arts and Letters)

Orphaned by the death of her financier father, William Collins Whitney, Dorothy Payne Whitney in 1904 became heir to a large portion of his $50 million fortune. She was only 17 years old and without direct access to her inheritance until she reached her majority four years later. Until then she lived with her oldest brother, Harry Payne Whitney, at his house at 57th Street and Fifth Avenue, where she had been born and had spent the greater part of her childhood. Her father had given this house to his son after his new house at 871 Fifth Avenue was completed. Harry was married to Gertrude Vanderbilt, the daughter of the late Cornelius Vanderbilt II, whose widow lived directly across the street.

During the two-year period of mourning that followed her father's death, Dorothy readied for her debut to New York society, spending most of her daylight hours with the best French,

Entrance Hall. (Collection of the American Academy of Arts and Letters)

FIRST FLOOR ENFILADE OF ROOMS. (Collection of the American Academy of Arts and Letters)

music, and dancing instructors in the city. Gertrude and Harry enlightened her on the many negative aspects of being a well-known heiress, a subject about which her sister-in-law was particularly knowledgeable. Before her marriage, Gertrude had written: "You don't know what the position of an heiress is! You can't imagine. There is no one in all the world who loves her for herself. No one. She cannot do this, that and the other simply because she is known by sight and will be talked about . . . everyone she loves loves her for what she has got, and earth is hell unless she is a fool and then it's heaven . . . The fortune hunter chases her footsteps with protestations of never-ending devotion and the true lover (if perchance such a one exists) shuns her society and dares not say the words that tremble on his lips."

Even though Gertrude had been delivered from this peril by marrying into a family almost as wealthy as her own, her marriage was still an unhappy one. This may be the reason that the intelligent and sensible Dorothy Whitney turned away from traditional society suitors and was attracted to men who were idealistic and wanted to do something helpful for mankind.

In January 1906, she made her debut in the Whitney ballroom. Worthington Whitehouse, the society bachelor of the day, led the cotillion with

STAIRCASE. (Collection of the American Academy of Arts and Letters)

her to the music of the Nathan Franco Orchestra. The cotillion favors were tomahawks and Red Riding Hood capes for the ladies, and for the men, feathered Indian headdresses or fur caps. Even though these rustic items might seem incongruous in a gilded Edwardian ballroom, they were typical of the favors given to guests at events like this. Two notable guests were Alice Roosevelt and her fiancé, Nicholas Longworth.

During her first season Dorothy went to a battery of balls, receptions, teas, and house parties. At one of these, held at the home of E. H. Harriman, she met a serious young man in the diplomatic corps named Willard Dickerman Straight. Straight was born in Oswego, New York, in 1880 to parents who were both schoolteachers. His father, Henry, contracted tuberculosis and died in 1885. Two years later his widow, Emma, learned that she was suffering from the same disease. Leaving her children with two spinster friends in Oswego, Emma left for the dryer climate of Yuma, Arizona, looking for a cure. She died there the following year.

Her son Willard, thought to be a difficult child, being both willful and unruly, turned out to be a brilliant student at Cornell University. After graduating, he went to China and worked for E. H. Harriman, the railroad tycoon who was trying to build a worldwide transportation network. Straight's proficiency in

RECEPTION ROOM. (Collection of the American Academy of Arts and Letters)

Dining Room. (Collection of the American Academy of Arts and Letters)

his job was based on his thorough understanding of the Chinese way of doing business, which allowed him to close deals advantageous to American interests. Later he worked for J. P. Morgan, where he successfully floated a $300 million loan between Western bankers and the Chinese government.

Straight was not the typical society suitor then competing for Miss Whitney, which may have won the race for him, as the heiress had already turned down many proposals from men her family found preferable. After a long courtship, Willard and Dorothy were married in Geneva, Switzerland, on September 7, 1911.

Two years later, after the birth of their second child, they purchased property on Fifth Avenue at 94th Street and asked Straight's good friend William Adams Delano, of the firm of Delano & Aldrich, to design a house on it. The firm was then primarily known for its handsome country houses in restrained and elegant Georgian and federal designs. Concurrent with the Straight commission, Delano & Aldrich was designing the federal revival Knickerbocker Club down the avenue at 62nd Street, and both structures were stylistically similar in detail and execution. The club specifically had been scaled to blend with the single-family residential character of the neighborhood. Of the Straight house, Delano writes in his memoirs: "If I do say so, it's a well-planned and lovely house; once inside it seems much larger than it is." Among the most interesting aspects of the design were the bull's-eye windows on the fourth floor, which were similar to those on the Bayard Thayer House, on Beacon Street in Boston, designed by Ogden Codman in 1912.

LIBRARY. (Author's Collection)

The interior of the house contained rooms of rare beauty that were equally restrained as the facade. Past the small vestibule was a round, marble-floored entrance hall with delicately painted rondels embellishing its Adam-style domed ceiling. Directly ahead through an open arch was the principal staircase with its marble treads and delicate wrought-iron balustrade. On either side of the entrance were paneled oval dressing rooms, each with a distinctive stone mantelpiece. Facing the park then was an Adam-style reception room and a small study; a federal revival dining room and service pantry filled the eastern end of the first floor.

The large rooms for entertaining were on the second floor. A spacious hall, often used as a ballroom or music room, separated the library on the Fifth Avenue side of the house from the drawing room. All three of these well-proportioned spaces were paneled in dark woodwork. There was ample space for family and guests on the third and fourth floors, while the household staff was hidden in rooms behind the roof balustrade. On top were a roof solarium and garden designed to take full advantage of the park views.

Straight died in Paris at the end of World War I, leaving a widow with three small children. About the only thing of value he bequeathed Dorothy were his shares in *The New Republic*, the paper he co-founded with Herbert Croly in 1914. The family continued to use 1130 as a New York

Second Floor Detail. (Author's Collection)

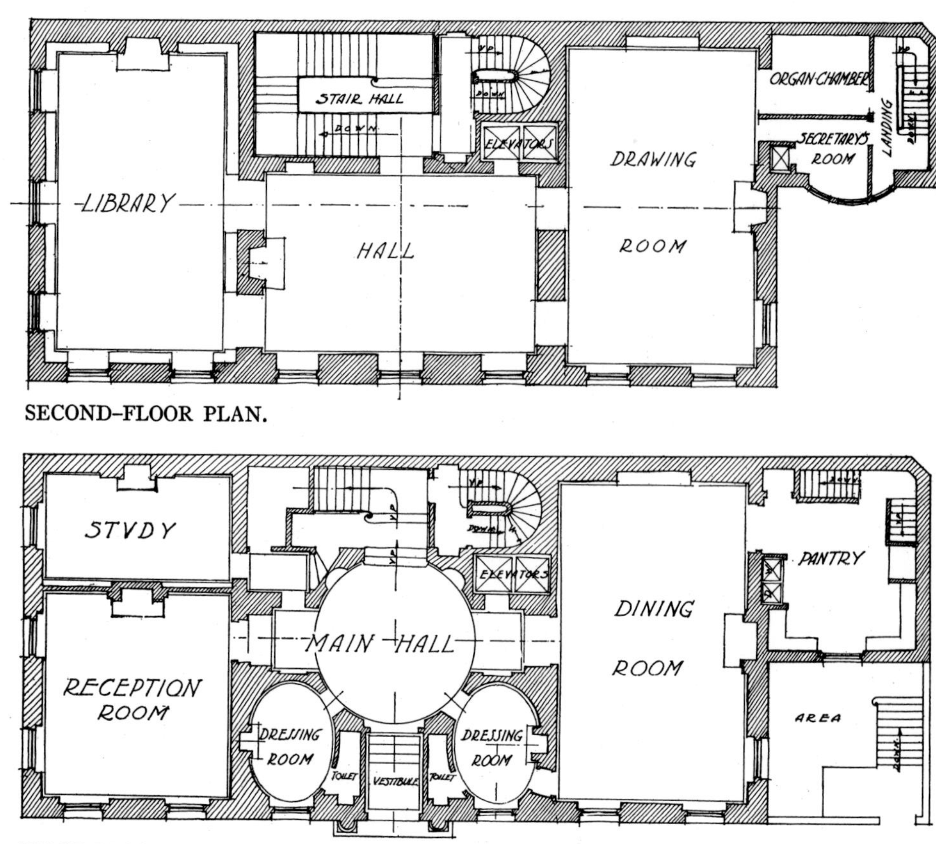

First (bottom) and Second Floor Plans. (Collection of the American Academy of Arts and Letters)

base until 1927, when Dorothy moved her family permanently to England. Originally sold to Judge Elbert H. Gary, and housing his important art collection, it was later occupied by the legendary hostess Mrs. Harrison Williams. In 1953, it became the home of the National Audubon Society until it was purchased by the International Center of Photography in 1974. All of these owners respected the beautiful Delano & Aldrich interiors and made no changes to them.

At the beginning of the 21st century the structure was acquired by commodities magnate Bruce Kovner for $17.5 million. The new owner engaged the architectural firm of Swanke, Hayden, Connell & Partners to proceed with a much-needed renovation. At the beginning of 2004 the firm's meticulously executed exterior work was completed. Unfortunately, it appears that most of the original interiors were gutted during the renovation process to create new interior spaces.

Morton F. Plant House

1051 Fifth Avenue

Guy Lowell, 1916

Morton F. Plant House

Exterior. (Courtesy of the New-York Historical Society)

With the invasion of commercial activity and the accompanying traffic noises it produced, transportation czar Morton F. Plant felt compelled to leave his Fifth Avenue mansion at 52nd Street and search for more peaceful surroundings farther north. In 1916, he and his second wife, Mae Cadwell Manwaring Plant, moved to a new house on the northeast corner of Fifth Avenue and 86th Street. Along with the benefit of a quieter neighborhood, this house had the advantage of Central Park views.

The limestone mansion designed by Guy Lowell was a cool patrician interpretation of a late Italian Renaissance palazzo. The only thing reminiscent of the earlier 52nd Street house was the use of a heavily carved rinceaux frieze underneath the cornice. The 86th Street entrance was set between two attached Doric columns that supported a full entablature and

STAIRCASE. (Courtesy of the New-York Historical Society)

balcony. The tall windows of the second floor were surmounted by alternating triangular and segmental pediments. At the top of the house, Lowell opted for a wrought-iron roof balustrade rather than a more traditional one made of stone. The delicately filigreed ironwork allowed more light to penetrate into the fifth-floor servants' rooms.

Plant did not have long to enjoy his new home; he succumbed to pneumonia late in 1918. His widow received a large portion of his $50 million estate, including the 86th Street town house. Within a year, she married the socially prominent Colonel William Hayward. Born in Nebraska, where his father was for many years a state senator, Hayward had moved to New York in 1912 to become a partner in a high-profile law firm. During World War I he organized and commanded the first African American regiment in the state of New York. After it was deployed in France, the regiment received citations from the French government for valor. Hayward was also a keen big game hunter and world explorer. During her marriage to Hayward, Mae acquired her Newport villa, Clarendon Court.

Soon after their marriage, Mae hired noted decorator Arthur S. Vernay to refit the interiors of 1051. He chose an eclectic mix of styles, which included an Elizabethan library, an Adam drawing room, and a high Georgian dining room. These then were filled with an extraordinary collection of paintings, antique furniture, porcelains, and decorative art

DRAWING ROOM. (Courtesy of the New-York Historical Society)

DINING ROOM. (Courtesy of the New-York Historical Society)

LIBRARY. (Courtesy of the New-York Historical Society)

MASTER BEDROOM. (Courtesy of the New-York Historical Society)

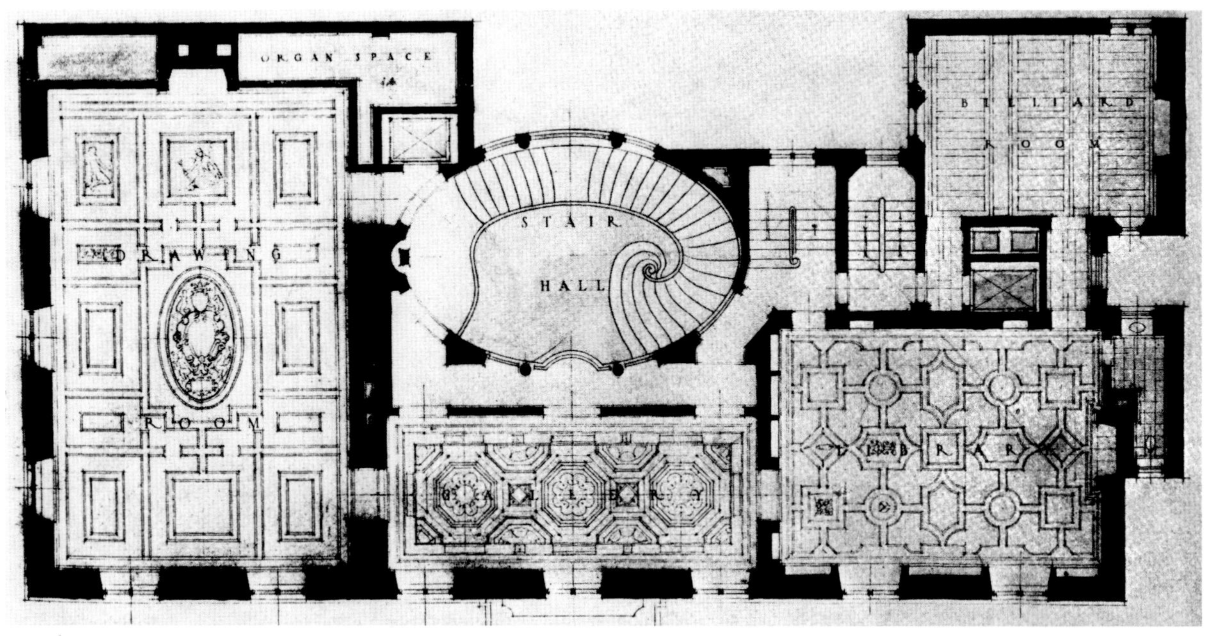

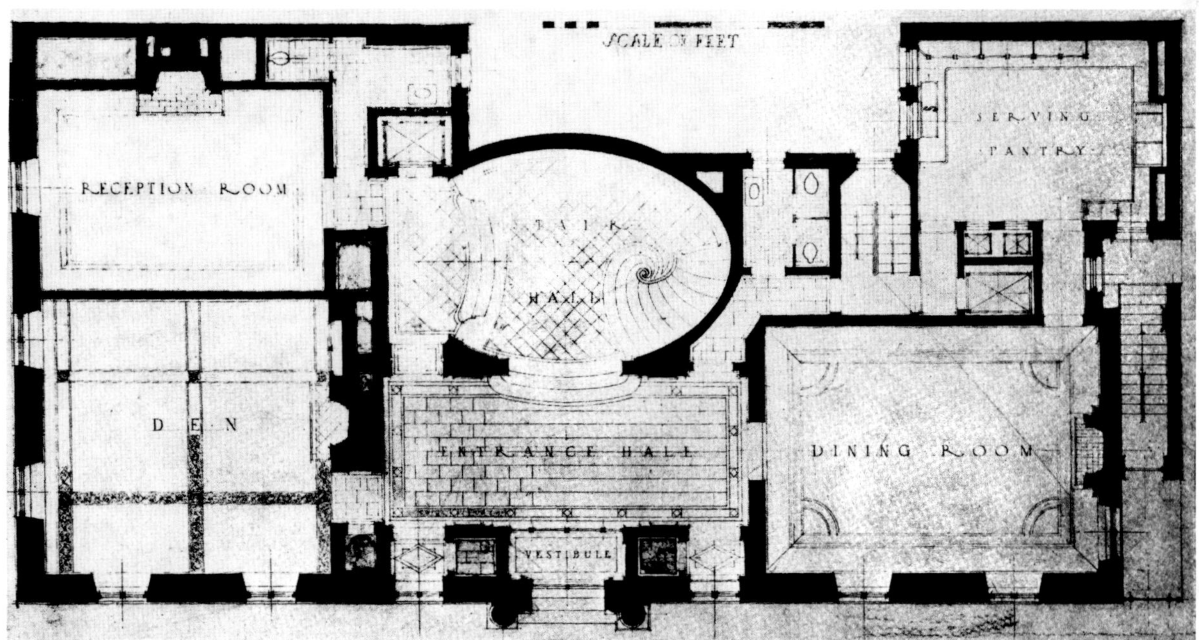

First (bottom) and Second Floor Plans. (Author's Collection)

pieces. All the rooms were tastefully designed, but the grand two-story staircase hall best exemplified the lush interiors of those postwar years.

After the colonel's death in 1944, Mae married the financier, banker, and economist John E. Rovensky. Of the four men she married, three were millionaires. Mae Cadwell Manwaring Plant Hayward Rovensky died at Clarendon Court in Newport in 1956. Her will revealed that she had spent most of her accumulated wealth and had left an estate of less than $4 million. Since she had outlived her childless son, most of the estate went to charity. Her city house soon was torn down and was replaced by an apartment building.

George Blumenthal House

50 East 70th Street

Trowbridge & Livingston, 1916

George Blumenthal House

EXTERIOR. (Courtesy of the Museum of the City of New York)

BY THE END of the World War I, New York had replaced London as the center of the financial world, and the major European banking houses rushed to open offices there, if they did not already have one. Astute institutions had established this connection much earlier. The powerful Rothschild family had sent August Belmont to the United States as early as 1845. A half-century later, Lazard Frères, one of the most respected banking houses in France, made George Blumenthal a full partner with the responsibility of watching over its American interests.

Born in Germany in 1858, Blumenthal came to New York when he was 24 years old to join the private banking house of Speyer & Co. He stayed there for 10 years, perfecting his knowledge of American banking practices. He went over to Lazard Frères in 1893.

He and his wife, Florence, crossed the Atlantic so frequently during the course of a

SKETCH OF FACADE. (Author's Collection)

business year that they found it expedient to maintain residences in both New York and Paris, as well as a chateau near Grasse. The Blumenthals enjoyed a glamorous international lifestyle and had a wide circle of friends on both continents. The death of their only child in 1909 caused them to seek solace in collecting art and antiques. Immersing themselves in the rarefied world of auction houses and fawning art dealers, the couple developed a sure eye for paintings, bronzes, and decorative objects from the Italian Renaissance and 18th-century France.

In 1914, with their New York residence becoming increasingly overwhelmed by their burgeoning collections, Blumenthal engaged Goodhue Livingston to design a Florentine-style palazzo on the southwest corner of Park Avenue and 70th Street, acquiring the choice site from the Union Theological Seminary, which had recently moved to a location on 120th Street. The fully detached residence had a rusticated first floor with arched windows and a column-framed entrance set in the middle of the 70th Street frontage. The next two floors, defined by quoin stone trim, had square-headed windows supporting full entablatures. Hidden behind a balustrade was a tile roof that contained many small servants'-room windows.

The major interiors of the house were placed around a two-story, covered, cloistered courtyard. This large space was finished with antique

Patio. (Courtesy of the New-York Historical Society)

Drawing Room. (Courtesy of the New-York Historical Society)

structural pieces from the 16th-century Spanish castle of Vélez Blanco. In the center of it was a marble fountain attributed, at different times, to Donatello and Antonio Rossellino. On opposite walls were Brussels tapestries depicting the story of Mercury and Herse. An 18th-century Venetian ballroom and two Gothic reception rooms surrounded this courtyard on the ground floor. Accessible from the balconied loggias above were an antique velvet-walled drawing room, a 15th-century vaulted Italian library, and a stone-sheathed Gothic dining room, complete with its own mezzanine-level minstrel's gallery. All of these rooms were filled with 16th- and 17th-century paintings by artists such as Francia, Titian, Justus of Ghent, and Bartolommeo di Giovanni. Also on this floor was Blumenthal's private study, which was furnished like a small jewel box brimming with exquisite furniture, bronzes, and paintings, which included an Annunciation from the school of Fra Angelico, a lunette by Cima da Conegliano, and a Virgin and Child by a student of Jean Bourdichon. The mantelpiece displayed the arms of Pierre II, Duke of Bourbon, and those of his wife, Anne of France, daughter of Louis XI.

At the top of the staircase leading to the third floor there was a rather abrupt transition from the

Ballroom. (Courtesy of the New-York Historical Society)

Dining Room. (Courtesy of the New-York Historical Society)

Patio. (Courtesy of the Metropolitan Museum of Art)

Study. (Courtesy of the New-York Historical Society)

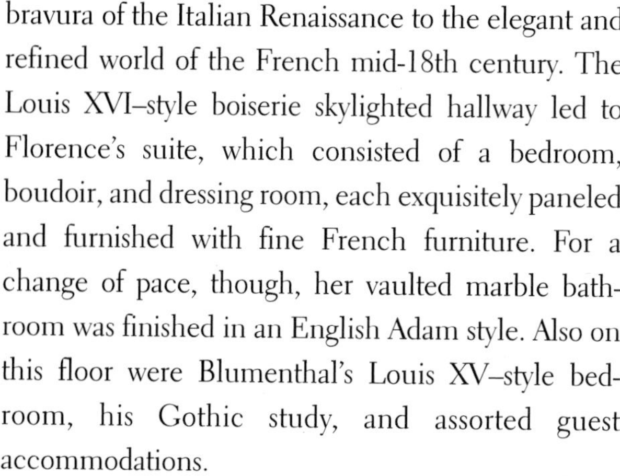

bravura of the Italian Renaissance to the elegant and refined world of the French mid-18th century. The Louis XVI–style boiserie skylighted hallway led to Florence's suite, which consisted of a bedroom, boudoir, and dressing room, each exquisitely paneled and furnished with fine French furniture. For a change of pace, though, her vaulted marble bathroom was finished in an English Adam style. Also on this floor were Blumenthal's Louis XV–style bedroom, his Gothic study, and assorted guest accommodations.

The house's single concession to contemporary art was the whimsical sea world mural by Paul Thevenaz that surrounded the basement swimming pool. The only other known Blumenthal purchases of modern art were three Matisse drawings, which the couple immediately donated to the Metropolitan Museum of Art.

Blumenthal was elected president of the Metropolitan Museum of Art in 1934, after having served on its board for over 23 years. Six years earlier he had given the museum $1 million with the stipulation that the funds could not be used for any kind of maintenance purpose, only for new acquisitions. During his lifetime Blumenthal also donated over $2 million to Mt. Sinai Hospital, and in 1937 a valuable collection of imported first editions went to the New York Public Library. His many benefactions were not limited to this side of the Atlantic; during the 1920s he gave 1 million francs to the Sorbonne, $60,000 to the Public Assistance Hospital in Paris, and 8 million francs for art scholarships at the Louvre. For these and other philanthropic endeavors the French government elected both the Blumenthals to the Legion of Honor.

Third Floor Hall. (Courtesy of the Metropolitan Museum of Art)

Third Floor Sitting Room. (Courtesy of the Metropolitan Museum of Art)

MRS. BLUMENTHAL'S BEDROOM. (Courtesy of the Metropolitan Museum of Art)

MR. BLUMENTHAL'S BEDROOM. (Courtesy of the Metropolitan Museum of Art)

Mrs. Blumenthal's Bath. (Author's Collection)

SWIMMING POOL. (Courtesy of the Metropolitan Museum of Art)

Soon after his wife's death in 1930, Blumenthal closed the Paris house and auctioned its contents. Five years later, he wed Mary Clews, the widow of fellow New York banker Henry Clews. In June 1941, the 83-year-old Blumenthal died at his New York house surrounded by the works of art he loved. Although officially retired at the time of his death, he still retained his directorships in the Continental Insurance Company, the Fifth Avenue Bank, and the Niagara Fire Insurance Company. He left life tenancy of 50 East 70th Street to his widow. After her death, the Renaissance art and antiques in the house were donated to the Metropolitan Museum of Art, along with a sizable monetary bequest. Blumenthal had originally considered the idea of establishing his house as a branch of the museum, but having worked so closely over the years with its prickly bureaucracy, he realized the impossibility of that idea. Aside from life tenancy privileges that she ultimately declined to accept, Mary Clews Blumenthal received $1.5 million plus 54 percent of the residuary estate. Nineteen percent of the estate went to Mt. Sinai Hospital, with the remainder divided between Blumenthal's nephew in London and the Federation for the Support of Jewish Philanthropic Societies. The internationally respected banker is now probably best remembered for the Blumenthal Patio (Vélez Blanco Patio) at The Metropolitan Museum, a much modified installation, with only the original Spanish components of the courtyard from his demolished New York City house.

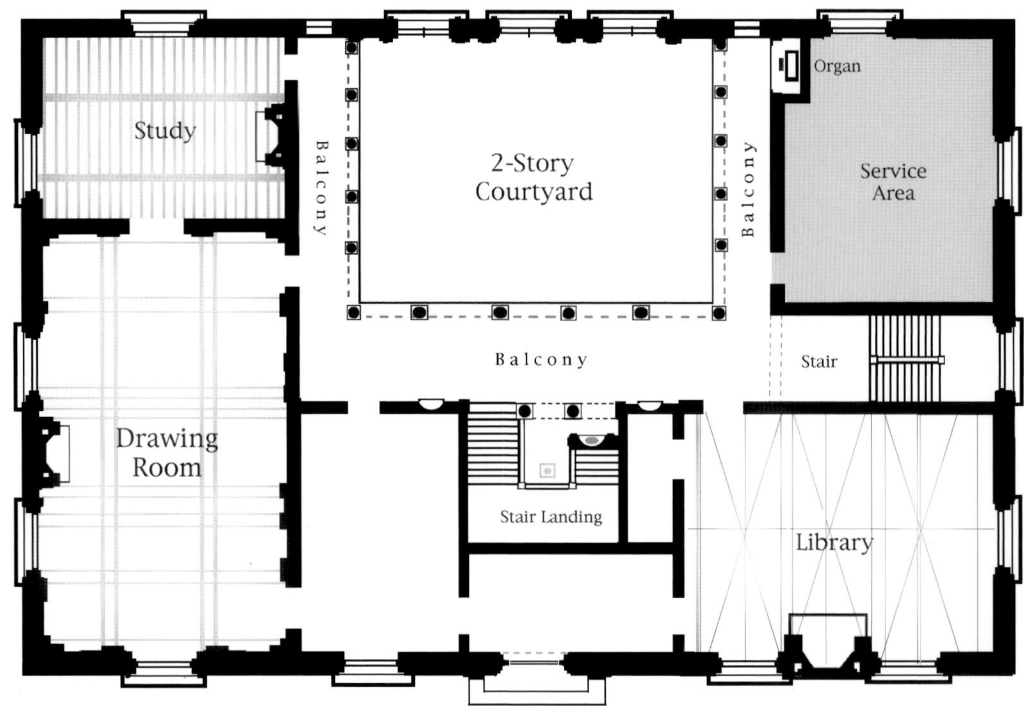

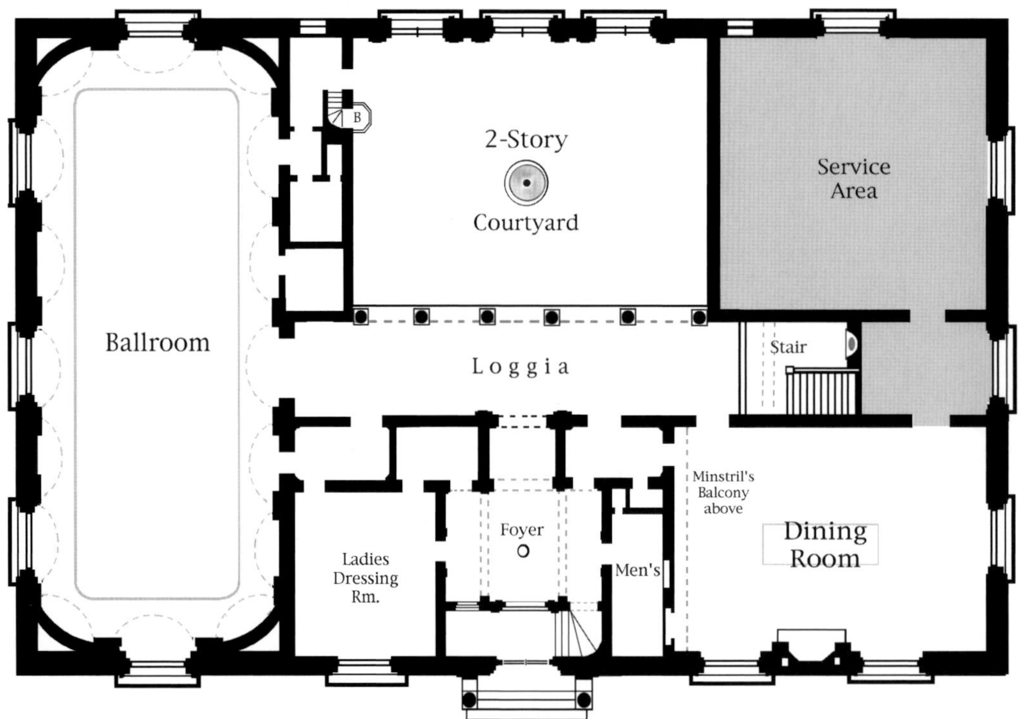

First (bottom) and Second Floor Plans, approximations. (Richard Marchand)

C. Ledyard Blair House

2 East 70th Street

Carrère & Hastings, 1917

C. Ledyard Blair House

Exterior. (Collection of the American Academy of Arts and Letters)

C. Ledyard Blair was the grandson of John Insley Blair, founder of the private banking house of Blair & Company. When it was first organized, the bank was heavily linked to the Gould railroad interests, particularly when it underwrote a $50 million bond issue for the Gould-owned Western Pacific Railroad. Later it was involved with the financial management of the Denver and Rio Grande Railroad, and the Western Maryland Railroad.

After graduating from Princeton in 1890, Ledyard Blair joined the family bank and was almost immediately handed directorships in several important railroads, as well as for the allied Clinchfield Coal Corporation. In 1920, Blair & Company merged with W. Salomon & Company, and he was named chairman of the board.

Blair was an accomplished yachtsman who was elected commodore of the New York Yacht Club in 1910. His pride and joy was the 254-foot motor yacht *Diana* that he commissioned at the beginning of the century. The commodore's seafaring ability was demonstrated in 1914 when he successfully piloted the North German Lloyd liner *Kronprinzessin Cecilie* into Bar Harbor, Maine. The ship had sailed from New York on July 28 and was headed for Plymouth, England. She carried over $14 million of American gold and silver, which was for payment of loans to American industry from France and England. War was declared in Europe just as the ship was nearing Plymouth, and Captain Polack was ordered to turn the ship around and return to neutral American waters. As the liner raced back across the Atlantic, the captain asked Blair, a passenger on the ship, where he could slip his ship into American waters away from New York or Boston, whose port entrances and routes would be watched by the British. Blair suggested the Maine resort, as he knew the waters around it very well because his father had a summer house there. Early in the morning of August 4, the ship and its treasure sailed safely into the harbor under Blair's direction.

The following year Blair purchased the Queen Anne-Gothic-style Josiah M. Fiske house on the southeast corner of Fifth Avenue and 70th Street, directly across from the newly completed Henry Clay Frick residence. Blair's property overlooked the open end of the Frick garden, which allowed it unusually generous Central Park views. He had the old-fashioned Fiske house torn down and replaced it with an elegant mansion designed by his neighbor's architect, Thomas Hastings. For the awkward 30-by-150-foot site, Hastings came up with a clean Modern Renaissance facade with a rusticated ground floor topped by smooth ashlar walls divided into three sections. The center of the 70th Street facade had seven sets of tall glazed French doors that were topped by alternating pediments and carved floral panels. Twin-bay pavilions defined by

ENTRANCE DETAIL.
(Collection of the American Academy of Arts and Letters)

fluted Corinthian pilasters flanked the center. The Tuscan-columned entrance-door surround and three crisply modeled wrought-iron balconies supplied the only features that projected from the mass. A partial roof balustrade and several panels of delicately carved Louis XVI decoration topped the composition. The building, because of its solid, cube-like mass, could have easily ended up looking flat and uninteresting, but in Hastings' talented hands it became one of the finest examples of early 20th-century neoclassicism ever built in the city. Its restrained but well-articulated detailing gave the structure an air of refined self-assurance.

The ground floor contained an oval entrance hall with staircase, a billiard room, and a reception room. The largest room on this level was the light-filled sitting room, which had two windows facing Central Park and another two facing the Frick

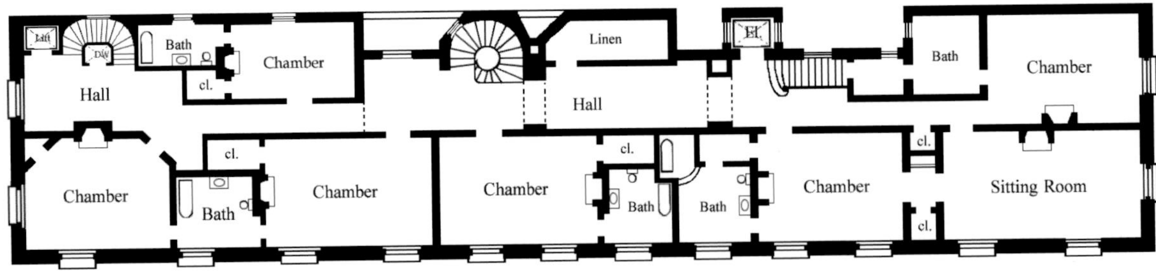

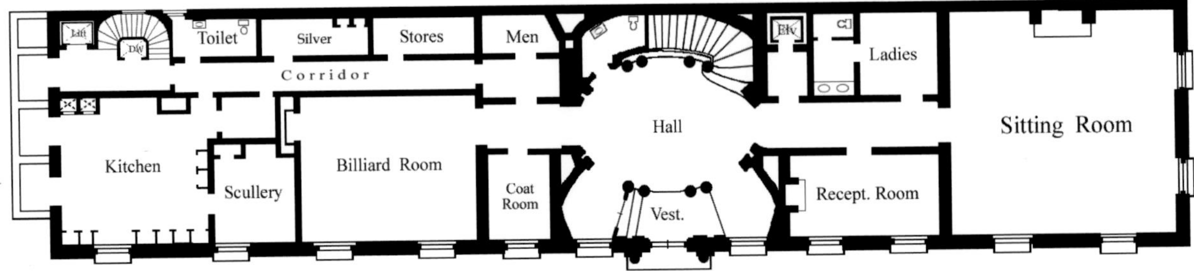

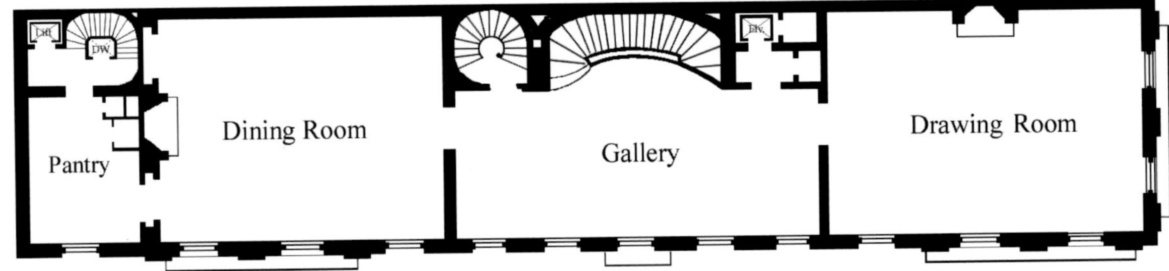

First (bottom) Second (middle) and Third (top) Floor Plans. (Richard Marchand)

garden. One flight up was a large gallery center hall with five windows that overlooked 70th Street. Flanking this were a drawing room and dining room, each built to the full 30-foot depth of the house. On the next two floors were nine bedrooms and bathrooms, plus a sitting room and Blair's wife's boudoir.

The Blairs enjoyed the house but were constantly traveling, either by private yacht or railroad car, to one of their three country houses: Blairsden, their estate in Peapack, New Jersey; Honeysuckle Lodge, their summer cottage in Newport; and Deepdene, a 28-room house in Bermuda. After the death of his wife in 1931, and 16 years after he had had it built, Blair sold the 70th Street house to developers, moving himself to a much cozier apartment on Park Avenue. It was soon replaced by an apartment house.

Francis Palmer–George F. Baker Jr. House

75 East 93rd Street

Delano & Aldrich, 1917; addition, 1928

FRANCIS PALMER–GEORGE F. BAKER JR. HOUSE

EXTERIOR. (Collection of the American Academy of Arts and Letters)

IN 1927, when George F. Baker Jr. purchased the large house on the northwest corner of Park Avenue and 93rd Street, little did his new neighbors know that this would be the first of many acquisitions in the area by members of the Baker family. Delano & Aldrich had designed the federal revival red-brick-and-marble house, constructed 10 years earlier for financier Francis Palmer, whose grandson, Charles Bailey, believed he made the money to build it by financing British war bonds during World War I. It had the distinction of being the northernmost mansion ever erected on Park Avenue.

In 1928, Baker purchased the adjacent property to the north and brought back Delano & Aldrich to design a combined ballroom and service wing. Finding the new addition less than adequate, he soon bought the brownstone at 69 East 93rd Street and had it replaced by a garage and guest extension. Both additions had large

ENTRANCE DETAIL. (Author's Collection)

windows that overlooked the central garden court. In 1929, George Baker Sr., then president of the First National Bank (now Citibank), purchased 67 East 93rd Street as the site for his retirement home. His daughter, Florence Baker Loew, completed the family enclave when she had Walker & Gillette design a regency-style town house down the block at 56 East 93rd Street. Architecturally, the Baker family dominated the block, with the only other important residence being the 18th-century classical revival Virginia Graham Fair Vanderbilt house, designed in 1930 by John Russell Pope, at number 60.

The George Baker house, with its completed additions, was certainly the grandest of any residence built on Park Avenue. The building has three stories, plus a high mansard roof that

STAIRCASE. (Author's Collection)

DINING ROOM. (Courtesy of the New-York Historical Society)

contains two additional levels. The most luxurious thing about this almost starkly simple house is the walled garden that separated it from its western neighbors. The spacious interiors were designed in the most restrained late-18th-century English neoclassicism one could imagine. Designed with a refined taste and originality, the rooms were a tribute to the skills of Delano & Aldrich. The only room to break from the strict decorative scheme was the ballroom; its walls were decorated with plaster palm trees reminiscent of those found in the Palm Room at Spencer House in London, designed by John Vardy in 1757.

There has been a persistent rumor that a railroad siding was built beneath 75 East 93rd Street, granting George Baker direct access to his house from his private railroad car. His grandson, who lived in the garage extension until the early 1970s, said he had never heard of it until a telephone repairman told him that a cable on which he was working ran down to the siding. On the other hand, Metro-North Railroad officials have specifically said that no such siding currently exists beneath the building. The only physical evidence that today might substantiate its existence is a non-operative elevator button that designates a stop somewhere below the cellar.

The story is plausible, because Baker was a director of several railroads as well as a director of AT&T, General Electric, United States Steel, and the General Motors Corporation. He abhorred publicity and never gave an interview or issued a public statement of any kind during his long career. In October 1929, Baker stood with J. P. Morgan Jr., trying to stabilize the stricken economy, and they were able to mobilize $250 million within the first 24 hours. Both men were doing exactly what their fathers had done during the panic of 1907, unfortunately with less success. In 1931, after the death of his father, Baker inherited $60 million from the estate.

Baker was an enthusiastic yachtsman. He was elected commodore of the New York Yacht Club and was a member of the syndicate that owned the *Enterprise*, the boat that defeated Sir Thomas Lipton's *Shamrock V* in the 1930 America's Cup race.

In May 1937, Baker was sailing on his yacht with a party of friends heading for Honolulu from the Fiji Islands when he became seriously ill. A doctor from a passing liner boarded the yacht in mid-ocean and assisted Baker's own physician, already on board, in performing an emergency operation. The Coast Guard converted a cutter into a hospital ship, picked up the director of the Honolulu Public Health Service and additional medical personnel, then sped to intercept the banker's yacht, which was some 300 miles away; needed serums were air-dropped. Upon hearing the news of her husband's illness, Baker's wife chartered a plane to take her on the 5,500-mile trip from New York to Hawaii. Despite these efforts, the 59-year-old Baker died of peritonitis soon after reaching Honolulu.

His widow continued to live in the Park Avenue house until the outbreak of World War II. In 1958, the main body of the house and the ballroom wing were sold to the Russian Orthodox Church Outside of Russia, but the family retained the garage and guest wing for many years thereafter. With the exception of a few alterations to the courtyard, the church has made few changes to the structure either inside or out and it continues to look much as it did when the Bakers were in residence.

Edith Fabbri House

7 East 95th Street

Egisto Fabbri and Grosvenor Atterbury, 1917

EDITH FABBRI HOUSE

EXTERIOR. (Linda Hall Library)

ERNESTO FABBRI was a junior partner at Morgan, Harjes, in Paris, where he and his wife Edith lived for seven years. Spending long holidays visiting relatives in Italy, Edith fell in love with Florentine architecture. When they returned to the United States in 1914, their house on East 62nd Street, which had been given to them soon after their marriage by Edith's mother, Margaret Louisa Vanderbilt Shepard, no longer suited them. The Fabbris wanted the grace and restrained elegance of Italy transplanted to the Upper East Side of Manhattan. Purchasing a lot on East 95th Street for this purpose, they gave the project to Ernesto's brother, Egisto Fabbri, an aristocratic amateur architect who had been designing churches in Italy for several years. New York-based Grosvenor Atterbury was hired as the architect of record. He was to oversee all of the construction details while leaving all stylistic decisions to Fabbri.

ENTRANCE HALL. (Collection of the New York Public Library)

Immediately inside the doors, a marble-floored vestibule has steps leading up to wrought-iron inner doors that access the main hall. Both the vestibule and the hall are lit by the French doors that open onto the fenced courtyard. The entrance hall, like many of the rooms of the house, has a floor of handmade tiles imported from Florence. All the pilasters and arches of the room are of dark gray stone and make a striking contrast with the simple whitewashed walls. A pair of dark, simply modeled wooden doors lead down three steps to the dining room with its vaulted ceiling and massive stone fireplace. At the front of the house is a reception room that has a late-16th-century Renaissance ceiling.

The two principal rooms of the house are on the second floor. Facing the street off the central hall is a somewhat narrow drawing room with a coffered wooden ceiling. Across the hall is the two-story library, whose paneling came from the Ducal palace in Urbino and was shipped to New York in two separate vessels during the opening days of the World War I. The coat of arms on the ceiling is said to have been executed by Raphael. The library's immense marble fireplace is flanked by two male figures carved in the style of Brunelleshi. Secreted in the panels of molded wood at the eastern end of the room is a large pipe organ.

LIVING ROOM. (Collection of the New York Public Library)

DINING ROOM. (Collection of the New York Public Library)

LIBRARY. (Collection of the New York Public Library)

The first entertainment given in the house was the coming-out party for the Fabbris' daughter on March 12, 1917. There was some concern about the house being completed in time. The party was given on schedule, but because of the war, the family opted to make their daughter's debut two evenings of classical music rather than a ball. Musical events would continue to be a tradition in the Fabbri household.

Edith Fabbri loved the monastic atmosphere of the place. As Egisto customarily designed religious structures, this was a well-justified emotional response. Pleased with the results, she asked her brother-in-law to design a summer house in Bar Harbor, Maine. Edith divorced her husband and continued to live in the house until 1949. That year she donated it to the Episcopal Church, which used it as a religious retreat under the name of "The House of the Redeemer." It still exists as such today.

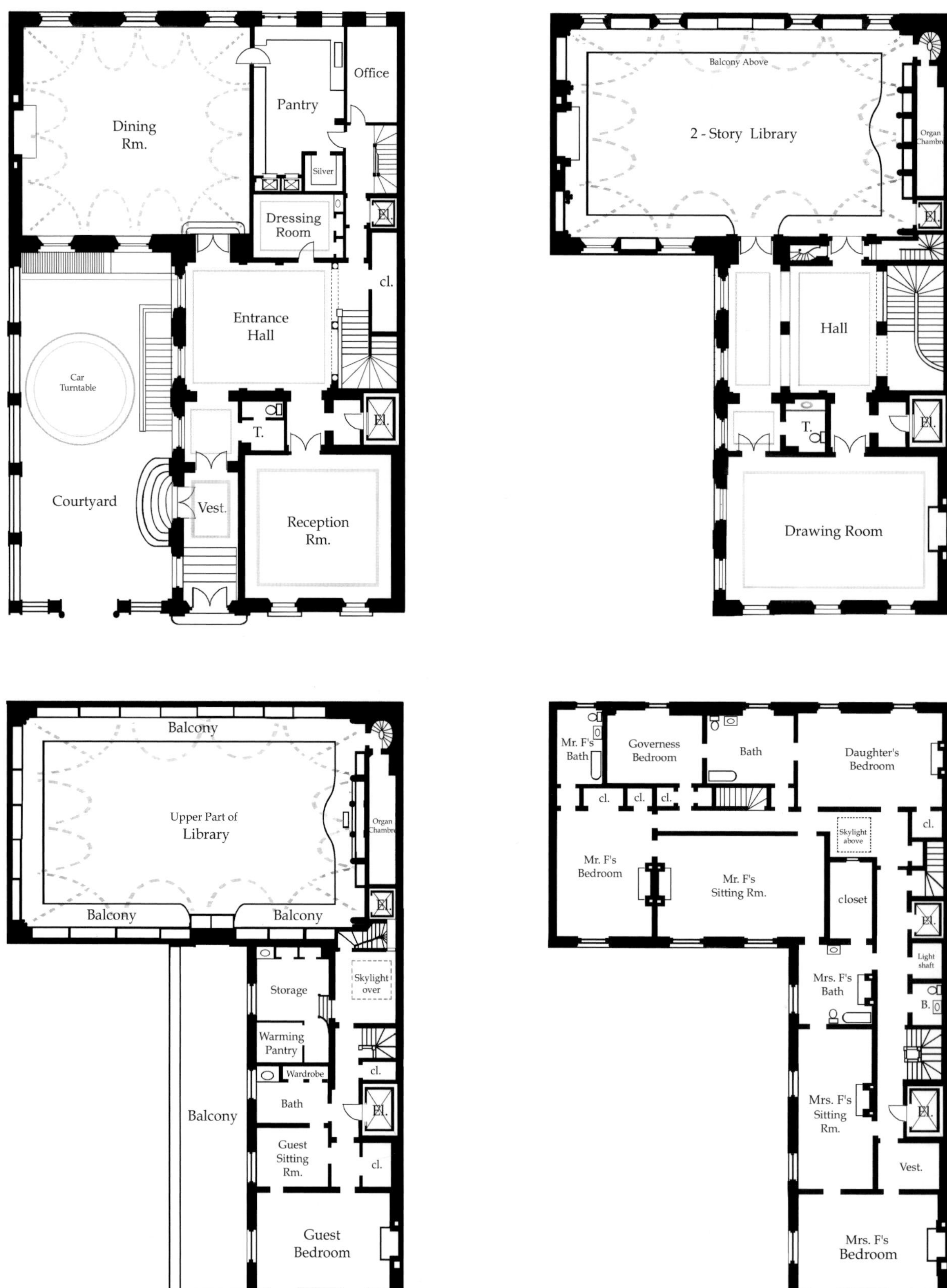

FIRST THROUGH FOURTH-FLOOR PLANS (UPPER LEFT TO LOWER RIGHT). (Richard Marchand)

Arthur Curtiss James House

39 East 69th Street

Allen & Collens, 1917

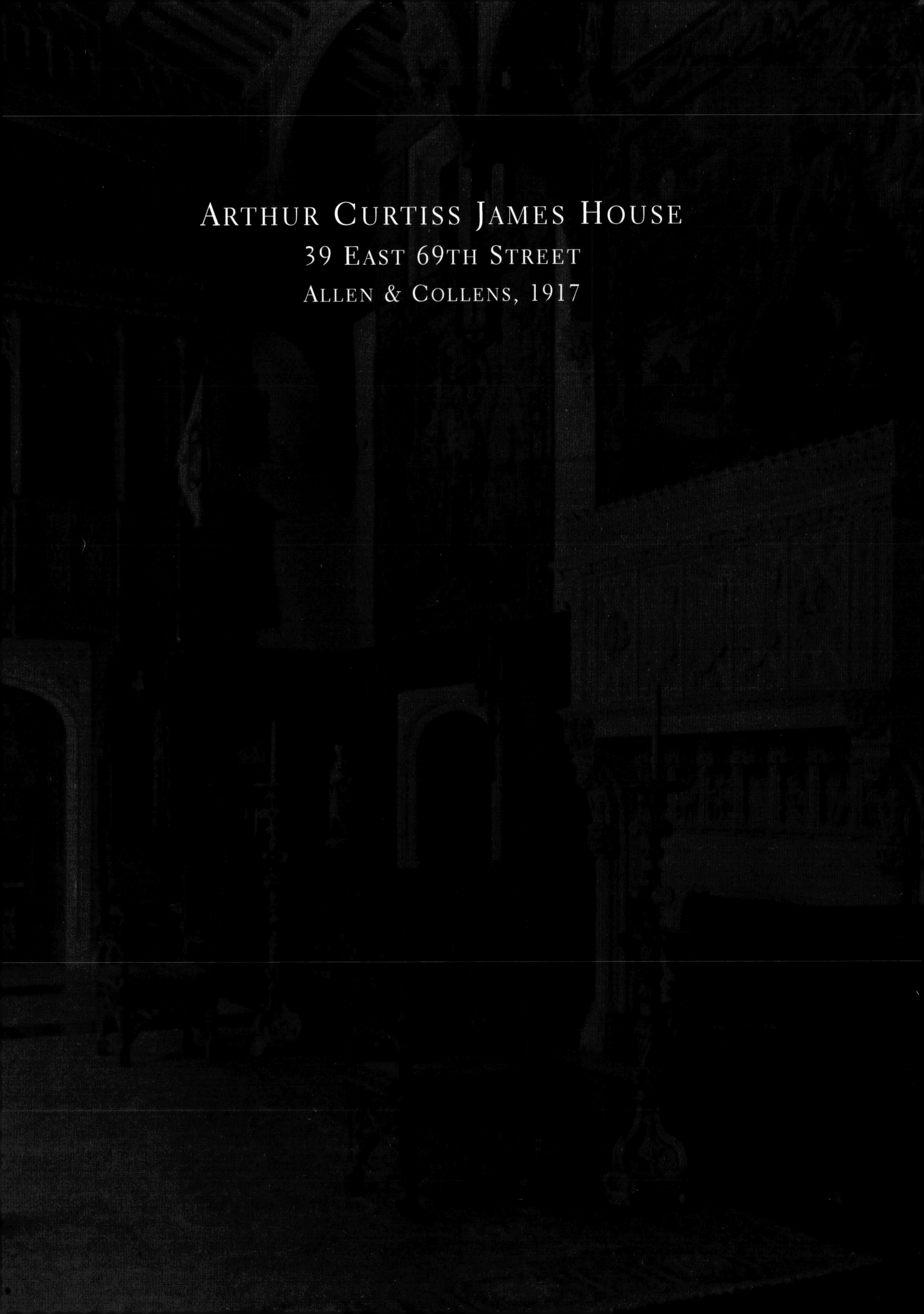

Arthur Curtiss James House

Exterior. (Avery Library, Columbia University)

As the George Blumenthal house was rising on its half of the Union Theological Seminary Park Avenue block front, railroad owner Arthur Curtiss James was simultaneously having a house constructed on the southern half. Designed by Allen & Collens in the English Renaissance style, the gray marble James house took two years to erect. The detached building did not completely fill its 100-foot-wide site, leaving room for a garden on its northern side.

The house paid homage to the great Renaissance houses developed in England at the end of the 16th and the beginning of the 17th centuries. The architects cleverly synthesized design elements from several English county houses of the period to create a highly imaginative composition successfully set within the urban context of New York. The entrance to the house, with its paired columns framing an arched doorway, is borrowed from the south

EXTERIOR–REAR VIEW. (Courtesy of the Museum of the City of New York)

front of Hatfield House, Hertfordshire, while, at the back of the house, the protruding bay windows with their pierced parapets were taken from Blickling Hall, Norfolk. Whereas the two English houses are of brick with stone trim, the James house was veneered completely with stone in the fashion of Hardwick Hall in Derbyshire. The enormous scale of the mullioned windows, particularly on the first floor, is also reminiscent of Hardwick. Overall, the James house captures the moment in the development of English architecture when the classical was on the ascendent and Tudor-Elizabethan excesses were surpressed.

The Romanesque and Byzantine-style entrance hall had walls finished in Botticini marble, with the columns, arches, and floors in a combination of Languedoc, gray Sienna, and Formosa marbles. The Tennessee marble treads of the staircase had been artificially worn to give an aged effect. The adjoining two-story great hall, with its beautifully trussed wooden ceiling, dated from the early Tudor period. A limestone mantelpiece was placed in the center of the north wall, and Flemish tapestries were hung on the upper walls. Continuing along the front of the house was a Georgian-style library with an adjacent oak-paneled den. Along the rear, the dining room was paneled with carved English limewood, and marble columns framed the entrance to an adjoining conservatory.

STAIR HALL. (Courtesy of the New York Historical Society)

At the top of the staircase on the second floor, a guest room with an adjoining dressing room had access to a balcony overlooking the great hall. The rest of this level was devoted to large suites for both Mr. and Mrs. James. These included separate bedrooms, baths, and dressing rooms, and a boudoir for the lady of the house. The third floor had a large gallery transverse hall that opened onto an equally long tiled solarium that held a central fountain. Elsewhere on this level were three guest rooms, a boudoir, and five staff rooms. Other staff accommodations were located in two different mezzanine levels, as well as in the basement.

Writer James W. Gerrard named Arthur Curtiss James as one of the 59 men who "owned" America. Born to great wealth, he inherited his father's $26 million fortune in 1907. Because the shy James shunned publicity, he never became well known. George Gould, James Hill, and Edward Harriman were better known, but James controlled more track than any of them—he was able to travel from coast to coast without ever having to leave his own railroad network. Aside from his transportation empire, James held substantial interests in copper, silver, and gold mines.

Though a confirmed Republican, James supported Franklin Delano Roosevelt in his battle

GREAT HALL. (Courtesy of the New York Historical Society)

DINING ROOM. (Author's Collection)

DINING ROOM DETAIL. (Author's Collection)

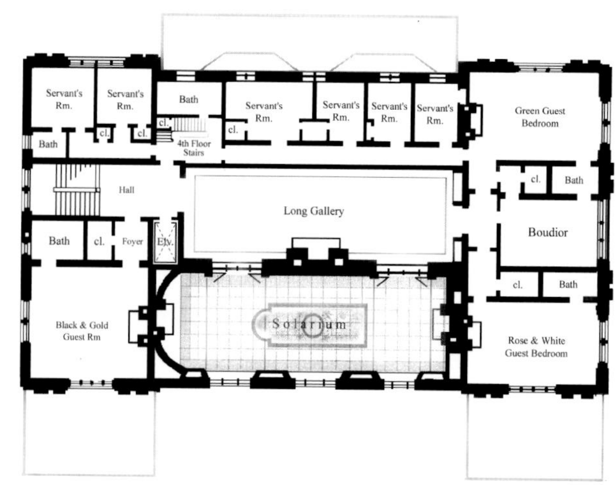

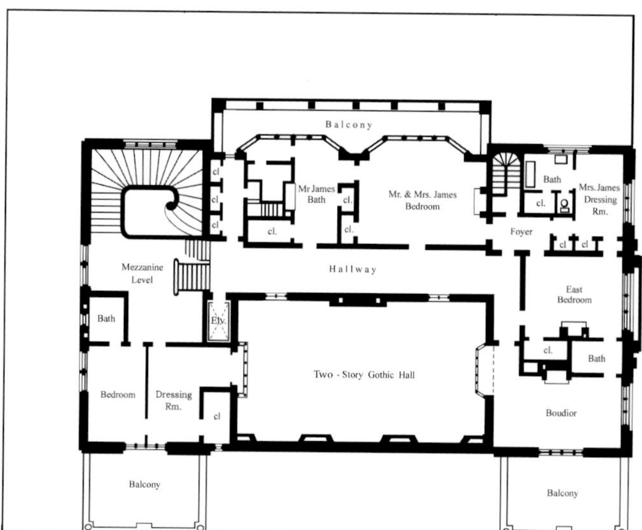

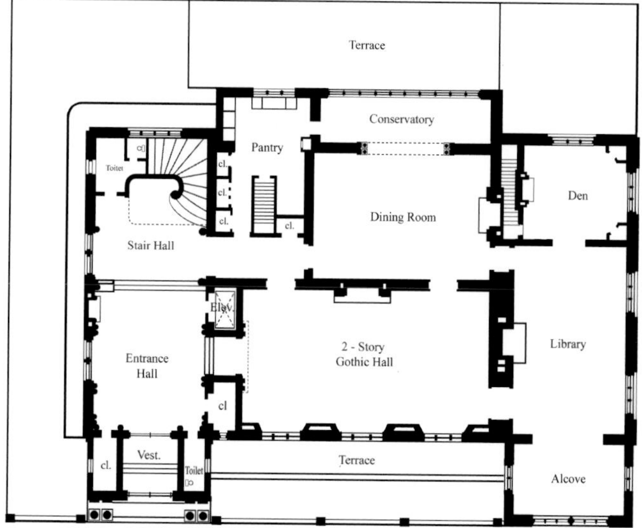

FIRST, SECOND, AND THIRD FLOOR PLANS (BOTTOM TO TOP).
(Richard Marchand)

against Prohibition. His desire to fight it might have originated with an incident in 1926, when a Coast Guard cutter in Long Island Sound fired on his yacht, suspecting it to be a rumrunner. James, a former commodore of the New York Yacht Club, depended on his yacht to transport him from New York City to his Hudson River estate, his Newport villa, and a winter house in Coconut Grove, Florida.

During his lifetime, James gave away millions of dollars to educational and charitable institutions, with the stipulation that the gifts remain anonymous. Civic minded, he was a member of the management group of the Metropolitan Opera, a director of the Philharmonic orchestra, and a director of the Botanical Gardens of New York City. With his wife, Harriet Parsons James, he donated a settlement house, called "Christodora House," on New York's Lower East Side.

Although he suffered severe financial reverses during the depression, James managed to retain control of his transportation empire. He retired from the active management of his railroad interests in 1939 to pursue recreational and philanthropic endeavors. In June 1941, the 75-year-old multimillionaire succumbed to pneumonia, just three weeks after his wife suffered a fatal heart attack in their New York City house. After giving 10 percent of his estate to nieces and nephews, the childless James left the remainder to establish a foundation for religious and educational purposes. Soon after his death, the house was torn down to make way for an apartment building.

Cornelius Vanderbilt III House

640 Fifth Avenue

John B. Snook and C. B. Atwood, 1878

Renovated by Horace Trumbauer, 1917

CORNELIUS VANDERBILT III HOUSE

EXTERIOR, C. 1880. (Author's Collection)

THE SAGA of 640 Fifth Avenue began in 1878, when William Henry Vanderbilt, son and principal heir of Commodore Cornelius Vanderbilt, engaged architect John B. Snook and decorator C. B. Atwood of the prestigious Herter Brothers firm to design and execute plans for twin mansions on the avenue. The finished building occupied the entire block between 51st and 52nd streets on the west side of Fifth Avenue. The northern half was occupied by residences for two of William's daughters; the southern half was reserved for Vanderbilt and his wife, Maria Louisa Kissam Vanderbilt.

This residence was designed at the end of the Victorian movement in America. Its rich neo-Grec brownstone facade was alive with decorative detailing, such as balconied window projections and intricately carved entablatures above the windows on the second story. An elaborately carved floral frieze ran in tandem with

GREAT HALL, C. 1880. (Author's Collection)

the windows on the third floor, and similar decorative detailing ran across the first-story level at the top of the windows. A perforated parapet balustrade topped all of this exuberant detailing.

The mansion's interiors were even more elaborately conceived. Overpowering in their intensity, the major interior spaces were filled with stone and mosaic walls and floors, and the most important rooms were decorated with murals by Jules-Joseph Lefebvre. Draperies and upholsteries were of textured velvets and silks in rich jewel tones. The furniture, constructed of exotic woods, was often inlaid with ebony and mother-of-pearl. A marble-and-bronze-clad central hall ran up to a stained-glass ceiling by John La Farge. The collection in the art gallery predominantly comprised important works by French academic painters, such as Bouguereau, Tissot, and Meissonier. M. S. Euen, the author of *Mr. Vanderbilt's House and Collection*, privately printed by Vanderbilt, opined that everything inside 640 "sparkles and flashes with gold and color. . . . with mother-of-pearl, with marble, with jewel effects in glass . . . and every surface is covered, one might say weighted, with ornament."

After Vanderbilt's death in 1885, the house continued to be inhabited by his widow. At her death 11 years later, his youngest son, George Washington Vanderbilt, inherited the mansion. By the end of the century, the house seemed dowdy. Most of the younger Vanderbilts' peers had long

Art Gallery, c. 1880. (Author's Collection)

ago subscribed to the new classical design vernacular espoused by prominent architectural firms such as Carrère & Hastings and McKim, Mead & White. George soon made a series of changes to his father's house. He began by eliminating a few of the decorative excesses on the exterior, at the same time replacing the balustrade that surrounded it with something more classical that held baroque lanterns at each corner. Soon after this expensive work was completed, the City of New York decided to widen Fifth Avenue, forcing Vanderbilt to remove this new balustrade completely. That, coupled with the heavy debt incurred with the building of his enormous Biltmore estate in Asheville, North Carolina, compelled him in 1905 to stop renovations. Soon thereafter he leased the house to Henry Clay Frick.

George Vanderbilt died in Washington, D.C., in 1914. Because he left no direct male heir, per his father's will, 640 was passed on to his eldest nephew. Cornelius Vanderbilt III was the oldest son of George's oldest brother, Cornelius II. Neily, as family and friends always called him, was an unexpectant recipient because his father had disinherited him for marrying Grace Wilson, a society belle of the era.

After Cornelius II's death, Neily's younger brother, who inherited the lion's share of his father's estate, gave Neily an additional $6 million, thereby bringing his inheritance up to the level of his sisters and younger brother, Reginald. That money, combined with his wife's personal fortune, enabled this branch of the Vanderbilt family to live quite well in a Fifth Avenue house at 677, two blocks north of his grandfather's mansion. But with Grace's burgeoning social career, defined by her position as the leading Mrs. Vanderbilt, it was fortunate that they inherited the much larger house at 640.

Drawing Room, c. 1880. (Author's Collection)

As George Vanderbilt had sided with the senior Vanderbilts in their dislike of Grace, the younger Mrs. Vanderbilt had not stepped foot in the house since long before her 1896 marriage. On her first tour of the property after her husband's inheritance, Grace reputedly dubbed it "the Black Hole of Calcutta" and immediately called in one of society's favorite architects, Horace Trumbauer, to transform the house, cellar to attic.

The exterior changes included removal of all the first- and second-story double-hung windows and their accompanying surrounds and replacing them with balustraded French doors set in classical frames. The elaborate, heavily carved frieze work of the first and third floors was removed, and the house was extended and enlarged in the back. Probably the most obvious change was the addition of a single-story entrance pavilion that was attached to the northern end of the Fifth Avenue facade. The brownstone veneer remained but was reinterpreted in an 18th-century vernacular.

Inside, the heavy Herter Brothers interiors were completely gutted and replaced with the elegant and bright French 18th-century rooms so loved by "Her Grace." A marble-lined foyer led into a soaring French Caen stone–lined great hall from which emanated most of the principal rooms for entertaining in the house. These included a Regénce-inspired oak-paneled library in which Grace served tea in the afternoons under a late-17th-century tapestry representing Alexander the Great's visit to Diogenes in Corinth. There was also an art gallery that continued to display William Henry Vanderbilt's collection of Millets, Meissoniers, and Corots. Nearby, the family dining room had beige-and-gold 18th-century paneling that had come from Europe via their 677 Fifth Avenue home. For larger dinners, the Vanderbilts used 640's main dining room, whose Louis XV

EXTERIOR, C. 1940. (Courtesy of the Museum of the City of New York)

paneling had niches that held wine-cooling fountains and buffets of red Siena marble. A dining table that could extend to seat 60 stood in the center of an enormous modern Savonnerie carpet. For larger groups, Grace had this table removed and used numerous smaller tables instead.

The music room had finely detailed Louis XVI boiserie and a *parquet de Versailles* floor that was considered too beautiful to cover. The adjoining ballroom, with its paneling anchored by gilded Corinthian pilasters, was the largest room in the house. At a Vanderbilt ball, as many as 1,000 people might be invited to dance on its highly polished parquet floor.

The upper floors comprised family and guest bedrooms, along with Grace's famous pink boudoir and her husband's paneled walnut study with an adjacent soundproof engineering laboratory. In the basement were the kitchen, servants' dining room, laundry, and wine cellar, and bedrooms for most of the male staff members. The female servants were housed four flights away under the roof. The Vanderbilts generally employed a household staff of about 30, who were at their busiest during the non-stop entertaining that enveloped the household during the all-important winter season.

For really important affairs a red carpet was rolled out from the front door, over the sidewalk to

GREAT HALL, C. 1920. (Private Collection)

BALLROOM, C. 1920. (Private Collection)

MUSIC ROOM, C. 1920. (Private Collection)

Dining Room, c. 1920. (Private Collection)

Family Dining Room, c. 1920. (Private Collection)

Library, c. 1920. (Private Collection)

the street. Supervising the front-of-the-house staff was the family butler, Gerald, who was so distinguished in appearance that arriving first-time guests, unfamiliar with their host, often confused the two. Alongside Gerald were six footmen, grandly arrayed in "Vanderbilt maroon" livery, consisting of jackets with gold-braided trim over matching knee britches and white stockings with black patent-leather pumps. To complete the 18th-century illusion, these footmen were required to either powder their own hair or don wigs. Maids in black dresses with frilly starched organdy capes and aprons carried hats, coats, and umbrellas to large dressing closets, which were designed to accommodate up to 700 coats. On a silver tray in the entrance hall, each male guest would find a little white envelope bearing his name. Inside he would find the name of the lady he would be escorting into dinner, or midnight supper if it were a ball.

Grace Vanderbilt's high Edwardian scale of entertaining never slackened, even during the darkest days of the Great Depression. Aside from her lavish balls, musicales, and dinner parties, as many as 100 people might drop by for tea during the season, and 1,000 would come to pay their respects on Christmas Day. She was given a daily roster of who was staying in each guest room, and her often overtaxed staff would sometimes confuse incoming and outgoing guests' luggage. Her husband thought 640 resembled the family's business headquarters, Grand Central Terminal.

Vanderbilt began to find this nonstop entertaining draining. His parents had perhaps been right all along; he and Grace were unsuited to each other. Soon he began retreating to his yachts, where he would often find solace at the bottom of a bottle. At the beginning of World War II, Vanderbilt donated his oceangoing yacht, the *Winchester*, to the Canadian government to use as a submarine chaser. He then leased a much smaller boat that he kept more or less permanently moored in Miami, where he died in 1942.

Vanderbilt's fortune was hard hit by the depression. In 1940, to raise capital, he sold 640 to the Astor Estate Office, with the proviso that his wife would be able to remain there until one year after his death, paying the Astor Estate Office a nominal rent. The house, whose neighborhood was already being commercialized at the time of the Trumbauer renovation, was then totally engulfed by towering skyscrapers. Even so, Grace was reluctant to leave the scene of her many social triumphs. Because of the war, the new owners of the property held off taking possession until 1945. In the fall of that year, refusing to leave the avenue that she had dominated for so long, Grace purchased the William Starr Miller mansion at 86th Street and Fifth Avenue. The following year, 640, the last of the great Vanderbilt mansions on the avenue, became victim to the wrecker's ball, replaced by a diminutive commercial structure that was little more than a taxpayer.

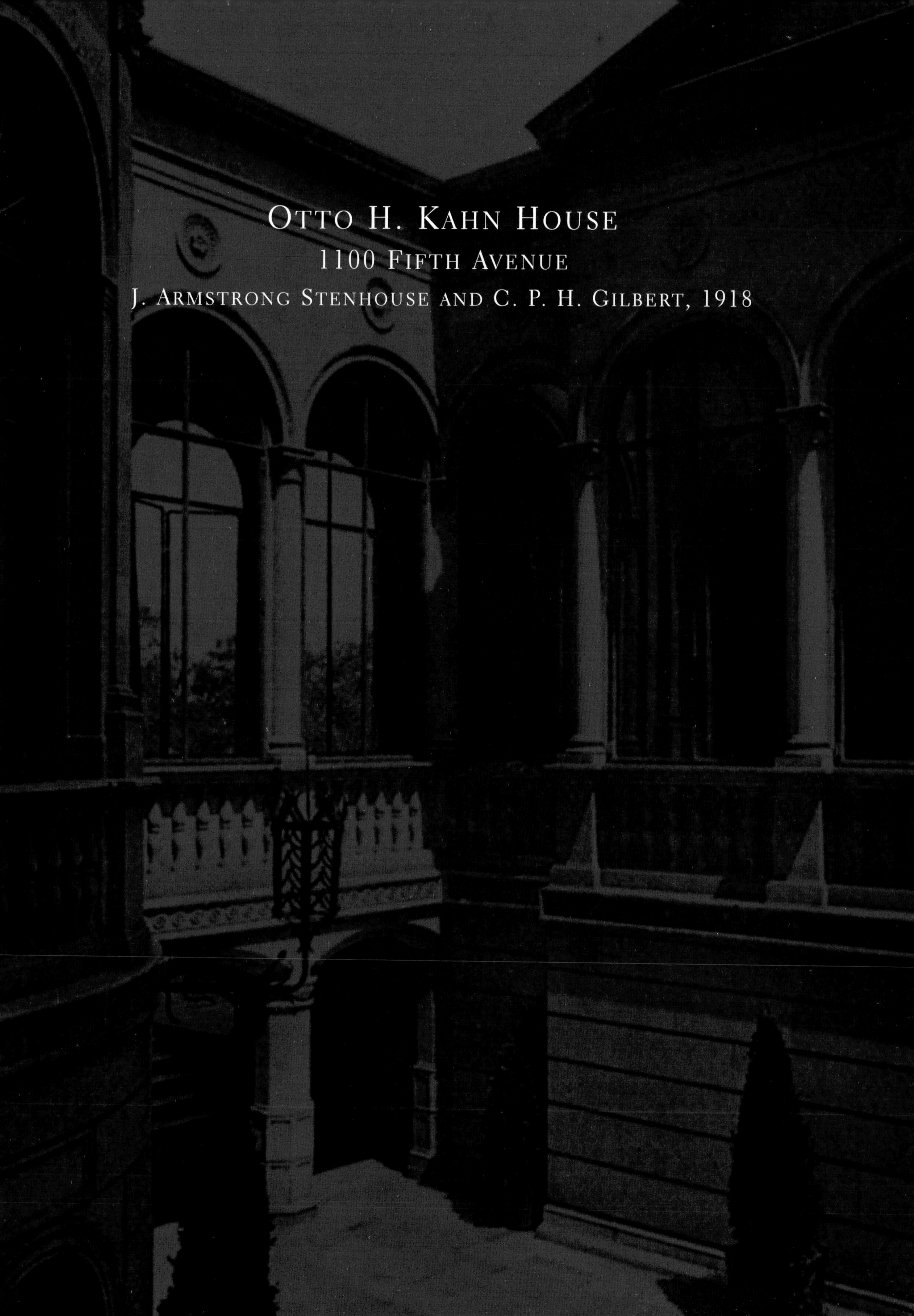

Otto H. Kahn House

1100 Fifth Avenue

J. Armstrong Stenhouse and C. P. H. Gilbert, 1918

Otto H. Kahn House

Exterior. (Courtesy of the Museum of the City of New York)

Because of delays in importing materials from Europe during World War I, many New York houses begun just before or during the war were not completed until the end of the decade. One of these houses was the Italian Renaissance palace that Kuhn, Loeb partner Otto Kahn was building on the northeast corner of 91st Street on Fifth Avenue. Kahn had purchased the 100-by-145-foot plot for $675,000 from his soon-to-be neighbor Andrew Carnegie. In 1912, British architect J. Armstrong Stenhouse was hired to design the building, and as Stenhouse did not have a New York license, C. P. H. Gilbert was asked to be the associate architect.

Otto Hermann Kahn, who was born in Mannheim, Germany, gained a reputation as an astute banker-first in London, then later in New York, where he immigrated in 1893. His first position in New York was at the private

COURTYARD. (Author's Collection)

banking house of Speyer & Company. Through business contacts he met Abraham Wolff, a senior partner at Kuhn, Loeb, and eventually married Wolff's daughter, Addie, while simultaneously becoming a junior partner at her father's bank. His spectacularly successful association with the bank did not end until his death some 40 years later.

After he and his new wife returned from an extended wedding trip, they moved into a house on East 68th Street and established their country home in Morristown, New Jersey. Both houses were gifts from the bride's father. When the 68th Street townhouse became too small for the Kahn family and their growing social obligations, they decided to build something considerably larger. The 65-room mansion on 91st Street that the couple commissioned was one of the largest private houses ever erected in the city. Construction began in 1913 but, because of the war, took five years to complete.

The two lower floors of the Renaissance-inspired house have a rusticated treatment, whereas the two floors above are of smooth masonry, all of imported French Caen stone. On the 91st Street side, there are two great wooden-doored carriage entrances that lead into an enclosed carriageway. This internal porte cochere, with its finely crafted coffered ceiling, was staffed by a liveried coachman whenever a member of the family was in residence. The facade of the second floor, the piano nobile, has tall, balustraded windows with alternating triangular and segmental

STAIRCASE. (Author's Collection)

Salon. (Courtesy of the Convent of the Sacred Heart)

pediments. Between these windows are slender twin Corinthian pilasters that support a small unifying cornice. At the north end of the Fifth Avenue facade is a small single-bay extension. The balustraded terrace above it leads to a large inner courtyard that guaranteed light and air to the inner rooms.

The exterior of the house was far enough along by February 1915 that *The New York Times* commented, "The Kahn house is nearing completion and is a noteworthy addition to the magnificent residences north of 59th Street. Although incomplete, Mr. Kahn has given it a decoration of merit on flying the American flag from one of the upper windows overlooking Fifth Avenue." With the coming American involvement in the war, Kahn wanted there to be no question where his allegiance lay. As chairman of the Metropolitan Opera, he requested that all German productions be eliminated from its repertoire. The banker played such an important role in the financing of the opera house that many quipped that his first two initials really stood for "opera house."

The Kahn house is enormous, with each of its principal floors having 13,000 square feet of floor space. From the interior carriageway, one enters a large hall with high windows that look into a courtyard. The ceiling is coved and vaulted, and the floor and walls are stone. The east end of the hall terminates at the family elevator and doors leading to the service areas of the house. The other end axis has a short flight of steps that led to an Adam-style reception room, an office, and a billiard room. On a table in the center of the hall, a large silver bowl was used for depositing calling cards.

A Florentine-style staircase led to the principal entertainment rooms on the second floor, where

DINING ROOM. (Courtesy of the Convent of the Sacred Heart)

GOTHIC ROOM. (Courtesy of the Convent of the Sacred Heart)

LIBRARY. (Courtesy of the Convent of the Sacred Heart)

the ceilings are 20 feet high. Through the large center hall, with its ornate stone mantelpiece, is a 30-by-50-foot-long Georgian library overlooking Central Park. In the center of this Palladian-style, walnut-paneled room, the Kahns had large matching desks that faced each other. Addie's was always immaculate; her husband's was usually piled high with papers and ledgers. Over the mantelpiece hung Rembrandt's *Portrait of a Jewish Student*. The adjoining Gothic room was used as a gallery for some of the Kahns' art collection, as well as for a reception room for dinner guests. In the northwest corner of the room is a spiral staircase that connected with Kahn's private sitting room, from which he used to secretly look down to see when the important guests arrived: only after they had would he make his entrance. Next to the paneled dining room, with its Grinling Gibbons—inspired carved cascades, is the Louis XVI salon. The antique gilded boiserie that graced this space came from the 18th-century Hôtel d'Humières in Paris. The last major room on this floor is the Adam-style ballroom. The ceiling has a broad central groin vault, with barrel vaults on either side, all of which are covered with subtle, but elaborately detailed, Adamesque plasterwork. The marble mantelpiece has a center oval medallion with floral swags and carvings that represent Cupid with Bacchus. Mirrored blind arches in the room hold large decorative bronze sconces, which, with the crystal chandelier in the center ceiling vault, illuminated the room on gala nights. After a private performance of *Chauve-Souris* that

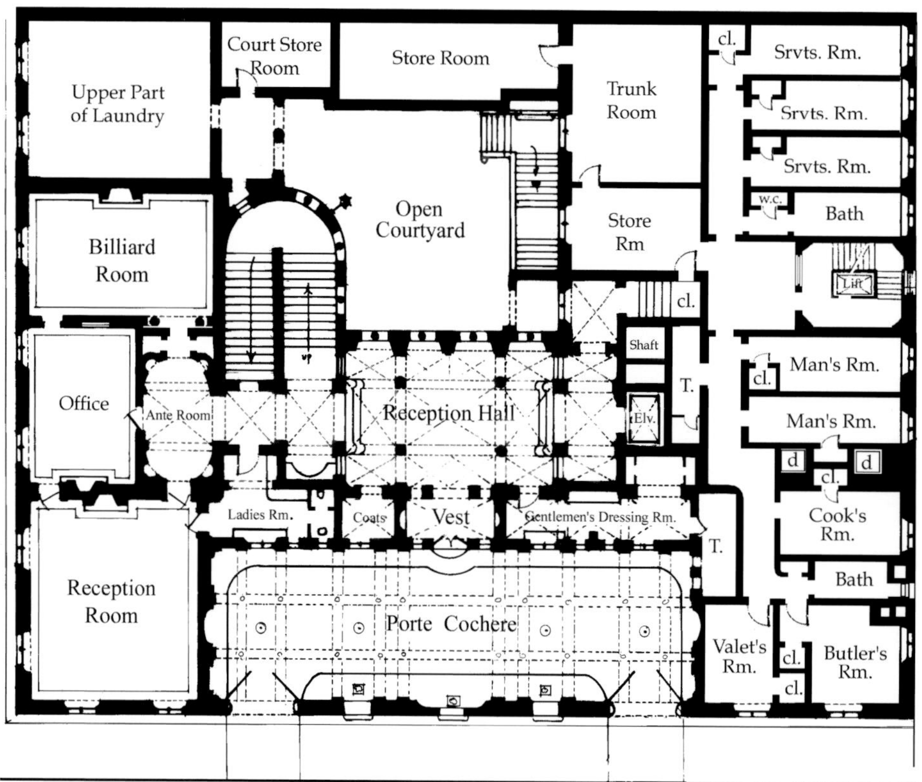

FIRST FLOOR PLAN. (Richard Marchand)

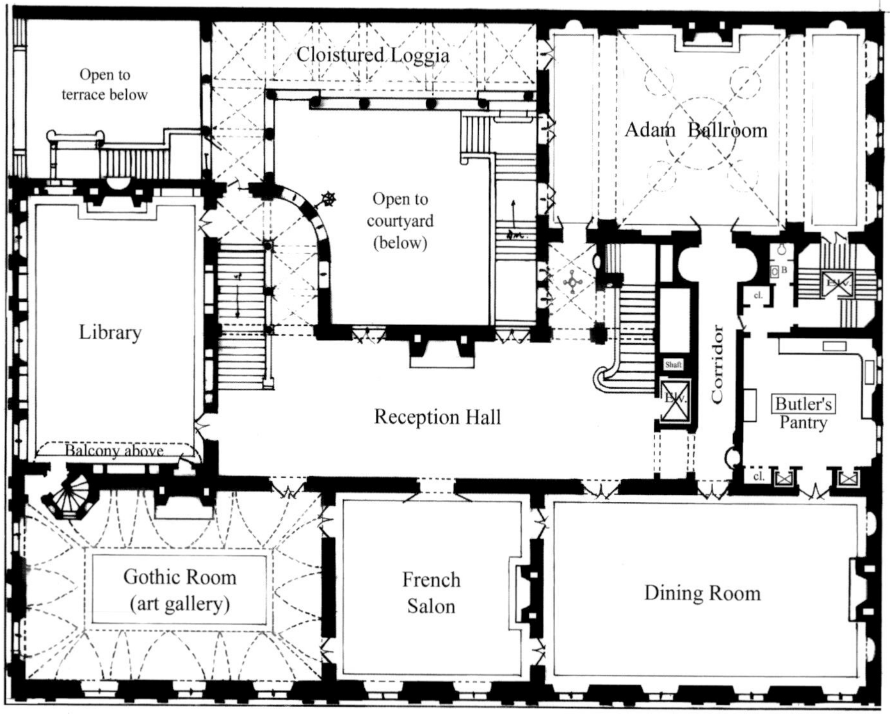

SECOND FLOOR PLAN. (Richard Marchand)

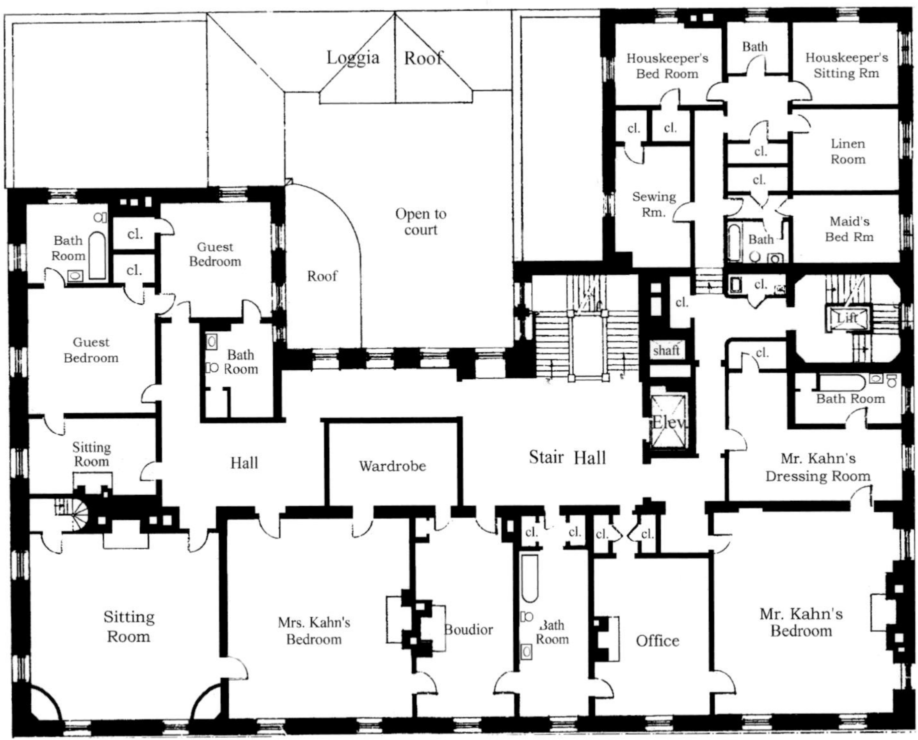

Third Floor Plan. (Richard Marchand)

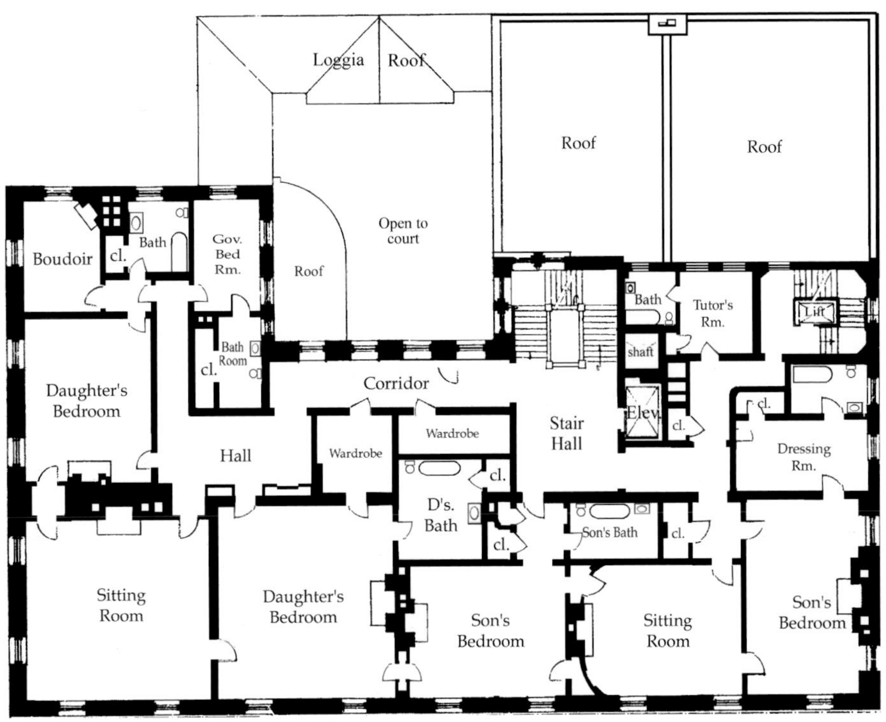

Fourth Floor Plan. (Richard Marchand)

Mr. Kahn staged in this room in 1922, he received a letter stating that Balieff "raved over your house. People in the company who had been in some of the imperial houses in Petrograd, said that yours was the finest house they had seen."

The third floor was predominantly filled with suites for the Kahns. His consisted of a bedroom, dressing room, bathroom, and private office. Addie had a bedroom, a boudoir, and a bathroom that contained a tub veneered in lapis lazuli. They both shared a sitting room that faced the park. Completing the third floor were two guest rooms, each with bathroom, plus a small shared sitting room. The next floor housed rooms for the four Kahn children. Guests of the children would be ushered into the house by a footman and then escorted to an elevator, where a servant would push the button for the fourth floor—they took no chances losing someone within the labyrinth of the house. On the roof is a balustraded terrace accessed from an arched loggia that looks much like a small Italian garden house. The main room behind this facade is an artist's studio with an adjoining penthouse apartment. This was used by a series of struggling artists whom Addie enjoyed helping, the most notable being the Russian artist Savely Sorine. The rest of the fifth floor was delegated to servant bedrooms.

Kahn, who liked large-scale entertainments, kept the house thronged with guests, who were doubly fortunate in that they were able to view one of the finest art collections in the city. Among the works that used to hang in the house were Frans Hals's *Family Group*, Rembrandt's *Philemon and Baucis*, Botticelli's *Giuliano de Medici*, Lucas Cranach's *Venus and Amor*, and works by Bellini, Boucher, Canalletto, and Matisse.

On March 29, 1934, Otto Kahn died of a heart attack at his desk at Kuhn, Loeb. As word spread, a crowd gathered around the building, and the flag over the entrance was lowered to half-mast. Even the notorious anti-Semite J. P. Morgan Jr. came to pay his respects at the funeral. Soon after Kahn's death, his widow dispersed the art collection and sold 1100 Fifth Avenue to the Convent of the Sacred Heart, which still maintains it beautifully.

William Ziegler Jr. House

2 East 63rd Street

Sterner & Wolfe, 1920

William Ziegler Jr. House

Exterior. (Courtesy of the New York Historical Society)

Gladys Watson Ziegler had purchased three brownstones on East 63rd Street steps away from Fifth Avenue during World War I, when European decorative arts and materials could not leave the continent. In 1919, she tore down the brownstones and engaged Sterner & Wolfe to create an Italian Renaissance palazzo for the 75-foot-wide property, one of the last private palaces constructed in the city.

Gladys' husband, William Ziegler Jr., was the adopted son of William Ziegler, founder of the Royal Baking Powder Company and owner of the Price Baking Powder Co. His birth father, George Brandt of Chicago, was Willilam Ziegler Sr.'s half brother. At the time of his adopted father's death in 1905, the 13-year-old boy inherited some $16 million.

Finished in 1920, the house was executed in a severe Italian Renaissance style. Except for the

COURTYARD. (Courtesy of the New York Historical Society)

carved decoration around the arched front door, the only ornamentation on the building were two windows on the second story that were capped by broken-scrolled pediments centered by decorative cartouches. Service rooms with smaller windows were placed along the front of the house on the ground floor, and the principal rooms were placed around a 30-foot-square patio-style courtyard in the rear, completely secluded from the sidewalk and the view of any passers-by. A high, ornate wrought-iron fence ran along the entire front of the building.

The eclectic mix of rooms around the courtyard included a Georgian-style drawing room, an Italian Renaissance dining room, and an antique paneled Elizabethan library. The hallway and the elegant curved main staircase were encased in travertine marble. A large kitchen and pantry completed the floor. On the second floor, Gladys' expansive suite comprised a foyer, boudoir, bedroom, and bath. Adjoining this were her husband's bedroom and dressing room. Up another flight were the children's rooms, a day nursery, and guest rooms.

In the 1930s, the Zieglers sold the house to Norman Woolworth, who was a cousin of the five-and-dime king. After the Charles Lindbergh baby kidnapping, Woolworth had a large playroom constructed on the fourth floor so his children could play inside the house. In 1949, Woolworth donated the house to the New York Academy of Sciences, which uses the building to this day.

Staircase. (Courtesy of the New York Historical Society)

Dining Room. (Courtesy of the New York Historical Society)

LIBRARY. (Courtesy of the New York Historical Society)

KITCHEN. (Courtesy of the New York Historical Society)

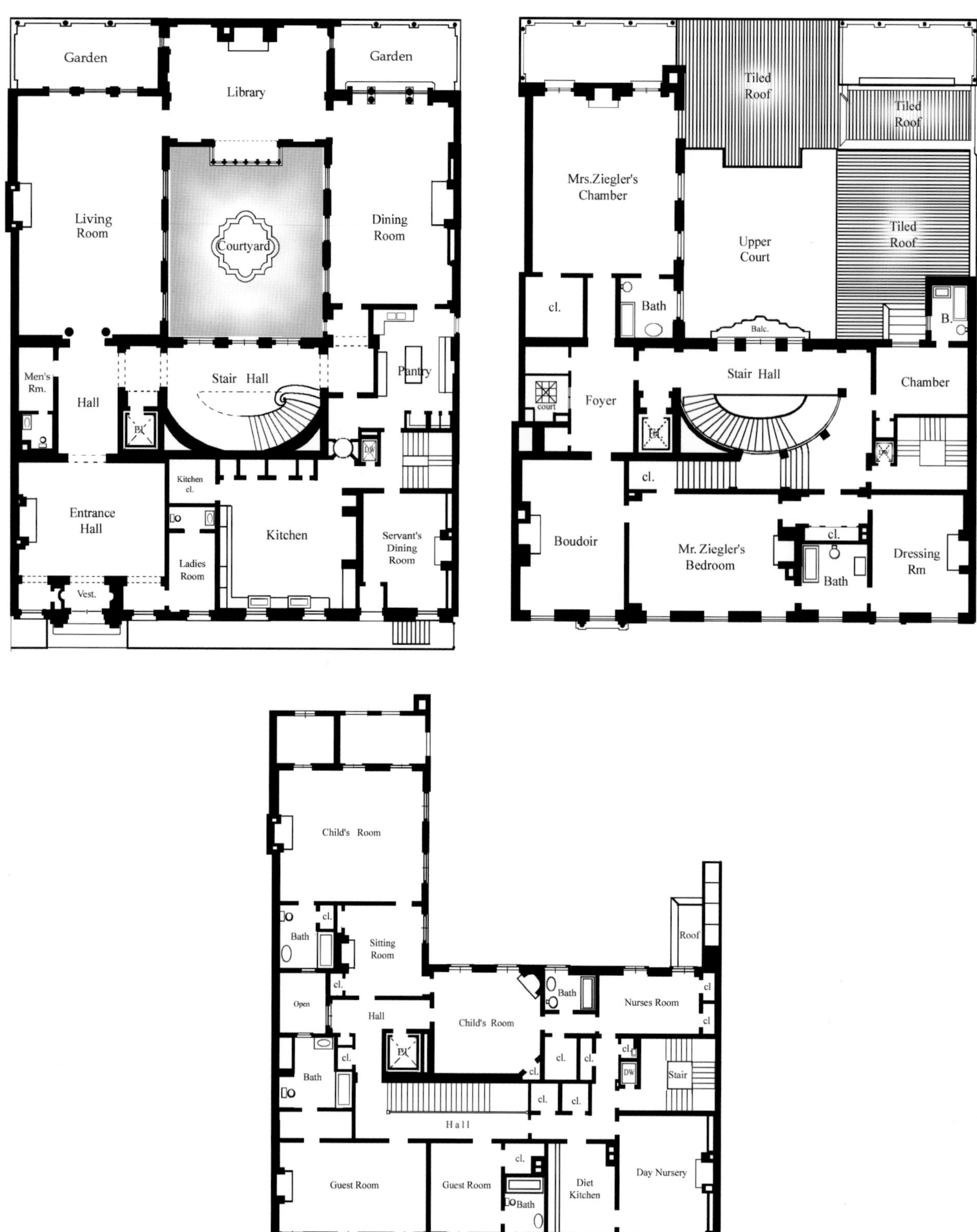

FIRST, SECOND, AND THIRD FLOOR PLANS (TOP LEFT TO BOTTOM). (Richard Marchand)

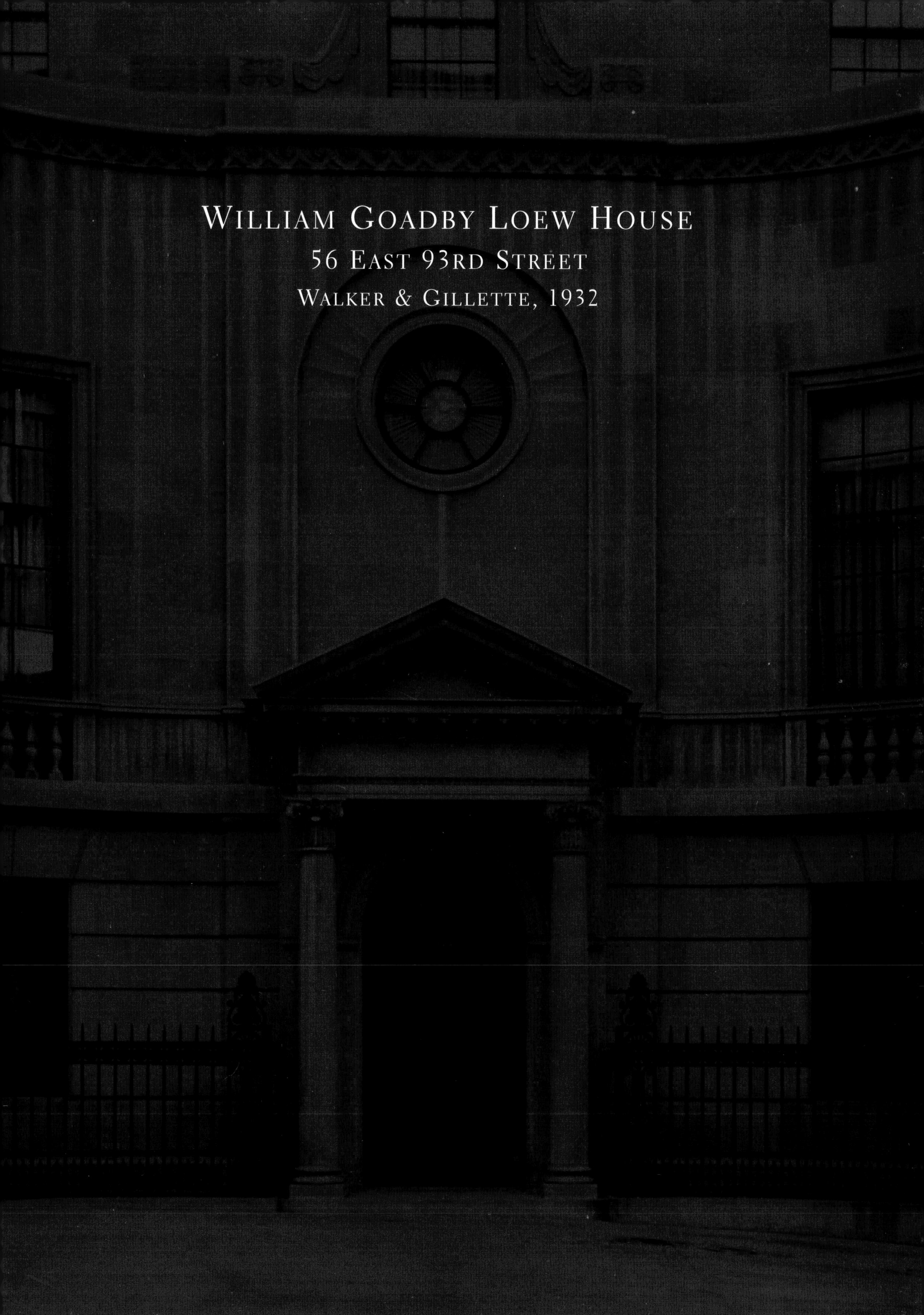

William Goadby Loew House

56 East 93rd Street

Walker & Gillette, 1932

William Goadby Loew House

Exterior. (Swanke, Hayden, and Connell)

This handsome English Regency–style mansion was architect A. Stewart Walker's final bow to an era. He and his partner, Leon Gillette, had been designing luxurious New York City town houses for over 25 years, and this was their last. In fact, it was the last private palace erected in the city. It was commissioned by Columbia University graduate William Goadby Loew, who in 1898 married Florence Baker, the daughter of George F. Baker, president of First National Bank. With the help of his father-in-law, Loew acquired a seat on the New York Stock Exchange, and in 1915 he founded the brokerage firm of Loew & Co.

The Loews, who had been living in Murray Hill, moved into the new house in 1932. The mansion's pedimented front door is placed in the center of a shallow entrance court created by the curving walls of its two projecting end pavilions. The building has a rusticated ground

ENTRANCE DETAIL. (Swanke, Hayden, and Connell)

floor with smooth ashlar walls above. At each end of the facade on the second-level projections, well-proportioned, balustrated Palladian windows are capped by a fan motif, which is repeated around the bull's-eye window above the entrance. Rondels are placed at either side of the Palladian windows, and a Vitruvian wave band tops the decorative program on this level. With the fourth floor hidden behind a solid parapet and a great portion of the third floor obscured by the projecting ends, the building's horizontal aspect is emphasized. This well-studied and fluid design created a building that looks less like a city house and more like a country villa. At the back of the house, above the basement service areas, Walker placed a "hanging garden" with a stone well-head surrounded by antique stone arches taken from a European cloister. The garden was accessed from both the dining and drawing rooms.

The mansion's dignified facade hid rooms that were equally refined. Sybil Walker, wife of the architect, was in charge of the interiors and her work complements that of her husband. The entrance hall has a black-and-white marble floor and polished Nubian marble columns. At the eastern end of the hall were entrances to a men's Jacobean-style reception room and an adjacent hexagonal-shaped ladies' reception room, each with it own toilet and large coat closets. At the other end of the hall, a curving

GARDEN ENTRANCE. (Swanke, Hayden, and Connell)

DINING ROOM. (Author's Collection)

ENTRANCE HALL. (Author's Collection)

LIVING ROOM. (Author's Collection)

Library. (Author's Collection)

staircase leads up to the main rooms for entertaining on the piano nobile.

A drawing room, running the entire width of the rear extension of the structure, had Georgian pine paneling taken from Longford House in England and was illuminated by a Waterford crystal chandelier. Carved swags by Grinling Gibbons adorned its chimney breast. On the walls hung *Mr. Barwell and His Son* by Sir Joshua Reynolds and *Lady Neave* by Thomas Lawrence. Across a large second-floor hallway were a blue-and-gold-paneled library and a classically styled Georgian dining room. Above the marble mantelpiece in the dining room hung Reynolds's *Lady Elizabeth Lee*, and on either side of the fireplace were matching double-eagle consoles originally from the collection of the Earl of Carnarvon at Highclere Castle. An important 19th-century silver table garniture by Paul Storr graced the mahogany dining table.

Florence Loew was an accomplished horsewoman and owned a stable of fine horses. She also enjoyed fox hunting and for many years was the only female master of the hounds in the United States. Always smartly turned out, she and her husband were regularly included on New York City's best-dressed lists. Leaders in fashionable society, the Loews entertained lavishly in town as well as at Stoneacre, their summerhouse in Newport, Rhode Island, and at Loewmoor, their estate in Old Westbury, Long Island. After Florence died in 1936, her husband continued to live in the house until his death almost 20 years later.

Theatrical producer Billy Rose spent $350,000 for the house in 1956. After his death a decade later, the building was purchased by the Republic of Algeria as its United Nations mission. Later the house became the Smithers Alcoholism Treatment Center and is currently owned by the Spence School.

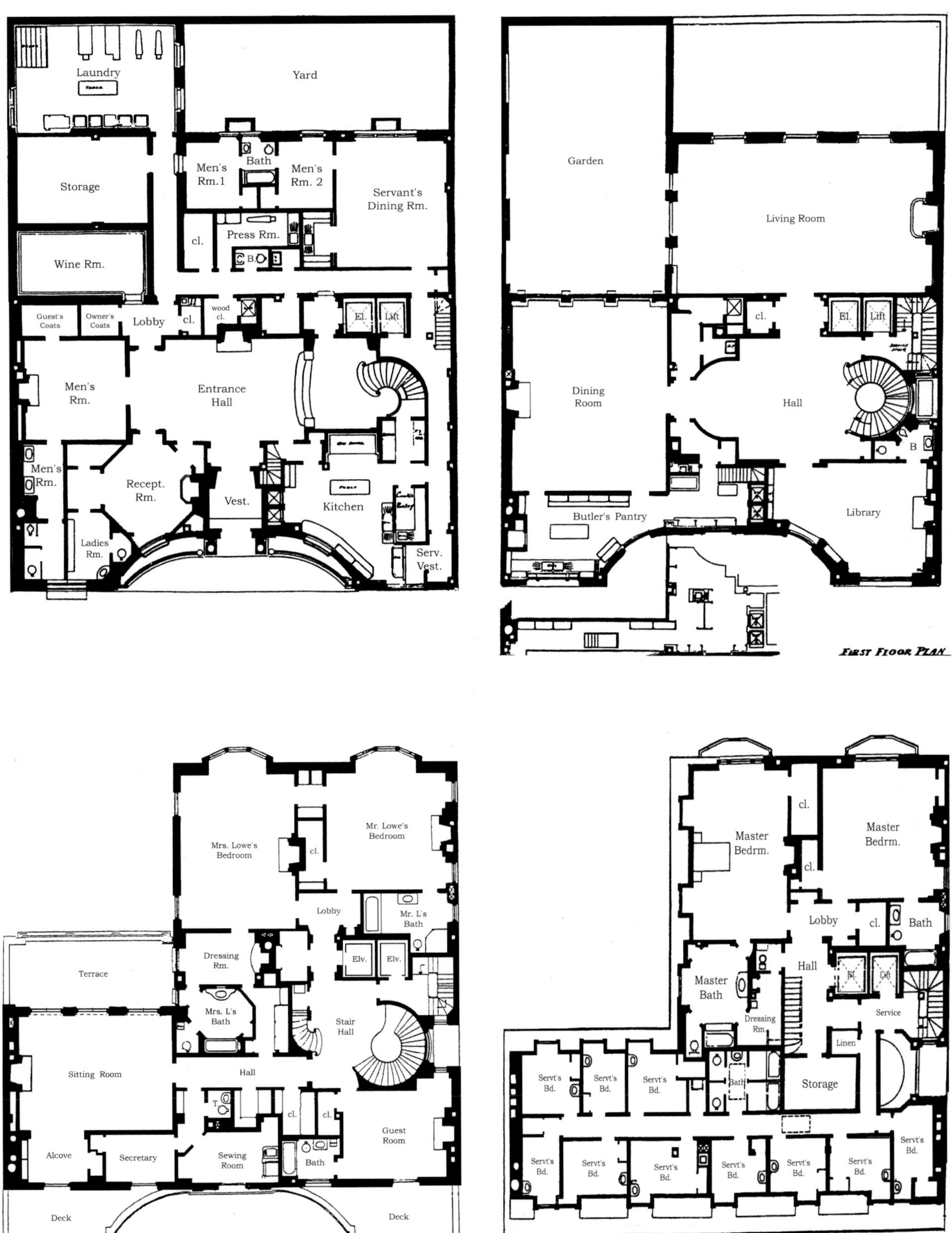

Ground through Third Floor Plans (upper left to lower right). (Richard Marchand)

The Architects

Allen & Collens, Boston

A native of Boston, Francis R. Collens (1843–1931) graduated from Amherst at the age of 20 but did not begin his architectural studies until 1876, when he enrolled in a two-year program at MIT. He then went to Paris to study at the Ecole des Beaux-Arts and returned to Boston in 1880 to open an office with Arthur Kenway. When this alliance ended 10 years later, Collens worked alone until he formed a partnership with Charles Allen in 1904. This partnership lasted more than 20 years and produced such works as the Mead Memorial Chapel at Middlebury (Vermont) College, the Taylor Art Building and Memorial Library at Vassar (1904), Women's Hospital at 110th Street (1906), Union Theological Seminary (1910), the Arthur Curtiss James house at Park Avenue and 69th Street (1916), and the Riverside Church (1929).

Babb, Cook & Willard, New York

Walter Cook (1843–1916) was born in New York and was a grandson of James C. Ireland, an early architect in the city. Cook attended Harvard and the Ecole des Beaux-Arts (1869). When he returned from France, he established himself with the firm of Babb, Cook & Willard (later Cook & Willard). They designed the DeVinne Press Building, the Choir School at St. John the Divine, and the New York Life Insurance Company Building. Their residential commissions included the J. O. Hoyt house at 310 West 75th Street (1897) and the Andrew Carnegie mansion at Fifth Avenue and 91st Street (1901).

Carrère & Hastings, New York

John Mervin Carrère (1858–1911) and Thomas Hastings (1860–1929) met as students at the Ecole des Beaux-Arts. They returned to the United States to work in the offices of McKim, Mead & White, and in the mid-1880s, they left that firm to open their own practice. Their former employers had specialized in building styles derived from the Italian Renaissance, but Carrère & Hastings produced many neoclassic buildings based on French precedents. The Modern French–style, limestone-faced Henry Sloane house (1896) on East 72nd Street, the first of its kind in the city, established a design philosophy that would often be repeated during the following decade. One of the firm's most important early clients was Henry Flagler, who gave them the Ponce de Leon Hotel commission in St. Augustine, Florida. Carrère was elected the chief architect of the Pan-American Exposition in Buffalo. He was also the co-founder and president of the Society of Beaux-Arts Architects. After Carrère's death in an auto accident in 1911, Hastings carried on the firm's work until his own death in 1929. Among their well-known civic structures were the New York Public Library (1911), the Manhattan Bridge and its ceremonial entrance (1912), and the Staten Island Ferry Terminal (1908). Among their residential works were the John Henry Hammond house at 9 East 91st Street (1906), the Christian Herter house at 819 Madison Avenue (1893), the C. Ledyard Blair house at Fifth Avenue and 70th Street (1917), and Henry Clay Frick's block-long Fifth Avenue mansion between 70th and 71st streets (1911).

OGDEN CODMAN, New York

Ogden Codman (1863–1951) was born into a Boston family whose financial reverses during the mid-1870s led to their 11-year European expatriation. Thus, at a young age, Codman was exposed to the architecture of Europe. He returned to the United States in 1882 and enrolled in architectural training at MIT, but he quickly dropped out to apprentice at the Boston architectural firm of Andrews, Jacques & Rantoul. By 1891, Codman had opened his own office on Chestnut Street. He soon met Edith Wharton, with whom he would coauthor *The Decoration of Houses*, and he redecorated her Newport cottage "Land's End." Three years later, he received a commission to redecorate the second- and third-floor rooms of "The Breakers," the Newport mansion of Cornelius Vanderbilt II. Because most of his work was then being generated in New York, Codman decided to open an office there at 5 West 16th Street. This office flourished until the outbreak of hostilities in Europe at the beginning of World War I. Almost all of his interior finishes were imported from France and England, so Codman's work came to a virtual standstill. After the war he chose not to reopen his office but instead moved to France. There he soon began designing "La Leopolda," his home on the Riviera. His most notable New York works included the Adam-style Frank K. Sturgis house at 17 East 51st Street (1910), the neoclassic J. Woodward Haven residence at 18 East 79th Street (1911), and his own home at 7 East 96th Street (1912).

DELANO & ALDRICH, New York

William Adams Delano (1874–1960) and Chester Aldrich (1871–1940) met while working at the offices of Carrère & Hastings. They each had studied at Columbia and at the Ecole des Beaux-Arts. The firm of Delano & Aldrich was officially formed in 1903, and one of its first commissions was for the house at Kykuit, the Rockefeller estate in Pocantico Hills, New York, a job they received because Mrs. Rockefeller was born an Aldrich. The office was renowned for its classical country houses, such as the James A. Burden house, Woodside, in Syosset, Long Island (1916), and the Otto H. Kahn house, Oheka, in Cold Spring Harbor, Long Island (1917). They also designed the Walters Art Gallery in Baltimore (1910), the Colony Club on Park Avenue in New York (1916), and the home of the Union Club, also on Park Avenue (1932). In the city they designed numerous houses, including the Harold I. Pratt house at 58 East 68th Street (1920), the Francis Palmer–George F. Baker house at 75 East 93rd Street (1917–28), the Willard Straight house at 1130 Fifth Avenue (1915), and the William Woodward house on East 86th Street (1916). After Chester Aldrich's death in 1940, the surviving partner continued the practice until the mid-1950s.

ROBERT W. GIBSON, New York

Born and educated in England, Robert W. Gibson (1854–1927) moved his architectural practice to the United States in 1881. Six years later, he became a naturalized citizen. His early reputation rests with his

Dutch Colonial Revival–style buildings, including the West End Collegiate Church at 77th Street and West End Avenue (1892) and the Protestant Welfare Agencies building at 281 Park Avenue South (1894). He also designed the Museum Building at the New York Botanical Gardens (1898) and the New York Clearing House (1896). His only known New York City mansion was the English Palladian–style Morton F. Plant house at 52nd Street and Fifth Avenue (1905).

C. P. H. GILBERT, New York

Born in New York City, Charles Pierrepont H. Gilbert (1863–1952) attended Columbia University and the Ecole des Beaux-Arts. He returned to the United States to begin his career designing buildings in the mining towns of Arizona and Colorado. Around 1885 he left for New York, where he designed buildings on the developing Upper West Side. He became known for his urban houses in Manhattan and in Brooklyn's Park Slope District, as well as country houses on Long Island and in Westchester County. As his city residential commissions started declining after Word War I, Flagg replaced them with projects for apartment buildings. His notable works include the Thomas Adams Jr. house in Park Slope (1888), the E. C. Converse house at 3 East 78th Street (1895), the Isaac D. Fletcher house at 2 East 79th Street (1899), the Mortimer Schiff house in Oyster Bay, Long Island (1900), the Henry Seligman house at 30 West 56th Street (1890s), and the J. R. DeLamar house at 233 Madison Avenue (1905).

MAURICE HÉBERT, Paris

"On the Hudson" (1907), the Charles H. Schwab house on Riverside Drive between 73rd and 74th streets, is Hébert's only known New York City work.

HUNT & HUNT, New York

Richard Howland Hunt (1862–1931), the eldest son of Richard Morris Hunt, was born in Paris and later studied at MIT and the Ecole des Beaux-Arts. After finishing his formal education, he apprenticed as a draftsman in his father's office, where he later became an associate. After Richard Morris Hunt's death in 1895, his son continued his work. In 1901 he was joined by his younger brother Joseph Hunt (1870–1924), and the office name was changed to Hunt & Hunt. Joseph was born in New York and graduated from Harvard in 1892. He studied at Columbia University for two years and then transferred to the Ecole des Beaux-Arts, where he stayed until 1900. Joseph Hunt was elected a director and president of the Municipal Arts Society and was the secretary of the Federation of Fine Arts from 1904 to 1915. Among the firm's many projects were the 69th Street Armory (1904), the First Precinct Police Station (1911), and several buildings for Vanderbilt University. Their residential work included Castle Gould, the Howard Gould Estate in Sands Point, Long Island (1909), and Idle Hour, the William K. Vanderbilt house in Oakdale, Long Island (1899). In the city they designed the home of Mrs. O. H. P. Belmont at 477 Madison Avenue (1909), the William J. Schieffelin house at 5 East 66th Street (1900), and the Marble Twins, created for George Washington Vanderbilt at 645 and 647 Fifth Avenue (1905).

RICHARD MORRIS HUNT, New York

Richard Morris Hunt (1827–97) is considered by many to be the father of American architecture. Born in Brattleboro, Vermont, at a young age his mother took him to live in Europe. He was the first American to study architecture at the Ecole des Beaux-Arts in Paris. On his return to the United

States in 1855, he opened an office in New York City. His first major project was the Studio Building on West 10th Street (1858), in which he opened his own atelier, where he instructed a new generation of American architects. His pupils included Henry Van Brunt, Frank Furness, and George Browne Post. During the 1880s, Hunt began designing houses for the Vanderbilt family. The first completed was the William K. Vanderbilt house at 660 Fifth Avenue (1882). Other notable Vanderbilt commissions were "Marble House" (1892) and "The Breakers" (1895), both in Newport, and "Biltmore" (1895), George Vanderbilt's 250-room house near Asheville, North Carolina. Hunt's New York City houses included the Henry Marquand house at 8 East 68th Street (1884), the Ogden Mills house at Fifth Avenue and 69th Street (1887), the Elbridge Gerry house at 2 East 61st Street (1894), and the Astor mansion at 840 Fifth Avenue (1895). Unfortunately, all of Hunt's major New York residential works have been demolished.

LORD, HEWLETT & HULL, New York

Austin W. Lord (1860–1922) was born in Minnesota and studied at MIT. He then attended the American Academy in Rome before joining the offices of McKim, Mead & White. In 1886, James M. Hewlett (1868–1941) entered Columbia's School of Mines after completing his work at the Brooklyn Polytechnic Institute. Hewlett then went to France to study at the Ecole des Beaux-Arts for four years. In 1895 he began his career in partnership with Austin Lord and Washington Hull (1866–1909). Hull, who had also studied at the Polytechnic Institute and Columbia, began his career as a draftsman in the offices of C. C. Haight and then McKim, Mead & White. Lord, Hewlett & Hull commissions included the Stapleton School on Staten Island, the Parish House of Grace Church in Brooklyn, the Bronx County Building, the Brooklyn Masonic Temple, and many country houses. The Fifth Avenue home of Senator William Andrews Clark was their most important project in Manhattan (1908).

GUY LOWELL, Boston

Born in Boston, Guy Lowell (1870–1927) graduated from Harvard in 1892 and went on to study architecture at MIT. From 1895 to 1899, he attended the Ecole des Beaux-Arts. He established his practice in Boston and, because of his family connections, his success was almost immediate. He designed many educational buildings in New England, including structures at Phillips Academy, Harvard University, Simmons College, and Brown University. He was also responsible for many fine homes in the vicinity of Boston, although the Boston Museum of Fine Arts is probably his best-known work in the area. Lowell also designed country estates on Long Island, but his only known residential work in Manhattan was the Morton F. Plant house at 1051 Fifth Avenue. He is better known in New York for the County Courthouse on Foley Square (1926).

MCKIM, MEAD & WHITE, New York

Charles Follen McKim (1847–1909), William Rutherford Mead (1846–1928), and Stanford White (1853–1906) headed up what was probably the most influential architectural firm in the history of New York. McKim studied at the Ecole des Beaux-Arts from 1886 to 1870. He then returned to New York, were he began working in the office of Henry Hobson Richardson. In 1873 he left Richardson to go into partnership with Mead. His new partner was born in Brattleboro, Vermont, and educated at Amherst before traveling to Florence to study the buildings of the Renaissance. In 1879, Stanford White, who also apprenticed in Richardson's office, joined the firm. Included in their vast volume of work are structures as far-flung as the New York Life building in Kansas City (1890) and the American Academy in Rome (1914). Closer to home are the Metropolitan Club (1894), the Tiffany & Co. building at 37th Street and Fifth Avenue (1906), and the Gorham Company building at 390 Fifth Avenue (1905). One of their largest commissions was for the original Madison Square Garden, which sat on the block bounded by 26th and 27th streets, Madison Avenue, and Park Avenue (1891). On the structure's roof garden, Stanford White was shot to death by the husband of a former lover. The office continued after White's death and the deaths of the other two founders. Their enormous New York City residential portfolio contains residences such as the Henry Villard houses at 451–457 Madison Avenue (1885), the H. A. C. Taylor house at 3 East 71st Street (1896), the Stuyvesant Fish house at 25 East 78th Street (1900), the Joseph Pulitzer House at 11 East 73rd Street (1900), the Charles Dana Gibson house at 127 East 73rd Street (1903), the Payne Whitney house at 972 Fifth Avenue (1906), the William K. Vanderbilt Jr. house at 666 Fifth Avenue (1907), and the Morris Newbold House at 15 East 79th Street (1918).

NATHAN C. MELLEN

Nathan Mellen Practiced in New York from 1889 to 1917. Many of those years were spent as a partner in the firm of Mellen, Westell & Kirby who participated in the design for the Cathedral of St. John the Divine. Mellen also designed the Edward J. Berwind house (1896), located on the southeast corner of Fifth Avenue and 64th Street.

GEORGE BROWNE POST, New York

After attending military school in his hometown of Ossining, New York, George Browne Post (1837–1913) went on to study civil engineering at New York University. Later he entered Richard Morris Hunt's atelier on West 10th Street. In 1860, Post decided to go into practice, so he opened an office in partnership with Charles D. Gambrill (1832–80). This office closed at the onset of the Civil War because both men enlisted in the army, where Post rose to the rank of colonel. After the war, he returned to New York to open his own architectural practice. His projects included the Equitable Life Assurance Building (1870), the Union Trust Building, the Pulitzer Building (1890), the New York Stock Exchange (1903), and the College of the City of New York (1905). Post became known for his engineering abilities; he was a pioneer in the use of steel framing for tall buildings. Aesthetically, however, his work never attained the sophistication of Hunt's. Post was esteemed by his peers, who elected him president of both the Architectural League of New York (1893–97) and the American Institute of Architects (1896–99). His two major Manhattan residential commissions, the Cornelius Vanderbilt II house (1882) and the Collis P. Huntington house (1892), were sited diagonally across from each other at 57th Street and Fifth Avenue. Post was the only architect included in Ward McAllister's list of the 400.

JAMES GAMBLE ROGERS, New York

James Gamble Rogers (1867–1947) was born in Kentucky, studied at Yale, and spent five years in Paris training at the Ecole des Beaux-Arts. Upon returning to America in 1897, Rogers opened an office in Chicago, where he stayed for seven years. From 1904 to 1907 he was a partner in the Boston firm Hale & Rogers, after which he established his own office in New York. This office was later incorporated and taken over by his son. His many commissions included the Butler Library at Columbia University (1904) and the Yale Club (1915). His two most important New York City residential works were the Edward S. Harkness house at 1 East 75th Street (1908) and the Jonathan Bulkley house at 600 Park Avenue (1911).

SCHICKEL & DITMARS, New York

William Schickel (1850–1907) was a native of Germany and completed his architectural studies there before immigrating to New York in 1870. He was first employed as a draftsman in the offices of Richard Morris Hunt. He later entered a 20-year partnership with Isaac E. Ditmars (1850–1934). Ditmars was born in Nova Scotia but as a youth moved to New York to complete his education. He started his career in the office of John F. Miller. Schickel and Ditmars opened their office at 111 Fifth Avenue and became widely known for their churches and institutional buildings. These included the Cathedral of the Sacred Heart in Newark, New Jersey; the Church of St. Ignatius Loyola at Park Avenue and 84th Street; St. Monica's Church at Lexington and 79th Street; the John Constable Building; and the German Hospital and Training School for Nurses. Their two most important residential commissions were for the homes of brothers Louis Stern, at 993 Fifth Avenue (1887), and Isaac Stern, down the avenue at number 858 (1894).

FREDERICK J. STERNER (STERNER & WOLFE), New York

Frederick Junius Sterner was born in England but immigrated to New York at the age of 16 in 1882. After studying architecture in the city, he moved to Denver, Colorado, where he opened a partnership with a man named "Varian" in 1910. The firm designed Colorado Springs' Antlers Hotel and the William J. Palmer estate, Glen Eyrie (1910), as well as other estates in the area. In 1910 Sterner returned to New York, where he remained in practice until his retirement in the early 1920s. His New York residential works included a Jacobean-style house for Stephen C. Clark at 21 East 70th Street (1910), his own home at 154 East 63rd Street (1914), and the William Ziegler residence at 2 East 63rd Street (1919).

TROWBRIDGE & LIVINGSTON, New York

Trowbridge & Livingston was one of the most prolific New York firms at the beginning of the 20th century. Samuel Breck Parkman Trowbridge (1862–1925), a native of New York, was educated at the local public schools. He went on to study at Trinity, where he graduated in 1886, and then spent three years at Columbia. In 1889, the Architectural Institute sent him to supervise the erection of the American School of Classical Studies in Athens. From there he went to Paris to complete his formal education at the Ecole des Beaux-Arts. Upon returning to New York in 1896, he apprenticed for five years in the offices of George Browne Post. In 1901 he opened his own practice with partner Goodhue Livingston, who had also studied at Columbia and met Trowbridge while both were working for Post. Among the firm's commissions were the B. Altman department store (1907), Bankers Trust (1913), J. P. Morgan and Co. (1914), the St. Regis Hotel (1904), Chemical Bank (1907), the Mellon National Bank in Pittsburgh (1924), the Mitsui Bank in Toyko (1920s), and the Red Cross Headquarters in Washington, D.C. (1917). In 1909 they received a Medal of Honor from the AIA for their work on the Henry Phipps house at 1063 Fifth Avenue. Trowbridge was a founder and trustee of the American Academy in Rome, and in 1913 he served as president of the Architectural League of New York. Other residential commissions in the city were the William Salomon house at 1020 Fifth Avenue (1904), the C. D. Jackson house at 4 Riverside Drive (1908), the George S. Brewster house at 746 Park Avenue (1909), the George Blumenthal house at 50 East 70th Street (1917), and the John S. Rogers house at 53 East 79th Street (1917).

HORACE TRUMBAUER, Philadelphia

Horace Trumbauer (1868–1938), a self-made man, was born in rural Bucks County, Pennsylvania. He later moved with his family to Philadelphia's suburban Jenkintown, where he was educated at the local public schools. At the age of 14 he quit school and begin his architectural apprenticeship in the Philadelphia offices of G. W. and W. D. Hewitt. In 1890 he opened his own practice. Two years later, at the age of 24, he received the commission to design Grey Towers, the William Welsh Harrison house in Glenside, Pennsylvania. The success of this project led to other residential commissions from the Elkins and Widener clans of Philadelphia. Although known for his city and country houses, Trumbauer designed commercial projects such as the Widener Building (1915) and the Public Ledger Building (1927), both in Philadelphia. His largest commission was for design and execution of the campus for Duke University in Durham, North Carolina (1927–31). The architect received an honorary M.A. from Harvard after completion of the Widener Memorial Library in 1919. That same year, he began work on the Philadelphia Museum of Art and finished his work on the Free Library. Trumbauer also designed several Philadelphia hotels, including the St. James (1904) and the Ritz-Carlton (1912), and the Jefferson Medical College (1928). The firm's New York City residential commissions included the houses of George J. Gould at Fifth Avenue and 67th Street (1908), J. B. Clews at 1 East 85th Street (1908), James B. Duke at 1 East 78th Street (1912), James Speyer at Fifth Avenue and 87th Street (1914), Amory S. Carhart on East 95th Street (1920), Mrs. Alexander Hamilton Rice at 901 Fifth Avenue (1922), and Herbert N. Straus at 9 East 71st Street (1930).

WALKER & GILLETTE, New York

Leon N. Gillette (1878–1945) was born in Malden, Massachusetts. He began his architectural career at the Minneapolis firm of Bertrand & Keith, then went on to receive his certificate in architecture at the University of Pennsylvania. From 1901 to 1903, he studied at the Ecole des Beaux-Arts. Afterward, he took a position with Warren & Wetmore in New York. Three years later, he created his own office in partnership with Harvard graduate A. Stewart Walker. Among their many notable works are the Fuller Building (1929), the First National Bank Building (1933), and the East River Savings Bank (1929). Along with their commercial structures, the firm was known for their Long Island residential commissions: the W. R. Coe estate, Planting Fields (1919); the H. H. Rogers home in Southampton (1916), and Peacock Point, the Henry P. Davison house (1920). In 1910 the firm was awarded an AIA medal for apartment-house design. Their city residential projects included the Harry P. Davison house at 68th Street and Park Avenue (1917), the Thomas Lamont House at 107 East 70th (1921), the Harvey G. Gibson house at 52 East 69th Street

(1922), the Charles E. Mitchell House at 934 Fifth Avenue (1926), and the William Goadby Loew house on East 93rd Street (1932).

WARREN & WETMORE, New York

Whitney Warren (1864–1941) was born in New York City but moved to Paris at the age of 18 to study at the Ecole des Beaux-Arts. He would remain in France for 10 years. In 1896 he joined Charles D. Wetmore (1867–1941) in creating the firm of Warren & Wetmore. Wetmore was born in Elmira, New York, and graduated from Harvard in 1889. Notable New York nonresidential works include the New York Yacht Club (1900), Grand Central Terminal (1913), the Biltmore Hotel (1914), the Hecksher Building (1921), the Aeolian Building (1924), and the St. James Theater (1927). Warren was the founder of the Beaux-Arts Institute of Design and always considered the Louvain Library restoration in Belgium to be his favorite project. The firm's city houses included the James A. Burden Jr. house at 7 East 91st Street (1902), the Orme Wilson house at 3 East 64th Street (1903), and the R. Livingston Beekman house at 854 Fifth Avenue (1905).

Selected Bibliography

BOOKS

Alpern, Andrew. *Apartments for the Affluent: A Historical Survey of Buildings in New York.* New York: McGraw-Hill, 1975.

Amory, Cleveland. *The Last Resorts.* New York: Harper & Brothers, 1948.

———. *Who Killed Society?* New York: Harper & Brothers, 1960.

Andrews, Wayne. *Architecture in New York: A Photographic History.* New York: Harper & Row, 1973.

Aslet, Clive. *The American Country House.* New Haven, CT: Yale University Press, 1990.

Auchincloss, Louis. *The Vanderbilt Era: Profiles of a Gilded Age.* New York: Charles Scribner's Sons, 1989.

Baker, Paul R. *Richard Morris Hunt.* Cambridge, MA: MIT Press, 1980.

———. *Stanny: The Gilded Life of Stanford White.* New York: Free Press, 1989.

Balsan, Consuelo Vanderbilt. *The Glitter and the Gold.* New York: Harper & Brothers, 1952.

Beebe, Lucius. *The Big Spenders.* Garden City, NY: Doubleday & Co., 1966.

Boegner, Peggie Phipps, and Richard Gachot. *Halcyon Days: An American Family through Three Generations.* New York: Harry N. Abrams, 1986.

Braudy, Susan. *This Crazy Thing Called Love: The Golden World and Fatal Marriage of Ann and Billy Woodward.* New York: Alfred A. Knopf, 1992.

Brandt, Clare. *An American Aristocracy: The Livingstons.* Garden City, NY: Doubleday & Company, 1986.

Brough, James. *Consuelo: Portrait of an American Heiress.* New York: Coward, McCann & Geoghegan, 1979.

Brown, Eve. *The Plaza: Its Life and Times.* New York: Meredith Press, 1967.

Burden, Shirley. *The Vanderbilts in My Life: A Personal Memoir.* New Haven, CT: Ticknor & Fields, 1981.

Carnegie, Andrew. *Autobiography of Andrew Carnegie.* New York: Houghton Mifflin Co., 1920.

Chernow, Ron. *The House of Morgan: An American Banking Dynasty and the Rise of Modern Finance.* New York: Atlantic Monthly Press, 1990.

Churchill, Allen. *The Splendor Seekers: An Informal Glimpse of America's Multimillionaire Spenders—Members of the $50,000,000 Club.* New York: Grosset & Dunlap, 1974.

Codman, Florence. *The Clever Young Boston Architect.* Augusta, ME: Privately printed, 1970.

Coles, William A. *Classical America IV.* New York: W. W. Norton & Co., 1977.

Cowles, Virginia. *The Astors.* New York: Alfred A. Knopf, 1979.

Decies, Elizabeth Wharton Drexel, Lady. *"King Lehr" and the Gilded Age.* Philadelphia: Lippincott, 1935.

———. *Turn of the World.* London: Lippincott, 1937.

De Koven, Mrs. Reginald. *A Musician and His Wife.* New York: Harper & Brothers, 1926.

Desmond, Harry W., and Herbert Croly. *Stately Homes in America from Colonial Times to the Present Day.* New York: D. Appleton & Co., 1903.

Diamonstein, Barbaralee. *The Landmarks of New York.* New York: Harry N. Abrams, 1988.

Ferree, Barr. *American Estates and Gardens.* New York: Munn & Company, 1906.

Folsom, Merrill. *Great American Mansions and Their Stories.* New York: Hastings House, 1963.

Foreman, John, and Robbe Pierce Stimson. *The Vanderbilts and the Gilded Age: Architectural Aspirations, 1879–1901.* New York: St. Martin's Press, 1991.

Friedman, B. H. *Gertrude Vanderbilt Whitney: A Biography.* Garden City, NY: Doubleday & Co., 1978.

Garmey, Stephen. *Gramercy Park: An Illustrated History of a New York Neighborhood.* New York: Balsam Press, 1984.

Geis, M. Christina. *Georgian Court: An Estate of the Gilded Age.* Philadelphia: Art Alliance Press, 1982.

Goldsmith, Barbara. *Little Gloria . . . Happy at Last.* New York: Alfred A. Knopf, 1980.

Gray, Christopher. *Changing New York: The Architectural Scene.* New York: Dover Publications, 1992.

Harvey, George. *Henry Clay Frick: The Man.* New York: Charles Scribner's Sons, 1928.

Hewitt, Mark Alan. *The Architect and the American Country House, 1890–1940.* New Haven, CT: Yale University Press, 1990.

———. *The Architecture of Mott B. Schmidt.* New York: Rizzoli, 1991.

Hoyt, Edwin P. *The Goulds: A Social History.* New York: Weybright & Tally, 1969.

———. *The Vanderbilts and Their Fortunes.* Garden City, NY: Doubleday & Company, 1962.

Irvine, Chippy, and Alex McLean. *Private New York: Remarkable Residences.* New York: Abbeville Press, 1990.

Juergen, George. *Joseph Pulitzer and the New York World.* Princeton, NJ: Princeton University Press, 1966.

Kahn, E. J., Jr. *Jock: The Life and Times of John Hay Whitney.* Garden City, NY: Doubleday & Co., 1981.

Kavaler, Lucy. *The Astors: An American Legend.* New York: Dodd, Mead & Co., 1966.

King, Robert B. *Raising a Fallen Treasure: The Otto H. Kahn Home, Huntington, Long Island.* New York: Mad Printers of Mattituck, 1985.

———, with Charles O. Mclean. *The Vanderbilt Homes.* New York: Rizzoli, 1989.

La Farge, Mabel. *Egisto Fabbri: 1866–1933.* New Haven: Privately printed, 1937.

Lockwood, Charles. *Bricks and Brownstone: The New York Row House, 1783–1929.* New York: Abbeville Press, 1972.

Lowe, David Garrard. *Stanford White's New York.* New York: Doubleday, 1992.

Maher, James T. *The Twilight of Splendor: Chronicles of the Age of American Palaces.* Boston: Little, Brown & Company, 1975.

Mann, William D'Alton. *Fads and Fancies of Representative Americans at the Beginning of the Twentieth Century.* New York: Town Topics, 1905.

Mansfield, Stephanie. *The Richest Girl in the World: The Extravagant Life and Fast Times of Doris Duke.* New York: G. P. Putnam's Sons, 1992.

McCash, W. B., and J. H. McCash. *The Jekyll Island Club: Southern Haven for America's Millionaires.* Athens: The University of Georgia Press, 1989.

Metcalf, Pauline, ed. *Ogden Codman and the Decoration of Houses.* Boston: Boston Atheneaum, 1988.

Mitchell, Henry. *Washington: Houses of the Capital.* New York: Viking Press, 1982.

Morris, Lloyd. *Incredible New York.* New York: Random House, 1951.

O'Conner, Richard. *The Golden Summers: An Antic History of Newport during Its Years of Glory.* New York: G. P. Putnam's Sons, 1974.

Owens, Carole. *The Berkshire Cottages: A Vanishing Era.* Englewood Cliffs, NJ: Cottage Press, 1984.

Patterson, Augusta Owen. *American Homes of To-day: Their Architectural Style, Their Environment, Their Characteristics.* New York: Macmillan Company, 1924.

Patterson, Jerry E. *The Vanderbilts.* New York: Harry N. Abrams, 1989.

Pearce, David. *The Great Houses of London.* New York: Vendome Press, 1986.

Pearson, Hesketh. *The Marrying Americans.* New York: Coward Mc Cann, 1961.

Platt, Frederick. *America's Gilded Age: Its Architecture and Decoration.* New York: A. S. Barnes & Company, 1976.

Porzelt, Paul. *The Metropolitan Club of New York.* New York: Rizzoli, 1982.

Pratt, Richard. *David Adler.* New York: M. Evans & Co., 1970.

Price, Matlack. *The Works of Dwight James Baum, Architect.* New York: William Helburn, 1927.

Pulitzer, Ralph. *New York Society on Parade.* New York: Harper & Brothers, 1910.

Randall, Monica. *The Mansions of Long Island's Gold Coast.* New York: Hastings House, 1979.

Rector, M. H. *Alva: That Vanderbilt-Belmont Woman.* ME: Dutch Island Press, 1992.

Roth, Leland. *A Monograph of the Works of McKim, Mead & White, 1879–1915.* New York: Arno Press, 1977.

Sclare, Liisa, and Donald Sclare. *Beaux Arts Estates: A Guide to the Architecture of Long Island.* New York: Viking Press, 1980.

Sherman, Joe. *The House at Shelburne Farms: The History of One of America's Great Country Estates.* Middlebury, VT: Paul S. Ericson, 1986.

Shopsin, William C. *The Villard Houses: Life Story of a Landmark.* New York: Viking Press, 1980.

Sinclair, David. *Dynasty: The Astors and Their Times.* New York: Beaufort Books, 1984.

Sloane, Florence Adele, with Louis Auchincloss. *Maverick in Mauve: The Diary of a Romantic Age.* Garden City, NY: Doubleday & Company, 1983.

Stasz, Clarice. *The Vanderbilt Women: Dynasty of Wealth, Glamour, and Tragedy.* New York: St. Martin's Press, 1991.

Stein, Susan, ed. *The Architecture of Richard Morris Hunt.* Chicago: University of Chicago Press, 1986.

Stern, Robert A. M., Gregory Gilmartin, and John Massengale. *New York 1900: Metropolitan Architecture and Urbanism, 1890–1915.* New York: Rizzoli, 1983.

———, ———, and Thomas Mellins. *New York 1930: Architecture and Urbanism between the Two World Wars.* New York: Rizzoli, 1987.

Swanberg, W. A. *Pulitzer.* New York: Charles Scribner's Sons, 1967.

———. *Whitney Father, Whitney Heiress.* New York: Charles Scribner's Sons, 1980.

Sykes, Christopher Simon. *Private Palaces: Life in the Great London Houses.* New York: Viking, 1986.

Tauranac, John, and Christopher Little. *Elegant New York: The Builders and the Buildings, 1885–1915.* New York: Abbeville Press, 1985.

Tebbel, John. *The Inheritors: A Study of America's Great Fortunes and What Happened to Them.* New York: G. P. Putnam's Sons, 1962.

Towner, Wesley. *The Elegant Auctioneers.* New York: Hill & Wang, 1970.

Trager, James. *Park Avenue: Street of Dreams.* New York: Atheneum, 1990.

———. *West of Fifth: The Rise and Fall and Rise of Manhattan's West Side.* New York: Atheneum, 1987.

Vanderbilt, Arthur T. *Fortune's Children: The Fall of the House of Vanderbilt.* New York: William Morrow and Company, 1989.

Vanderbilt, Cornelius, Jr. *Farewell to Fifth Avenue.* New York: Simon & Schuster, 1935.

———. *Queen of the Golden Age: The Fabulous Story of Grace Wilson Vanderbilt.* New York: McGraw-Hill, 1956.

Van Rensselaer, May King. *Newport: Our Social Capital.* Philadelphia: Lippincott, 1905.

Wharton, Edith, and Ogden Codman. *The Decoration of Houses.* New York: Charles Scribner's Sons, 1914.

Wheeler, George. *Pierpont Morgan and Friends: The Anatomy of a Myth.* Englewood Cliffs, NJ: Prentice-Hall, 1973.

Wilson, Richard Guy. *McKim, Mead & White: Architects.* New York: Rizzoli, 1983.

Winkler, John K. *Morgan the Magnificent: The Life of J. Pierpont Morgan (1837–1913).* New York: The Vanguard Press, 1930.

———. *Tobacco Tycoon: The Story of James Buchanan Duke.* New York: Random House, 1942.

Wright, William. *Heiress: The Rich Life of Marjorie Merriweather Post.* Washington, D.C.: New Republic Books, 1978.

Zukowsky, John, and Robbe Pierce Stimson. *Hudson River Villas.* New York: Rizzoli, 1985.

PERIODICALS

American Architect
American Architect and Building News
American Homes and Gardens
The Architect
Architectural Record
The Architectural Review
Architecture and Building
Architecture, Arts, and Decoration
Brickbuilder
Country Life in America
The Inland Architect and News Record
Real Estate Record and Guide
Town and Country
Vogue

MANUSCRIPT COLLECTIONS

Museum of the City of New York
The New York Historical Society
New York Public Library
The Richard Marchand Collection
Avery Library, Columbia University
The Richard Morris Hunt Collection, The American Institute of Architects, Washington, D.C

Index

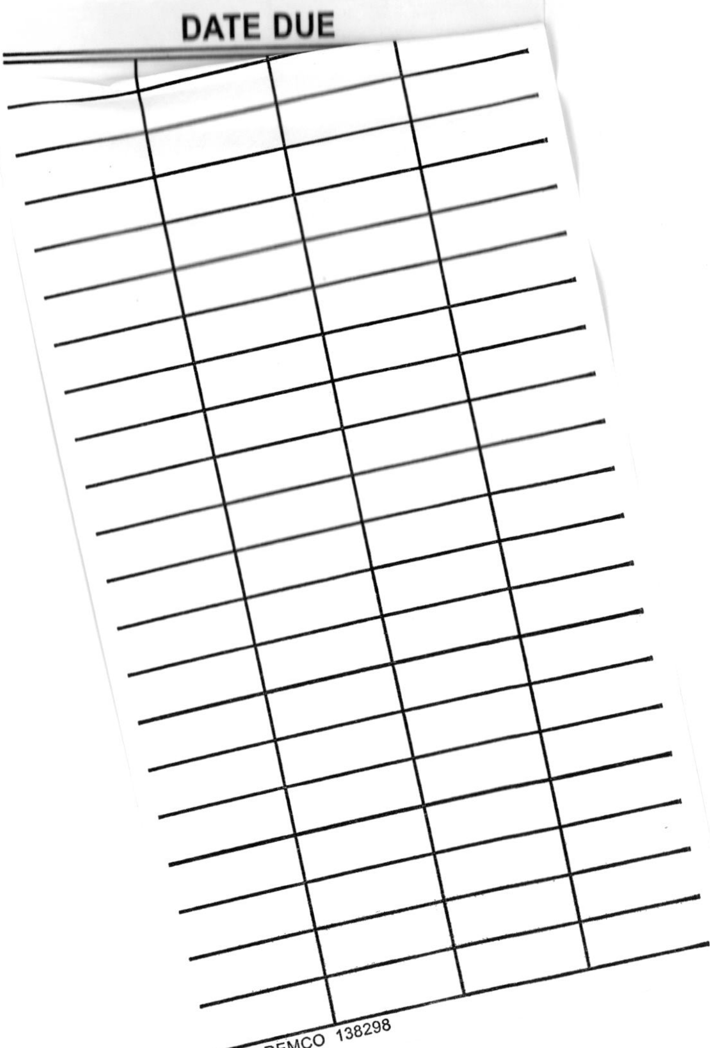
DATE DUE
DEMCO 138298

Winter Garden
St. Thomas Ch.
Vanderbilt Twin Houses
Union Club
St. Patrick's Cath.
Collegiate Church
Lyceum Th.
Windsor Arcade
American Th.
Times Bldg.
Harvard Cl.
Liberty Th.
Broadway
Delmonico's
Grand Central Station
Grand Central Palace
Automobile Blue Book Pub Co
Bryant Park
Empire Th.
Metropolitan Opera House
Manhattan Opera House
Union League Cl.
P.O.
Penna R.R.
Macy's
Herald Bldg.
Herald Sq.
Cornell Cl.
Chelsea Park
Tiffany
Gimbels
Greeley Sq.
St. Gabriel Park
Chelsea College
Daly's Th.
Armory
London Terrace
Mouquin's
Calumet Cl.
Gr. Opera Ho.
Y.M.C.A.
Little Church around the Corner
Chelsea Square
Madison Square Garden
St. Peter's Ch.
Fifth Ave Bldg.
Manhattan Club
Court House
Madison Square
Dr. Parkhurst Ch.
Emergency Hospital
Beth Haim
Flat Iron Bldg.
Metropolitan Bldg.
Bellevue Hospital
Arthur Ho.
Morgue
Carey Ho.
Roosevelt Ho.
Gramercy Park
West Washington Market
Gansevoort Market
Methodist Temple
St. Xavier
Natl. Arts Club
Bryant Ho.
Van Buren
Union Square
German Th.
N.Y. Lying in Hosp.
The Barracks
St. George
Stuyvesant Sq.
Union Sq. Th.
Tammany
Milligan Pl.
N.Y. Society Lib.
Old Commissioner's Office
Eye & Ear Infirmary
Tom Payne
Washington Sq.
Grace Ch.
St. Mark Ch.
Memorial Arch
Clinton Hall
Morton Ho.
M.E. Church
Stuyvesant
N.Y. University
Cooper Union
St. Clement Ch.
Colonnade Row
Astor Library
Middle Dutch Ch.
Tompkins Square
West St.
Police Headquarters
Monroe H.
St. Patrick
St. Alphonsus
One Mile House
The Ghetto
Hamilton Fish Park
Broadway
Park
Ericsson Ho.
Essex Market
Williamsburg
Criminal Court
Chinatown
W. H. Seward Park
Thalia Th.
Tombs
5 Points
Hall of Records
Chatham Sq.
Mariners Temple
H-U-D-S-O-N R-I-V-E-R